creative ESSENTIALS

OTHER BOOKS BY KAREN LEE STREET

Tattoos and Motorcycles
Honest

KAREN LEE STREET

WRITING AND SELLING
CRIME FILM SCREENPLAYS

creative ESSENTIALS

First published in 2013 by Kamera Books,
an imprint of Oldcastle Books
PO Box 394, Harpenden, Herts, AL5 1XJ
kamerabooks.com

A CIP catalogue record for this book is available from the British Library.

978-1-84243-974-6   (Print)
978-1-84243-975-3   (epub)
978-1-84243-976-0   (kindle)
978-1-84344-264-6   (pdf)

Typeset by Elsa Mathern in Franklin Gothic 9 pt
Printed and bound by CPI Group (UK) Ltd, Croydon, CR0 4YY

ACKNOWLEDGEMENTS

Special thanks to Hannah Patterson, Anne Hudson, the Kamera Books team, Peter Carlton, Keith Potter, Vicki Madden, Jackie Malton, Sally Griffiths, Philip Palmer, Jon Gilbert, Sam Johnston, Mike Fear, Craig Batty and Darren Hill.

CONTENTS

THE **MOTIVE**

This is not a book on film genre theory. Its aim is not to debate the difference between a film style, mode, technique and genre or to attempt to establish rules that define crime sub-genres. It has a very simple goal: to present a user-friendly approach to writing and developing crime genre screenplays that address audience expectations without sacrificing originality.

My own fascination with the crime genre started fairly early as my grandfather was a pulp fiction writer whose stories were published in *Dime Mystery Magazine*, *Black Mask* and Street & Smith's *Detective Story Magazine*. He gave me impromptu lessons on how to write crime fiction as he sat behind his Smith Corona, haloed in smoke from his ever-present 'writing cigar'. I have also written crime genre novels, but it's primarily my two decades of script development experience as a development executive, freelance script editor, and script evaluator for major film funding bodies in Europe and North America that prompted my interest in finding a useful way to approach 'writing the crime' in screenplay form. This work has entailed reading thousands of scripts, some very good, some very bad, most in need of further development.

FROM DIAGNOSIS TO SCRIPT DOCTORING:
THE FIRST PAN-EUROPEAN SCRIPT ANALYSIS SERVICE

It's one thing to critique a script and write a report about why that draft isn't working; quite different skills are required to actually figure out how to improve that script. The most practical experience I gained in 'script doctoring' was during my time as Head of Development at the European Script Fund and European Media Development Agency, where my role was to facilitate the development of all funded projects from selection to production. 'ESF' was the largest feature film development agency in Europe and is now the development funding arm of the MEDIA Programme, European Commission. We co-developed film and television projects from 18 countries by most of the key players in the European film industry, including Oscar-nominated and winning films such as *Farinelli*, *Daens*, *Children of Nature*, *All Things Fair*, *Poussières de Vie*, *Journey of Hope*, *A Chef in Love* and acclaimed features including *Breaking the Waves*, *Orlando*, *Elizabeth*, *Rob Roy*, *Naked*, *Carla's Song*, *Toto le Héros*, *Hilary and Jackie*, *The Cement Garden* and *Live Flesh*. I joined the company at its inception in January 1989 and set up the script submission evaluation system. It quickly became clear that common script weaknesses prevented projects from attracting initial development funding. It also became clear that many funded companies did not spend enough time on script development and either the project failed to secure production finance or went into production before the script was ready. I discovered that screenwriters are too frequently given script notes that are difficult to follow or that focus on minor problems rather than the bigger issues. This is exacerbated if the writer is receiving notes – often contradictory – from several people. To help counter this confusing process, I created the first pan-European script analysis service so that every funded writer and producer received detailed written feedback on their submitted script in a consistent, coherent format. These very detailed script analysis reports had a simple but effective structure designed to help the writer address the bigger issues first rather than getting muddled up in less important detail.

FATAL FLAWS AND GENRE CONFUSION

The script analysis service was hugely popular and helped to emphasise the importance of script development in the European film industry. And as we funded and analysed more scripts – over a thousand projects during my tenure – the most fundamental and 'fatal' script problems became apparent:

- An unclear concept (what is this story really about?)
- A promising idea overcome by cliché
- A writer and producer with different visions for the project, resulting in a weakened story
- Genre confusion

Looking more specifically at genre, script readers often labelled a project's genre as 'drama' on the report form, even if the screenwriter claimed it was a thriller, love story or mystery. Why? Because the reader couldn't identify the genre. Conversely, the genre might have been clear to the reader, but the script was considered derivative and therefore boring. So how does a screenwriter write a crime genre film with a recognisable identity without descending into cliché? That was the key question that prompted the research behind this book.

WHAT KIND OF STORY IS THIS?

One of the first problems a writer faces when setting out to write a crime screenplay is defining the nature of the beast. If you list five crime films and then do a search to see how they are categorised on various websites, most are assigned to several genres. For example, *Scarface* is defined as: crime, gangster and film noir (Howard Hawks's version) or action-adventure (Brian de Palma's version).

- *Double Indemnity*: crime, film noir, thriller
- *LA Confidential*: crime, mystery, film noir, police drama

- *Ocean's Eleven*: crime, thriller, heist film
- *The Shawshank Redemption*: crime, prison drama, buddy movie

If there is so much disagreement about how to categorise a produced feature film, how easy is it to define the genre, and indeed sub-genre, at script stage? And yet, this is what is often demanded by producers and funders who state they are looking for a gangster, heist or detective film, a prison or police drama, film noir, neo-noir, or a serial killer story. A starting point is to understand the conventions an audience (and therefore a producer) expects from a sub-genre. The next stage is to decide which conventions to adhere to and which might be subverted to bring something fresh to the genre. Very basically, if the crime genre is 'cake' and its sub-genres are types of cake, how many ingredients can you alter before you end up with bread or pie or dumplings? The goal is to write a script that is recognisable as a crime genre piece, but with new elements that make it exciting to read.

CRIME FILM BASICS, SHARPENING SKILLS, LEARNING FROM THE PROS

The crime sub-genres that will be considered in this book are: detective, police, film noir, gangster, heist, prison and serial killer. A brief historical overview of the sub-genre's development will be presented, as will its key conventions. These should provoke a light-bulb moment of recognition when considering classic crime genre films we know and love and may prompt the reader to think of other conventions. Examples will be provided that show how the creative use of genre conventions resulted in exciting rather than derivative cinema. (And there will be spoilers if you haven't seen some of the films. Repeat: there will be spoilers.)

A number of writing exercises will be included to help generate ideas, familiarise the writer with key crime genre story patterns, sharpen skills, and kick-start script revision. It's worth sticking to a strict time limit when undertaking a writing exercise, as writing at speed can stop self-censoring, help shift writer's block, and (from my experience of running writers' workshops) result in some great story ideas. Many of these exercises also work well as team writing endeavours that writers and filmmakers of every level seem to find enjoyable and thought-provoking.

In the final chapters, I'll sum up key points to consider before sending a crime film script (or any script!) to producers, co-producers or funders. Included in that section are the script pet peeves and some helpful advice from film industry readers, the 'threshold guardians' who first read your project. Following that are some short interviews with industry insiders – produced writers, script editors, crime film consultants, producers and heads of production funds – who share their thoughts on crime films, the types of projects they like, and why.

WHY THESE CRIMES AND NOT OTHERS?

This book is an introduction to the crime genre that should help a screenwriter understand various crime sub-genre conventions and get them thinking about how to use them creatively. There are other sub-genres not covered in this book that often deal with crimes, such as legal dramas, thrillers, social issue and espionage films, but these have their own distinct tropes. To paraphrase SS Van Dine's nineteenth rule from 'Twenty Rules for Writing Detective Stories' (September 1928, *American Magazine*), the motives for all crimes in detective stories should be personal. International plottings and war politics belong to a different genre such as war story or espionage thriller. The crime genre should feature personal crimes that reflect the audience's everyday experiences and give them a certain outlet for their own repressed desires and emotions. In other words, the audience gains pleasure from being as clever as the sleuth, as rebellious as the gangster, or as daring as the prisoner planning an escape, and there is, perhaps, more than a touch of wish fulfilment when the viewer participates in a really cracking crime movie.

THE **MODUS OPERANDI**:
AN APPROACH TO GENRE
FOR SCREENWRITERS

Writers are as willing as anyone to debate a genre's defining tropes, but can crime sub-genres be so easily defined and, more importantly, so easily written by simply ticking all the boxes? Must modern gangster films adhere to the same conventions established by their earliest predecessors or have gangster films evolved?

Filmmaking is a modern art compared to literature or theatre, and the complexity, scope and ways of communicating film stories are linked to the evolution of the technology needed to make films – and costs to produce them. The earliest films were simple experiments with the moving image and records of real events such as the Lumière Brothers' 1895 film of workers leaving their factory. *La Fée aux Choux*, probably the first narrative short film, was made in 1896 by Alice Guy-Blaché and, until 1913, all films were 'one-reelers' – a reel held 1,000 feet of film and played for 11–17 minutes, depending on projection speed. They were typically shot in one take with no editing; the stories were correspondingly simple. Experimentation with trick photography and editing encouraged more creativity in storytelling. The production of longer narratives such as Giovanni Patrone's *Cabiria* (1914) and, later that year, DW Griffith's 61-minute *Judith of Bethulia* allowed for more complex stories. DW Griffith went on to help establish techniques such as the use of close-ups, cross-cutting, the flashback, and fade-in/fade-out to enhance storytelling.

As advances in technology and technique inspired more complex ways of presenting a narrative, there was a ready-made supply of stories to adapt to the screen from literary and theatrical sources, including tales of highwaymen, murders, mysteries, and early detective stories. Publishers of periodicals had been publishing stories by 'type' for years. For example, Street & Smith Publications in New York City, founded in 1855, was one of the largest publishers of pulp fiction, dime novels and comic books in America, their low cost making them accessible to a wide audience. Street & Smith targeted fans of specific genres with periodicals such as *Sea Stories Magazine*, *Do and Dare Weekly*, *Mystery Story Magazine*, *All-Sports Library*, *Love Story Magazine*, *True Western Stories* and *Bowery Boy Weekly*. They changed their titles frequently to satisfy the tastes of their readership.

The successful writing and selling of genre stories through periodicals and paperback novels paved the way for the film genre stories and influenced the evolution of genre conventions. This is a key point. Genres evolve and continue to evolve – they are not static structures that stifle a writer's creativity as some 'anti-genre' writers seem to think. A useful approach to genre for screenwriters is outlined in Louis Giannetti's *Understanding Movies*, which focuses on the evolution of genre through four stages: primitive, classical, revisionist and parody; these genre progressions are inevitably linked to filmmakers' endeavours to use conventions creatively and to address changes in society and audience expectations.

Once a genre is established and progresses to the classical stage, it does not revert back to the primitive stage, but classical stage genre films are made concurrently with revisionist or parody films. A revisionist genre film may subvert certain conventions to surprise the viewer, but the genre recipe is not radically altered or there is risk of audience disappointment. New sub-genres sometimes arise from the revisionist stage of a genre, progressing from their own primitive to classical stage when specific conventions are established. A genre is ripe for parody as soon as its conventions are well known to an audience and playful manipulation of genre tropes makes the viewer feel clever for recognising these 'in-jokes'.

FIGURE 1: **THE FOUR STAGES OF GENRE**

The Primitive Stage:
The origins of a genre, when its key conventions are introduced and developed.

The Classical Stage:
A genre's conventions are recognisable to an audience and considered well-established; the genre is at the height of its popularity.

The Revisionist Stage:
Classical stage conventions are examined critically, re-evaluated, and revised, often due to societal changes.

The Parody Stage:
Key characteristics of the genre are satirised; parodies focus on genre tropes that are most recognisable to an audience.

Ultimately, this four-stage approach emphasises that genres evolve through the creativity of filmmakers and a genre's popularity with audiences. Genre tropes provide a useful framework for telling a particular type of story, but should not straitjacket a screenwriter into scripting overly derivative, clichéd screenplays.

JUDGE AND JURY:
GENRE, PUBLIC TASTE AND CENSORSHIP

The motion pictures, which are the most popular of modern arts for the masses, have their moral quality from the intention of the minds which produce them and from their effects on the moral lives and reactions of their audiences. This gives them a most important morality.

(The Motion Picture Production Code of 1930)

Why do we think of Hollywood when we talk about genre films? European filmmakers have made movies that deal with crime and criminals since the inception of cinema, but the sheer output of Hollywood studios was fundamental to the creation of genre pictures. When a studio had a commercial hit, it tended to produce numerous variations of the same story, hoping to replicate that success. In other words, public taste was key in establishing many genre conventions and film story paradigms. For example, boy might meet girl, lose girl, and win girl back because the audience wanted a happy ending to their romances, but what of the crime story? Crime is not meant to pay, so can stories about breaking the law end well for the criminal or show the bad guy in a sympathetic light? A brief overview of how the crime genre developed, particularly in Hollywood, should give some insight into how specific crime sub-genre conventions evolved from their primitive to classical, revisionist and parody stages.

ESTABLISHING THE CRIME SCENE:
EARLY PULP AND PRIMITIVE STAGE GENRE FILMS

Some of the first films made were crime films, which is hardly surprising given that the battle between the 'good guy' and the 'bad guy' has appealed to audiences since the earliest stories were told, written down, and performed. European directors, whether working in Europe or Hollywood, contributed significantly to the evolution of the crime genre, most particularly with short film serials, many of which were based on popular 'pulp fiction' of the day. At the forefront of the explosion in European pulp fiction at the beginning of the twentieth century was German publisher Eichler. Adolf Eichler first bought translation rights to Street & Smith's Buffalo Bill stories; when these proved to be best-sellers in Germany, he bought the rights to their Nick Carter character in 1906 and began publishing weekly crime stories. The Nick Carter detective stories were even more popular than the Westerns. Other publishers jumped on the pulp bandwagon, releasing Maurice Leblanc's tales of gentleman thief Arsène Lupin; Léon Sazie's master criminal Zigomar; and Fantômas, the 'Genius of Crime', by Marcel Allain and Pierre Souvestre. The public revelled in the adventures of these wily and seductive criminals and, due to their popularity, all became the protagonists of short film serials, beginning with Zigomar in 1908. These serials helped establish the symbiotic relationship between popular literature and film that continues to influence the development of genre films.

In the US, a number of early one-reelers focused on a simple crime being committed and the subsequent pursuit of the perpetrator. As early filmmakers experimented with the moving image and narrative, the chase sequence was an audience-pleasing way of combining activity and the 'cause and effect' of a simple narrative. Wallace McCutcheon and Edwin S Porter made quite a few short silent films, both separately and collaboratively, that focused on the activity surrounding a crime. One of McCutcheon's earliest films for American Mutoscope & Biograph was How They Rob Men in Chicago (1900), and Porter made the popular and commercially successful The Great Train

Robbery (1903), with its innovative editing and chase scene, for the Edison Manufacturing Company. Early Hollywood crime features set in the criminal underworld or telling the tale of an innocent coerced to the 'dark side' quickly gained popularity with audiences. *Lights of New York* (1928), Warner Brothers' first all-talking feature, had it all: innocent country lad conned into fronting an illegal New York City speakeasy, murderous gangster, chorus-girl with heart of gold. It cost only $23,000 to produce and grossed over one million dollars. The studios were keen to repeat their successes and why reinvent the wheel if a particular type of story is a crowd pleaser?

THE GOLDEN AGE OF PULP FICTION AND CLASSIC CRIMES

As film storytelling evolved and more crime films were produced, more specific sub-genre conventions were established. While early European gangster serials allowed the criminal to outwit the law and go on to commit another tantalising crime, in the majority of Hollywood primitive-stage crime films good prevailed over evil, the law was upheld, and the villain was conquered. A more realistic picture of the criminal world evolved along with Hollywood genre cinema. Writers and directors weren't as content as many studio executives to churn out the same film over and over. Theatre plays dealing with controversial social issues, containing profanity and featuring scantily clad actors, were performed in New York theatres; these shows contributed to the rise of so-called vice pictures and social-issue or 'preachment yarns'. The golden age of pulp fiction crime writing was a huge influence on the classical stage of Hollywood crime films; hard-boiled detective novels by influential crime writers Dashiell Hammett, James M Cain and Raymond Chandler were adapted for the screen and pulp fiction writers such as Ben Hecht, WR Burnett, and Jonathan Latimer turned screenwriter. When Prohibition, the Great Depression, and the actions of corrupt politicians and bankers helped make folk heroes out of gangsters who seemed to grab back what was stolen away from ordinary folk, Hollywood studios started making gangster films, producing 35 of them in the 1930–31 production season alone. Key conventions of the sub-genre were established during this classical stage when gangster films were at their most popular. But there was a backlash. This flurry of crime films resulted in an escalation of complaints from civic and religious organisations. They claimed that crime, vice and social-issue movies glamorised criminals; the film studios countered that movies were deterrents rather than incentives to criminal behaviour. The argument echoed the nineteenth-century debate about so-called 'Newgate novels' written by Charles Dickens and his contemporaries. These works were accused of valorising criminals and famously prompted murderer François Benjamin Courvoisier to claim that reading a Newgate novel 'made him do it'. Initially it was determined locally whether movies might be screened or banned and there was little that could be done to counter these regional decisions as the United States Supreme Court had ruled in 1915 that freedom of speech did not extend to motion pictures. The major studios wanted to get around this as banned films hurt their profits, but they also wanted to avoid direct government intervention; a code of standards for filmmakers seemed the best solution as the studios could potentially exercise more control through self-regulation.

ALIAS 'THE HAYS CODE'

William H Hays was appointed president of the Motion Picture Producers and Distributors of America in 1922 to improve Hollywood's image after a number of studio scandals. He first introduced 'The Formula' in 1924, which was a set of guidelines for movie content. Five years later, a Jesuit priest and a Catholic layman who were concerned about the negative influence sound films purportedly had on children drew up a code of standards that Hays embraced. After some negotiated revisions, the studio heads agreed the document and the Motion Picture Production Code of 1930 was established to 'govern the Making of Talking, Synchronized and Silent Motion Pictures'. It was adopted by the Association of Motion Picture

Producers and the Motion Picture Producers and Distributors of America, with the responsibility for supervising its enforcement going to the Studio Relations Committee. 'The Hays Code', as it became known, was not rigorously enforced initially, not least because the Studio Relations Committee team had to review about 500 films a year and did not have the power to insist on the alteration of film content. Crime and vice stories were winners at the box office and studios made no real attempt to adhere to the Code during the hard times of the Great Depression. One small concession was to preface a crime film with a disclaimer, a tactic that had been established with social-issue films critiquing the immoral activities and white-collar crimes of politicians, bankers, lawyers and businessmen. For example, gangster film *The Public Enemy* (1931) began with the text: 'It is the intention of the authors of *The Public Enemy* to honestly depict an environment that exists today in certain strata of American life, rather than to glorify the hoodlum or the criminal.'

The studios came up against the Catholic church again in early 1934 when Cardinal Thomas Dougherty found a Philadelphia billboard advertisement for a film so offensive he helped facilitate a boycott of motion pictures, which resulted in a much more stringent enforcement of the Motion Picture Production Code. An indication of the influence of the Code on content can be gleaned from its preamble, which states that, while motion pictures are primarily for entertainment rather than propaganda or education, they 'may be directly responsible for spiritual or moral progress, for higher types of social life, and for much correct thinking' and therefore the objective of the Code was 'to bring the motion picture to a still higher level of wholesome entertainment for all the people'. The Motion Picture Production Code's general principles exhorted that 'no picture shall be produced that will lower the moral standards of those who see it'; 'the sympathy of the audience should never be thrown to the side of crime, wrongdoing, evil or sin'; and 'law, natural or human, shall not be ridiculed, nor shall sympathy be created for its violation'. There was great concern that the apparent realism of cinema when compared with plays or books might more easily sway the 'lower classes' and young people towards a criminal lifestyle, as might their enthusiasm for film actors and actresses. Many of these debates continue. It was specifically forbidden to teach methods of crime, inspire imitation, and make criminals seem heroic or justified. A character could only be shown taking revenge if the film was set in 'lands and ages of less developed civilisation and moral principles'. Drug trafficking and the excessive use of liquor were not permitted. Brutal killings could not be presented in detail, and 'the technique of murder must be presented in a way that will not inspire imitation'. The specifics of theft, robbery, safe-cracking, arson, and the dynamiting of various locations were also not allowed.

Many of the crime shows on television today would have been inconceivable during the enforcement of the Hays Code due to the graphic nature of the violence; their purported potential to influence budding criminals; and specifics about detective work, processing crime scenes, and criminal law that might assist a perpetrator in avoiding arrest or imprisonment. Equally, many now classic 1970s Hollywood films that were nominated for, or won, Academy Awards, such as *The French Connection* (1971), *The Godfather* (1972), *Serpico* (1973), *Papillon* (1973), *The Godfather, Part II* (1974), *Chinatown* (1974), *Dog Day Afternoon* (1975), *Taxi Driver* (1976) and *Midnight Express* (1978), could not have been made in their produced form under the Hays Code, whether due to their extreme violence, depictions of drug smuggling, empathetic portrayals of criminals, unsympathetic representations of law-enforcement agents, or overly specific enactments of the crime itself. It's worth having a look at the full Motion Picture Production Code online to see what filmmakers were up against from 1934 to 1968, and to get an idea of the impact such strictures had on Hollywood cinema. It also gives a sense of how master filmmakers such as Alfred Hitchcock used these strictures creatively while working in Hollywood.

In *Rear Window* (1954), for example, Hitchcock seems to be poking fun at some of the Hays Code rules. Grace Kelly's single girl Lisa Fremont invites herself to stay overnight in the (only) bed of LB Jeffries, played by Jimmy Stewart. This does not go unnoticed by Detective

Lieutenant Doyle who sees the 'lightly packed' negligee that she later models rather provocatively; it's clear that pre-marital sex is on the cards. But first Fremont will play sleuth as Jeffries is convinced that probable dog-killer Lars Thorwald (Raymond Burr) has also murdered his wife. Jeffries' nurse Stella (Thelma Ritter) hypothesises that Thorwald chopped Mrs Thorwald into little pieces and planted her amongst the zinnias. Today we might see both the sex scene and the grisly murder, but Hitchcock merely suggests both events, which of course is much more in keeping with the film's themes, highly effective, and manages to stay the right side of the Code.

LAUGHING AT LAW AND ORDER: THE PARODY STAGE

Parody relies on audience recognition of a particular creative work, a style, a character or character type, or specific story conventions. Some of the earliest film comedies poked fun at inept agents of the law or criminals. Between 1912 and 1917, audiences laughed at the pratfalls of the Keystone Cops, a gang of bumbling policemen, in Mack Sennett's popular silent short films. The incompetent coppers were revived as secondary characters in later feature films and the phrase 'Keystone Cop' has become synonymous with 'headless chicken' physical ineptitude. In 1922, Buster Keaton parodied the melodramatic Westerns of William S Hart in his film *The Frozen North*, satirising the protagonist's typical redemptive arc of bad guy to good guy, his costume, and other key props. Audiences were quick to pick up on the parody and the film was a success. Many other parodies of Westerns have followed as so many conventions of the genre are well known to audiences.

But what about crime films? Detective films were ripe for parody as the very basic story structure was well established: a crime is committed, the detective gathers evidence and interviews suspects, the crime is solved due to the detective's superior ratiocination skills. Fast-talking, hard-drinking, quick-thinking, tough guy detectives as first established in pulp fiction and then immortalised on screen by actors such as Humphrey Bogart became such iconic characters they have inspired a multitude of comic imitators. Police procedurals also provide fertile material for parody, with a similar story pattern to detective films and the opportunity to mock agents of the law as pioneered in the Keystone Cops. The gangster genre has not been parodied as much as detective or police films, but gangsters have been extensively spoofed as secondary characters in films. Inept attempts at prison escapes and bumbling crooks trying to pull off a heist have proved popular internationally. Even serial killer films have been spoofed, primarily in anarchic or absurdist black comedies that often poke fun at the 'trigger' for the killer's first murder. While stupid criminals have been used for comic effect in many movies, it seems that even the most gruesome crimes are ripe for parody in the right filmmaker's hands. Successful genre parodies work on a nudge-nudge, wink-wink level; they play to an audience's familiarity with genre conventions, turning them into crowd-pleasing in-jokes.

HOLLYWOOD MAKEOVERS:
GENRE STAGES, ADAPTATIONS AND REMAKES

It should be clear from the overview of the four stages of genre that your potential audience cannot be ignored when writing a crime genre film. Hollywood studios have tried to second-guess public taste for decades in hopes of producing profitable films and this contributes to the large number of adaptations of popular literature, film sequels, and remakes of successful films. This approach can be frustrating for screenwriters trying to get a foot in the door with a great original script, but it's not easy to argue against the success of the Bond or Harry Potter franchises.

Too many screenwriters 'auto-complain' that any remake of a film or sequel is rubbish compared to the original. This may be true, but a screenwriter should be able to cogently articulate why the remake or sequel is rubbish. Just as a script reader must be able to justify his or her opinions about a script in a reader's report, filmmakers must also be able to pinpoint where a script isn't working and have good ideas about how to improve it in order to have a fruitful script development meeting. 'I don't like this character' or 'this scene is boring' are not helpful comments for a writer unless backed up by concrete ways to improve the character or scene. How might the film have been better? Was the problem in the components of the script, the casting, or the direction? It's part of a writer's job to be able to figure this out, for those are the skills that are needed if commissioned to do a script rewrite.

....

WRITING EXERCISE: RE-SPINNING THE YARN

Part A
Think of a crime film that has been remade. For example: *Scarface* or *The Postman Always Rings Twice*. Make a list of pros and cons for the original and the remake(s), focusing on the script rather than the allure of the actors. Consider all aspects of the protagonist, antagonist, the plot, structure, setting, dialogue, and so on. Is the remake a revisionist remake or a more faithful, classical stage remake? Or is it even a parody?

Part B
Think of a fairytale or folktale that contains a crime. Revise it into a (more) modern crime story or scene.

Example
Consider the 'execution scene' from the fairytale *Snow White* (Brothers Grimm version). The huntsman is ordered by the evil Queen to murder Snow White in the forest and cut out her heart as proof that she's dead, but he cannot do the deed as Snow White is so enchanting and good. He relents and lets Snow White escape into the forest, with the promise that she will never return to the kingdom. He delivers a boar's heart to the Queen, who consumes it believing it to be Snow White's.

The Coen Brothers' *Miller's Crossing* (1990) has a very similar scene. Tom Regan (Gabriel Byrne) is ordered by Mafia boss

Johnny Caspar to execute Bernie Bernbaum, his lover Verna's brother. He relents and allows Bernie to run away, on the promise that he leaves town. Regan's nemesis 'the Dane' drops Regan in it as no proof was delivered of Bernie's execution. Johnny Caspar demands that Regan retrieve Bernie's body from Miller's Crossing, and Regan is certain he is facing a bullet in the head from the two thugs accompanying him. However, in a twist, they find a dead man in the woods, with his face mutilated. Regan is off the hook but, in a second twist, Bernie turns up at his apartment and tries to blackmail him.

This 'revisionist' version of a classic fairytale scene gives the huntsman's dilemma to the main character of *Miller's Crossing* and makes the intended victim of the 'evil leader' a secondary character. In Disney's animated *Snow White and the Seven Dwarfs* (1937), the Huntsman is ordered to murder Snow White and bring her heart to the Evil Queen as proof of her death, but, as in the fairytale, he cannot do the deed, so overwhelmed is he by Snow White's magical goodness. Instead he takes the Evil Queen a pig's heart. In *Snow White and the Huntsman* (2012), the Huntsman is willing to murder Snow White because the Queen promises to bring his wife back from the dead. Snow White proves herself to be a far more capable character by escaping the castle and surviving in the forest. The Huntsman does not spare Snow White because of her saintly charm, but primarily because he discovers that the Evil Queen's promise is a lie; the situation is revised to reflect modern sensibilities.

....

THE CRIME **CONTINUUM**

The earliest primitive stage crime films were silent one-reelers of about 15 minutes or less. The stories conveyed were quite simple, often focusing on the perpetration of a crime and a chase sequence. As filmmakers became more ambitious and technology developed, so did the narratives. Short film serials gave way to multi-reel narratives that allowed for more complex tales and character development. The advent of sound made it easier to adapt more dialogue-heavy theatre plays for the screen and to include scenes with necessary exposition. Writers began to experiment with story scope and point of view, which we will look at in more detail later. The crime continuum (Figure 2) presents some key situations that surround the committing of a crime and some of the dramatic questions raised by these situations.

If we consider story scope in relation to the crime continuum, it's clear that crime stories can focus on just one element of the crime continuum or, at the other extreme, encompass the entire spectrum. These variations in scope necessitate different story structures and influence the overall level of dramatic tension. For example, a story that encompasses the entire continuum would tend to be epic in timescale (*Once Upon a Time in America* [1984] or *The Godfather* [1972]) with varying levels of tension, whereas focusing on one element from the continuum and applying a ticking clock (*Dog Day Afternoon* [1975] or *Cell 211* [2009]) normally results in a story with a much shorter timeframe and a higher level of tension throughout.

FIGURE 2: **THE CRIME CONTINUUM**

⬇ **Going Bad: Temptation to the 'Dark Side'**
Why did he/she become a criminal? Who influenced them?
What was the goal?

⬇ **The Planning and Preparations for the Crime**
What's the 'prize'? How will they get it? Will they go through
with it?

⬇ **The Crime is Committed**
The perfect crime or a botched job? Honour amongst criminals
or deception?

⬇ **The Getaway**
Perpetrator(s) covering their tracks or on the run. Will they
escape or get caught? Live or die?

⬇ **Law Enforcement: Cops vs Robbers**
The police called to action; will they catch the known perpetrator or usual suspect?

⬇ **Investigating the Crime**
Whodunit? Gathering evidence to find or convict the perpetrator.

⬇ **The Trial**
Guilty or innocent? The sentence.

⬇ **Behind Bars**
Life inside or the Great Escape?

⬇ **The Ex-Con: Reformed or a Repeat Offender?**
Temptation back to the Dark Side: will the criminal stay on
the straight and narrow or return to 'the life'? The pressure
to do one last job.

Various elements from the continuum can be combined chronologically or in a non-linear fashion to enhance mystery, increase tension, and keep the audience guessing. A classic heist story such as *Ocean's Eleven* (2001) might depict several elements from the crime continuum in chronological order. A film noir such as *Double Indemnity* (1944) might present those same elements in two timeframes to increase tension, with a much heavier focus on 'going bad' as the protagonist is seduced by the femme fatale. A more experimental, non-linear structure might unite non-chronological elements from the crime continuum in films such as *Point Blank* (1967) or *Pulp Fiction* (1994).

Consider how focusing on various aspects of the crime continuum facilitated the development of crime sub-genres such as the gangster, heist, detective, or prison dramas. Courtroom and legal dramas developed into separate genres with their own conventions, even if quite a few crime films have key courtroom scenes. The television series *Law & Order* meshed the police procedural and the legal drama to bring something new to both genres. Experimenting with the crime continuum can lead to innovative stories in terms of content and also structure.

WRITING TOOLS: THE IMAGE KIT

Put together a collection of images (print or virtual) in the following categories: characters, locations, animals, objects. An 'image kit' is a simple but useful tool for brainstorming ideas and sharpening writing skills. It may seem a little rudimentary, but writers with a wide range of experience and backgrounds have enjoyed working with an image kit in screenwriting workshops I've run, precisely because the idea is so simple and allows playful creativity without over-thinking. Using an image kit for various writing exercises allows the writer to be more spontaneous when creating characters and to experiment with story ideas without feeling overly precious about them. Freeing up the imagination can also help a writer to think beyond stereotypes when creating characters and situations. Putting together an image kit is a good reminder that film is a visual medium and of how much can be conveyed in a single image.

....

WRITING EXERCISE: CRIME AND CONFLICT

The following exercises use the crime continuum as a starting point. They can be tackled in one sitting or separately.

Part A
From your image kit:

- Choose two characters
- Choose a location
- Choose an object (prop)

Then:

- Give each of your characters a name and make one the protagonist, the other the antagonist. Assign four key character traits to each, a mix of positive and negative. For example: confident, quick thinking, lazy, parsimonious, envious. Your protagonist and antagonist may share traits if you wish.

- Choose an event from the crime continuum.

- Define your location according to your chosen event: a crime scene, the getaway destination, a prison (in the widest sense of the word).

- Define the object. It could be a weapon, an obstacle, a prize, a tool, an object of desire.

- Now, write a brief summary of a scene based on your chosen event, characters, location, and object. Have fun with it.

Example
- Protagonist: 'The Dude' – an ageing surfer. Genial, a slob, quick witted, lazy. Antagonists: 'Woo' – a small-time hired

thug. Aggressive, tidy, without scruples, physically fit. His sidekick – a dumb-blonde hoodlum. Aggressive, stupid, hyperactive, a follower.

- Event: the crime is committed.

- Location: a scruffy apartment as crime scene.

- Object: a rug (the Dude's most prized household possession).

- Woo and the dumb-blonde hoodlum rough up 'Jeffrey Lebowski', demanding money his wife Bunny owes their boss Jackie Treehorn. The Dude tries to tell them that he never uses his birth name and definitely isn't married, but the thugs persist. Woo then urinates on the Dude's treasured rug, which upsets him far more than the attack itself. The thugs finally realise that it's a case of mistaken identity and leave. The Dude is gutted by his ruined rug.

This scene from the Coen Brothers' comedy crime caper *The Big Lebowski* (which was loosely inspired by *The Big Sleep*) uses a crime (in the Dude's eyes) as an inciting incident. It would be quite a different story if the thugs broke in and stole the Dude's bowling ball, sending him on a quest to reclaim the sporting good essential for his favourite activity rather than recompense for a ruined rug that 'tied the room together'. Either way, the object, location, and the Dude's demeanour make it clear this will be a crime-comedy. At the scene's end we don't know if the overly laid-back Dude will do anything about his ruined rug, and are left wondering about the other Jeffrey Lebowski and his spendthrift wife, Bunny.

Part B

Develop your story outline further by adding additional events from the *crime continuum*. Try it chronologically first (committing the crime, then the getaway, for example). You might then experiment with a non-linear timeframe (the protagonist's release from prison; the getaway; the crime committed).

Think about how changing the order of events alters the dramatic tension and energy of your story. For example, if a man meets a married woman and there's strong sexual chemistry, that might be interesting. However, if the audience wants a crime story, rather than a love story, how long will viewers be satisfied with the flirtation if expecting a crime? And how much 'foreplay' is needed between the man and woman before she can convince him to murder her husband? Consider how *Double Indemnity* (1944) would work if told in a strictly linear fashion – would it be as gripping? Opening with insurance salesman Walter Neff's confession that he killed 'Dietrichson' tells us whodunit, even if we haven't met the victim yet. He then goes on to tell us his motive: a woman and money, but he didn't get either. We flash back in time and meet the femme fatale – Mrs Dietrichson – who is very interested in getting her husband insured. It's clear from the beginning that this is a murder story, not a simple romance, and we want to find out how Neff, an ordinary guy, is persuaded to kill Dietrichson. Neff himself guides us through the story, his voiceover smoothing over jumps in time and character development.

Part C
Let's consider what happens when any aspect of a crime goes wrong. What action might your protagonist take? What kind of story might this lead to? Give your imagination free rein.

- Revisit your protagonist, antagonist, location and prop from Part A.

- Choose an element from the crime continuum.

- Your antagonist will betray your protagonist, leading to negative repercussions for your protagonist (arrest, injury, being pursued by other criminals, harm to his/her family). Decide what those repercussions are.

- Your protagonist wants revenge – this is his or her goal – but he or she does not want to murder the antagonist. Think of a reason why.

- Come up with a plan. Outline a scene of planning/preparation. What objects might he/she need; what is the strategy?

- Outline the plan in action. Think of at least three steps.

- What is the resolution? What happens to the antagonist? Does your protagonist feel vindicated when he/she takes revenge?

Example

Consider the film *Point Blank*. A planned heist goes wrong when Mal Reece betrays his partner, Walker, shooting him and leaving him for dead at the money drop point (Alcatraz) and running off with the dough. But Walker recovers and goes in pursuit of Reece, determined to get his share of the money back. The story is told with flashbacks. This adds to the atmosphere of the piece.

....

WHODUNIT (OR WHOSE STORY IS IT?)

'Well, this is where you came in, back at that pool again, the one I always wanted.
It's dawn now and they must have photographed me a thousand times.
Then they got a couple of pruning hooks from the garden and fished me out... ever so gently.
Funny how gentle people get with you once you're dead.'

(Joe Gillis, Sunset Boulevard)

A crime is committed and the cops are called to the scene. The jaded veteran cop presumes that the local gangster is responsible and closes his mind to all other possibilities, but the idealistic rookie thinks the gangster is innocent and is determined to find the true killer...

A classic whodunit told from the hero's point of view. But what if the same story is told from the gangster's point of view and (for once) he really isn't the culprit? He may go on a mission to clear his name and to bring the true perpetrator to justice using the skills he has gained as a successful criminal. Or, what if the story is told by a girl-next-door type who transpires to be the true perpetrator and a classic unreliable narrator? Motive is key – was she being blackmailed, driven by revenge or greed, or is she just plain evil? What if the victim is also the protagonist, as in *Sunset Boulevard* (1950)?

A very simple crime story can be approached in a variety of ways by experimenting with point of view. The line between 'good guy' and 'bad guy' might be significantly blurred if we learn more about the

WRITING AND SELLING CRIME FILM SCREENPLAYS

FIGURE 3: **WHOSE STORY IS IT?**

TYPE OF MAIN CHARACTER

Protagonist: the principle or leading character.

Antagonist: the protagonist's main opposing character or adversary.

Hero (heroine): a central character with positive qualities with whom the viewer is expected to sympathise.

Anti-hero: a central character who lacks conventional heroic qualities or whose flaws obscure more positive qualities. A more realistic approach to the hero that blurs the line between hero and villain.

Villain: a character whose criminal or evil actions or motives are important to the plot.

Anti-villain: an antagonist who isn't purely evil and is 'flawed' by positive attributes or motives; his/her goal may be for the greater good, but their means for achieving it are criminal or evil. Just as the hero may become jaded or corrupted over time, the villain may become transformed into an anti-villain.

Source: derived from Oxford Dictionaries online.

---

antagonist's motive or backstory. The 'Cluedo Approach' – presenting everyone as a suspect and allowing the audience to play detective – can also be interesting.

Akira Kurosawa's crime drama *Rashomon* (1950) neatly points out how point of view and subjectivity influences story. The film focuses on a double crime – the rape of a samurai's wife and the murder of the samurai – and the contradictory accounts of events by four witnesses: the bandit/ rapist, the samurai's wife, the dead samurai (through a medium), and a wood-cutter who found the samurai's body.

Each different story leaves us wondering who is telling the truth and, conventionally, we are led to presume that the final version presented reveals what really happened.

Figure 3 indicates how a story might change if the protagonist were a hero, an anti-hero, a villain, or an anti-villain, and how sub-genres have developed through experimentation with point of view. As revisionist stage films have blurred the line between 'hero' and 'villain' by presenting more realistic rather than black and white characters, it's useful to first revisit some definitions. It's also worth bearing in mind that this diagram is a starting point rather than a comprehensive or definitive example of crime story character types or sub-genres; it should be used creatively as a springboard for coming up with other possibilities.

EXAMPLES

The intellectual or amateur detective hero would be a character like C Auguste Dupin, Sherlock Holmes, Miss Marple or Columbo, whereas the 'anti-hero' private detective would be a hard-boiled character like Sam Spade or Mike Hammer. Detective Harry Callahan from *Dirty Harry* (1971) is an example of an anti-hero cop willing to bend the law to capture a villain. Films such as *The Departed* (2006) and *LA Confidential* (1997) contrast idealistic or anti-hero cops with corrupt cops as the villains. Giving negative traits to 'good guys' and positive traits to 'bad guys' brings both originality and a stronger sense of realism to sub-genres. Television series *The Shield* (2002–08) took the anti-hero even further by focusing on the mixed morality of a group of police detectives led by Vic Mackey who were loyal to each other (initially) but were more than happy to break the law to capture their targets and to better provide for their families; Mackey's 'strike team' operated under a similar moral code to a Mafia gang, but did very successfully enforce the law (even while lining their pockets) and, overall, seemed morally superior to their adversaries, who tended to have no regard for societal or human law. Television series *Sons of Anarchy* (2008–) focuses on a biker gang that engages in various types of criminal activity including drugs and arms smuggling, porn, 'enforcement', and murder; like gangsters, the gang are villains and have their own specific 'club rules'. Police Chief Wayne Unser is a perfectly likeable anti-hero who chooses to work with them or turn a blind eye. Walter Hill's classic gang film *The Warriors* (1979) has the Coney Island 'Warriors' on the run after straight-up villain and psycho Luther murders the charismatic, visionary Cyrus and blames them. When Warrior warlord Cleon is arrested, second-in-command anti-villain protagonist Swan meets resistance from antagonist Ajax. Ajax is more of a villain-type as he believes that being a gang member is all about macho power and fighting, whereas Swan is rebelling against the privations of his upbringing and his un-starry future. We never quite know why Swan joined a gang, but he demonstrates leadership, strategic thinking, and has a sense of ethics, which makes him empathetic. In the army, his 'warrior' mentality might get him a medal, but on the streets he is likely to get a prison sentence.

The above examples show that the line between hero, anti-hero, villain and anti-villain can be quite blurry. Maybe these are outdated terms in some ways, but they are useful to point out that the protagonist is the main character, but not necessarily a *good* character. Equally, his or her antagonist isn't evil because he or she is putting pressure on the protagonist, even if the protagonist perceives the antagonist in a negative way. Gone are the days of the heroic man-in-white as protagonist and eventual victor against the villainous man-in-black who ends up in prison or shot dead. The main character, whether good guy or bad guy, tends to be far more complex.

Further to this, a protagonist or antagonist can also change 'categories' if he or she has a transformative arc. A redemptive or reformative journey might transform a character from villain to anti-villain (and perhaps anti-hero in the sequel) whereas a corruptive journey might have the protagonist shift from (innocent) hero to anti-villain to villain. The character may not actually change his or her moral code, but their true colours might be revealed to the audience as the story progresses. In the film *Tsotsi* (2005), the protagonist Tsotsi shifts from teen gang leader to anti-villain to anti-hero, redeemed by the responsibility of caring for the infant he accidentally kidnaps and confronting his own dehumanising childhood. In *Wall Street* (1987), up and coming stockbroker Bud Fox shifts from ambitious innocent to white-collar villain to anti-villain when he learns that greed isn't always good, but corporate villain Gordon Gekko is unlikely to change much. The criminal businessmen/villain protagonists were a type often played by actor Warren William in pre-Hays Code films such as *Skyscraper Souls* (1932) in which David Dwight, a wealthy banker, swindles and financially ruins everyone he knows until he is shot to death by his mistress who has lost everything thanks to Dwight. Post stock market crash, Depression era audiences were more than sympathetic towards the mistress's revenge. The television series *Revenge* (2011–) allows us to side with revenge-driven anti-hero protagonist Emily Thorne/Amanda Clarke as her antagonists are so nasty they make her desire for revenge seem justified even if she has little regard for the law whilst pursuing her goal.

....

WRITING EXERCISE: WHODUNIT AND POV

Part A
Revisit your image kit and choose two characters, a location, and an object.

- Choose a type of crime story from Figure 2.

- Give your characters names and make one the protagonist and the other the antagonist. Write a very short character sketch of each that makes it clear why he or she is either a hero, anti-hero, villain or anti-villain.

- Design a crime that utilises characters, location, and object. Be inventive.

- Now play the protagonist and narrate a scene – the execution of the crime – in the first person (present tense).

- Narrate the same scene in the first person (present tense) from the POV of the antagonist.

In weak scripts, the antagonist or secondary characters are used as props to facilitate plot and are not fully developed as convincing characters. Writing a scene, particularly any key scenes or problem scenes, from the point of view of various characters forces the writer to really consider motivation and what is at stake for each character. This simple exercise should strengthen character interaction and make the conflict more convincing.

Part B: Redemptive or Corruptive Journey
Now take either your protagonist or antagonist and consider how the crime committed might transform your character either positively or negatively. Have your character progress through three different roles. For example, a redemptive path would see a villain transform to anti-villain, and then an anti-hero. Think of two key events that might force your character to make a decision and take action that could possibly facilitate such a transformation. Write a first-person monologue of the scenes, dwelling on the character's internal conflict, any self-deception, or personal realisations.

....

THE CRIME CONTINUUM AND
THE PROTAGONIST'S JOURNEY

Experimenting with elements from the crime continuum and with character point of view can bring an original angle to a crime story. Events pertaining to a crime may corrupt or redeem a character – plot and character have a symbiotic relationship. The protagonist needs to have a goal, which in simplest terms is either to pursue or to get away from something or someone. During this chase or escape the protagonist reacts to unexpected occurrences or events outside his or her control; makes decisions that provoke events; and normally learns something through the whole experience or 'journey'. This journey is the backbone of the film, providing structure and often following a particular pattern.

Joseph Campbell's seminal work *The Hero With a Thousand Faces* explores his concept of the monomyth, an underlying story pattern that forms the basis of myths and the oldest heroic tales from cultures around the world. Campbell noted that the hero evolves in three stages: separation, initiation and return. After leaving his ordinary world, the protagonist answers the call to adventure and descends into the underworld where he is forced to undergo a series of tests and meets a variety of archetypal figures who might be allies or enemies. This struggle transforms the protagonist, allowing him to gain access to the ultimate boon and escape the underworld. The protagonist returns a hero, bestowing the prize upon his people.

Christopher Vogler applies Campbell's idea of the mythic hero's journey to that of a film protagonist in his book *The Hero's Journey*; this paradigm seems to work very well in animation features when the protagonist typically goes on a physical journey that mirrors the internal journey of self-actualisation and maturation.

FIGURE 4: JOSEPH CAMPBELL'S MONO-MYTH PARADIGM

Separation

- **The Call to Adventure:** the call often comes from the Herald, a character who may be judged evil by others.

- **The Refusal of the Call:** the hero may refuse the call at first, then reconsider or be forced by events to go on the adventure.

- **Supernatural Aid:** a protective Mentor may help train the hero for the adventure and provide tools, weapons or amulets.

- **The Threshold Guardian/Crossing the First Threshold:** after confronting a threshold guardian, the hero descends into the 'underworld' or a new, Special World.

- **Belly of the Whale:** the hero may pass into this new world after apparently dying (swallowed by a whale or being torn asunder) and then re-emerging into the Special World/Underworld.

Initiation

- **The Road of Trials:** the hero must survive a series of challenges, obstacles and meetings with powerful archetypal figures in the Special World. He may be helped by the Mentor figure.

- **Meeting of the Goddess:** the biggest trial may involve marriage or union with a Queen or Mother figure.

- **The Temptress:** the hero may meet with and reject a seductive, treacherous female figure.

- **Atonement with the Father:** the hero must make peace with an authority figure that seems at once tyrannical and merciful.
- **Apotheosis:** the hero's idea of reality may change or he may discover a new ability or feel ready to sacrifice himself for a larger cause.
- **The Ultimate Boon:** the hero has evolved enough to be able to claim the object, skill,or knowledge that will benefit his society/homeland.

Return

- **Refusal of the Return:** the hero may refuse the call to return to the Ordinary World to bestow the Ultimate Boon on his fellow man.
- **The Magic Flight:** or the hero may be pursued by antagonistic beings that want to prevent him from returning to the Ordinary World with the Ultimate Boon.
- **Rescue from Without:** forces from the Ordinary World may need to rescue the hero who has either refused the return or is prevented from leaving the Special World with the Ultimate Boon.
- **Crossing of the Return Threshold:** the hero returns to the Ordinary World and must accept his place in it.
- **Master of Two Worlds:** the hero gains the ability to perceive both the Special World and the Ordinary World.
- **Freedom to Live:** the hero bestows the Ultimate Boon on his fellow man.

But does this journey and its various steps apply to the *anti-hero* or *villain* protagonist of a crime film – the gangster, thief, prisoner, serial killer, or even the most self-destructive film noir protagonist? If we amalgamate the crime continuum and Joseph Campbell's mono-myth paradigm, it would seem that the anti-hero either attempts to break the rules of the Special World or tries to take the fast route to the prize, thus skipping important steps of the hero's transformative journey. This cheating does not tend to end well for him or her. *Figure 5* plays around with how the anti-hero or villain might respond to the call to adventure – or might attempt such an adventure before he or she is ready. The anti-hero or villain might fall at any hurdle during the journey.

FIGURE 5: **THE ANTI-HERO'S JOURNEY**

Going Bad: Temptation to the 'Dark Side'

The Anti-hero's Ordinary World: what might drive him or her to 'go bad'/break the law? Or is it a chance event?

The Call to Adventure: the anti-hero is tempted to join in criminal activity, perhaps by 'The Herald', an evil character in the eyes of society.

Or he might organise the illicit adventure himself.

Refusal of the Call: the anti-hero refuses to join in criminal activity, which causes suffering to him or those he cares about.

The Mentor: after the anti-hero accepts the call, he meets a mentor who provides special tools, a weapon, or amulet, and advice for the 'adventure': a crime to be committed.

The Planning and Preparations for the Crime

The Crossing of the First Threshold: the anti-hero may face a challenge from a threshold guardian – a gang member or minion of the 'Big Boss' – who protects the entrance to the Underworld from outsiders/the Law and tests the anti-hero's worthiness to participate in the criminal activity. Or he receives his first challenge from a representative of the law.

The Belly of the Whale: the anti-hero survives a violent and transformative event – whether a gang initiation or attack

---

from the Law – which makes him emotionally and physically ready for the criminal activity/life.

The Road of Trials: while participating in the crime/criminal activity, the anti-hero must survive a series of challenges, obstacles, and meetings with powerful Underworld figures and agents of the Law. He may be helped by the Mentor figure. He may succumb to any of these challenges and go down in a hail of bullets.

Meeting of the Goddess: meeting a girl from the right side of the tracks or loyalty to a mother figure has the potential to reform the anti-hero.

The Temptress: a femme fatale may bring about the anti-hero's downfall.

Atonement with the Father: the anti-hero must make peace with an authority figure: a rival gang leader, an agent of the law, a family member; failure to make atonement may lead to the anti-hero's death or an audacious attempt to claim the Ultimate Boon.

The Crime is Committed

The Ultimate Boon: the anti-hero attempts to claim or steal the big prize he covets.

The Getaway

The Magic Flight: despite opposition, the anti-hero seizes the Ultimate Boon (without earning it) and must flee its guardian/the Law; the antagonistic forces may prevail and he meets his end.

Law Enforcement: Cops vs Robbers
Investigating the Crime

Apotheosis: the anti-hero's success in grabbing the Ultimate Boon leads to his pinnacle of power and glory in the Underworld where he may become a 'Godfather'.

(Or) Master of the Two Worlds: the anti-hero escapes with the Ultimate Boon and re-enters society apparently reformed.
(Or) Freedom to Live: the anti-hero gives away the Ultimate Boon (to the rightful owner, someone needy, a good cause) and reforms.

⬇ **The Trial**
⬇ **Behind Bars**
Rescue from Without: the anti-hero's refusal to re-enter law abiding society (the Ordinary World) may lead to being 'rescued' by agents of the Law and sent to trial and prison.
Refusal of the Return: the anti-hero is given the opportunity to reform and re-enter law-abiding society, but refuses. He may attempt a prison break or become a 'Boss' on the inside.

⬇ **The Ex-Con: Reformed or a Repeat Offender?**
The Crossing of the Return Threshold: the anti-hero returns to the Ordinary World and must accept its laws.
(Or) Refusal of the Return: the anti-hero is given the opportunity to reform and re-enter law-abiding society, but refuses and returns to the 'Underworld'.

WRITING EXERCISE: JOURNEY TO THE CRIMINAL UNDERWORLD

- Create an anti-hero or villain protagonist. Give him or her a name, age and basic background along with at least six key character traits, three positive and three negative.

- Think of a crime he or she might get involved in.

- Put your protagonist through an anti-hero's journey, choosing options from each section of the crime continuum until you feel his or her journey should end, whether as a redeemed character... or in a hail of bullets, lost in the underworld forever.

BASIC CRIME GENRE **PROTOCOL**

'Each crime scene is different and may require a different approach to processing the scene. However there is a basic crime scene protocol that should be adhered to in all crime scenes. These basic functions or tasks are as follows: interview, examine, photograph, sketch, process.'

> (Illinois State Police M/Sgt Hayden B Baldwin,
> Crime Scene Processing Protocol)

What does an audience expect from the crime genre? Most obviously, the story will involve a crime, even if we do not see the crime committed or the immediate aftermath of the crime. Different sub-genres will focus on various aspects of different types of crimes and an audience will have specific expectations for each sub-genre. If these expectations are not met, the film may be considered unsatisfying. A useful approach to thinking about sub-genre conventions is outlined in Ken Dancyger and Jeff Rush's *Alternative Approaches to Scriptwriting*. The following is a variation on the points they suggest should be considered.

The Protagonist: The most general qualities of the main character tend to be the same within a specific genre/sub-genre. Is he or she active or passive; realistic or unrealistic; hero or victim? Character traits, goal, and psychological need should also be examined. For example: in the Western the protagonist tends to be heroic whereas the main character in the horror film is usually a potential victim.

Comedy characters are typically less realistic than revisionist stage police story characters.

The Antagonist: The general qualities of the antagonist must also be considered. His or her nature is linked to the genre's level of realism and to the qualities of the protagonist. If the protagonist is heroic, as in an action-adventure film or Western, the antagonist tends to be very powerful and evil or the battle between them would lack interest. If the genre is nightmarish (horror film and film noir) the antagonist is equally extreme. It's also relevant to consider secondary characters – are they helpers or hinderers? The sympathetic friend in the rom com tends to bear little resemblance to the false friend in a thriller or film noir, genres in which it's never clear who the protagonist can truly trust.

Type of Plot or Story Pattern: Certain types of plots and story patterns are normally associated with particular genres/sub-genres. The fate of the main character will differ in accordance with genre expectations. Boy meets girl, boy loses girl, boy wins girl back is the classic rom com story pattern at its most basic. A gangster story follows the rise and fall of the gangster whereas a detective story begins with the discovery of a crime, followed by the investigation, normally concluding with the mystery being solved.

Certain events tend to occur within each act of the film and key plot points are often of a similar nature in each sub-genre. For example, the inciting incident (sometimes called the 'disturbance', catalytic event, or the element of chaos) in Act I disrupts the main character's ordinary world and sets him or her on the journey of Act II. The murder of a friend, love at first sight, a kidnapping, the sighting of an alien spaceship, the appearance of a ghost – each of these inciting incidences suggests a particular genre and raises a specific dramatic question. The same applies to the 'point of no return' or 'locking in point', which typically occurs just before the end of Act I. The inciting incident of a heist movie might be a loan shark's ultimatum to the protagonist: repay his loan or die. The point of no return could be the offer of one last job and the decision to take it. Equally, these two events could be reversed. The reformed thief is invited to participate in a heist, but refuses. The point of no return is the loan shark's ultimatum, which forces the protagonist to agree to the job.

An audience will expect a particular type of resolution in Act III for a genre. Does it tend to be positive or negative? Does the main character reach his or her goal and discover what they need emotionally? Melodrama might be unhappy or tragic but, in a rom com, the boy typically gets the girl. Filmmakers have experimented with breaking this rom com 'rule', typically unsuccessfully as an audience expects a more uplifting resolution from the genre.

Note: to keep things simple, I will refer to the classic three-act structure rather than four acts, or eight sequences, or even more complex structural breakdowns.

Narrative Style: Does the genre have more objective or subjective drama? Are particular activities associated with the genre/sub-genre? For example, a Western usually features gun-fights and travel or chases on horseback; the hero is a man comfortable in the wilderness, with expert survival skills. Thrillers, heists and film noirs tend to have a high ratio of violence and an aggressive 'show down'. In melodramas, the violence is primarily emotional with the underlying tension that it might turn physical.

Timeframe/Pace: The passing of time is also a key factor when considering genre conventions. Does the story take place within one day or over a more expansive timeframe? Is there a ticking clock and deadline pressure? Is the pace frenetic or slower? Westerns often have expansive timeframes. In film noir the protagonist is often running out of time both in terms of plot and his interest in life. Action/adventure and thrillers tend to have a specific deadline or ticking clocks. A ticking clock may also be used as an obstacle in a comedy or romance. A key question in a biopic is how to compress time. The scope of the narrative should be considered in connection with the main character's goal and stakes.

Tone: Is the story's tone realistic, 'heightened', or completely fantasti-cal? Audiences expect a specific tone for most genres unless the film is a parody and then the genre's usual tone might also be a source of comedy. War and crime stories tend to be serious and realistic in tone, thrillers are suspenseful, and horror films nightmarish. The action-adventure film is fantastical in terms of the hero's physical feats, as is the musical with characters bursting into song and dance. Screwball comedies and satire have an ironic tone; love stories strive to be emotionally involving, whereas rom coms are more playful.

Setting and Mise-en-scène: The setting of a story includes the time period, location, and the circumstances in which it takes place. Broadly speaking, the setting provides the main backdrop for the story. In some cases, setting becomes a character itself and can set the tone of a story. *Mise-en-scène* refers to everything that appears before the camera and its arrangement – sets, props, actors, costumes and lighting. These elements are relevant to specific genres. For example, film noir is recognisable from dark, rainy, urban landscapes and an ominous atmosphere. A fantasy film has a more extraordinary setting or 'otherworldly' location.

Each crime sub-genre has its own specific conventions. Remember that the tropes noted in the brief overviews in the following chapters apply to the <u>classical stage</u> of that sub-genre; these are the conventions that writers experiment with to surprise an audience and bring something fresh to a genre. The most obvious change is to make the classic male protagonist – be it cop, detective, gangster, expert thief, prison inmate, or serial killer – a female, particularly if the woman is typically a victim in that genre. As already noted, these revisionist films reflect changes in society. A writer might also consider other defining factors such as the protagonist's sexuality, ethnicity, religion, or socio-economic background when updating the genre story. Some examples of revisionist films or approaches will be noted after the classical stage conventions, which may seem dated to those accustomed to revisionist stage films.

THE MASTER OF DEDUCTION:
THE DETECTIVE SUB-GENRE

'Do you promise that your detectives shall well and truly detect the crimes presented to them using those wits which it may please you to bestow upon them and not placing reliance on nor making use of Divine Revelation, Feminine Intuition, Mumbo Jumbo, Jiggery-Pokery, Coincidence, or Act of God?'

(British Detection Club oath, written by GK Chesterton)

The detective sub-genre focuses on an investigator's attempts to solve a crime, typically a high-stakes crime like murder. The sleuth may be a highly objective professional; a hobbyist who revels in the intellectual challenge; or an amateur with a personal agenda. The focus is on the mystery of the crime to be solved – 'whodunit', why and how – and the unique skills of the detective. It's crucial that the reader engages in the pleasure of solving the mystery, almost playing sidekick to the sleuth. These basic conventions were established in detective literature over 150 years ago and provided a basic 'formula' for detective films, which were first made in the early years of cinema. Studios embraced popular detective story adaptations as they came with a ready-made audience.

A screenwriter wishing to write in the detective sub-genre must be able to construct a gripping mystery that keeps the audience guessing, without resorting to cheats. The solution to the mystery must be hidden in plain sight so that, when a viewer thinks back to the beginning of the film, the clues were all there. A screenwriter must also be able to construct a fascinating detective, someone we wish to go on a sleuthing expedition with.

PRIMITIVE STAGE DETECTIVE FILMS: THE FILM SLEUTH'S LITERARY ROOTS

'The best place to hide anything is in plain view.'

(C Auguste Dupin, *The Purloined Letter*)

Edgar Allan Poe is credited with writing some of the earliest detective stories with his tales *The Murders in the Rue Morgue* (1841), *The Mystery of Marie Roget* (1842) and *The Purloined Letter* (1844); his 'ratiocinator', the Chevalier C Auguste Dupin, is the prototype private detective. The mysterious Frenchman assists the Prefect of the Paris police with difficult cases, but is an independent agent. Dupin is highly intelligent, observant, rational, rather condescending, well-versed in esoteric studies, and deemed peculiar by most. He is solitary but for a single friend, the unnamed narrator of the tales, and lives on his own in a decayed mansion in Paris, which indicates some reversal in his financial fortunes. That dark blot on his past is never explained. Poe's ratiocinator with his nocturnal habits, meerschaum pipe and supportive sidekick inspired the creation of Sherlock Holmes and numerous detectives of both sexes. *The Murders in the Rue Morgue* was first filmed in France in 1914 and re-adapted for the screen a further three times after that.

Female detectives were established in literature not long after Kate Warne became the first female hired by the Pinkerton Detective Agency in 1856, well before Sherlock Holmes and Dr Watson appeared in print in 1887. Marian Halcombe undertakes an investigation in Wilkie Collins's *The Woman in White* (1860) as does Eleanor Vane in *Eleanor's Victory* (1863) by Mary Elizabeth Braddon. Mrs G in *The Female Detective* by Andrew J Forrester Jr is often noted as the first female detective in fiction, quickly followed by Mrs Paschal in *The*

Experiences of a Lady Detective (1864). In 1926, Agatha Christie introduced her sleuth Miss Marple, the protagonist of 12 crime novels and 20 short stories, many of which have been adapted for television and the big screen.

But the most popular fictional detective with filmmakers is Sir Arthur Conan Doyle's Sherlock Holmes, who has appeared as a character (in many forms) in well over 200 film and television projects to date. Silent short film *Sherlock Holmes Baffled*, made by Arthur Marvin and initially released in 1900, is often considered the earliest detective film. The first detective film serial, *Nick Carter, le Roi des Détectives*, was produced in France in 1908 by Société Française des Films Éclair; the collection of six short films was directed by Victorin-Hippolyte Jasset. The serial was inspired by *Nick Carter Weekly*, one of the many pulp detective magazines produced by Street & Smith publications, but Nick Carter's adventures were set in Paris.

CLASSICAL STAGE DETECTIVE FILMS:
THE GOLDEN AGE OF DETECTIVE LITERATURE AND FILMS

'A really good detective never gets married.'

(Raymond Chandler)

During the 1920s and 1930s, often considered the golden age of detective literature, rules for writing in the genre were compiled by aficionados, such as SS Van Dine's 'Twenty rules for writing detective stories' (1928) and Ronald Knox's 'Decalogue' (1929). Inevitably, classic detective film tropes were influenced by these 'commandments', as many classic detective films also had literary roots. Pulp detective fiction gained a wide audience with reasonably priced paperbacks and detective story magazines that gave a number of talented writers an outlet for their work. Hollywood studios were quick to buy up the rights to popular detective stories, knowing there would be a ready-made audience for adaptations of best-selling pulp fiction. SS Van Dine's Philo Vance detective novels were the inspiration for 15 feature films (1929– 47); *The Canary Murder Case*, produced by Paramount Pictures in 1929, was the first detective talkie. Erle Stanley Gardner's Perry Mason novels were adapted into six murder mystery whodunits (1934–37) by Warner Brothers. *The Thin Man* murder mystery series (1934–47), based on *The Thin Man* novel by Dashiell Hammett and produced by Metro-Goldwyn-Mayer, was witty with elements of screwball. Film serials of the time also featured female detectives. Warner Bros made nine films from 1936–39 featuring news reporter and amateur detective Torchy Blane. RKO Pictures made six films from 1932 to 1937 based on Stuart Palmer's schoolteacher detective Hildegarde Withers.

The 1940s brought the iconic tough-guy detective to the screen. Dashiell Hammett, inspired by his time working for the Pinkerton Agency, introduced the hard-boiled 'gumshoe' Sam Spade in his detective novel *The Maltese Falcon* (1930), which was adapted into a film starring Humphrey Bogart in 1941. Raymond Chandler further popularised the hard-boiled detective story through short stories published in *Black Mask* and through a series of novels featuring tough private eye Philip Marlowe, a number of which were adapted into motion pictures such as *The Big Sleep* (1946) and *Murder, My Sweet* (1944). Mickey Spillane continued the hard-boiled detective tradition with his first novel *I, the Jury* (1947) featuring private detective Mike Hammer, which was adapted for the screen in 1953, as were several of his other best-selling novels. Mike Hammer was also the protagonist of several television series, beginning in 1958.

CLASSIC DETECTIVE SUB-GENRE CONVENTIONS

'You're so bright working on your own, you penny-ante gumshoe. You thought you saw something big and you tried to horn in.'

**(Police Lieutenant Pat Murphy to private detective Mike Hammer,
Kiss Me Deadly)**

'It may irritate you, Inspector, but sometimes women have superior minds. You'll simply have to accept it.'

(Miss Marple, *Murder Most Foul*, 1964)

Protagonist: The master of ratiocination sleuth. The classic cinema detective operates outside the police force as an unaffiliated adviser; through his own private agency; or as a hobby. There are, of course, police detectives, but the focus of this detective/police story hybrid is enforcing the law whereas a detective story may simply focus on the 'puzzle' to be solved. This differentiation between private and police detective is often critical in terms of the plot and the rules of an investigation, particularly as private investigators do not always follow the letter of the law and seem driven by a somewhat obsessive need to unravel any mystery. A police detective may take liberties with the law, but he or she risks punishment from his superiors for failing in his duty. With this differentiation in mind, police detective films will be examined along with police stories.

The detective's greatest weapons are acute observation, deductive reasoning, knowledge of human motive, and a passion for solving intellectual puzzles. There are several classic types of detective, which spring from sleuths popularised in literature. The male detective tends to be something of an outsider, an urbane, cynical character with a whiff of the lone cowboy about him. The intellectual or gentleman detective may have outsider status due to limited social skills, certain eccentric qualities, extreme objectivity, and a hyper-focus on intellectual pursuits. The street-smart, hard-boiled private eye finds it difficult to sustain personal relationships due to his over-exposure to violent crime and jaded attitude. He may have lost a job with the police for a personal vice or an inability to follow the rules. Cynicism rather than objectivity makes him aloof.

Unlike some other crime sub-genres, there is a classic tradition of female protagonists, as established in detective stories and novels, typically called 'cosy mysteries'. Classic female detectives tend to live alone in a small town, village, or suburban setting, what might be considered a more domestic environment. While they have all of the intellectual skills of the male detective, their loner status, eccentricity and skills were initially given negative labels such as busybody spinster, meddler or snoop, even if their intellect proved them intellectually superior to the criminal. Both the male and female detectives may have an unusual hobby that flags their obsession with detail, intelligence, and ability to enjoy their own company.

Antagonist: The perpetrator of the crime. The antagonist tends to keep his or her identity concealed for as long as possible, hoping to escape detection and get away with the crime. There is a subtle battle of wits at play with the protagonist; the perpetrator may have done everything possible to conceal their connection to the crime and crime scene by covering his or her tracks or hiding evidence. There must be a genuine struggle between the protagonist and antagonist. The more powerful the protagonist, the stronger the antagonist should be. A criminal mastermind is a worthy foe for a renowned detective. This classic arch-villain is typically male, arrogant about his intellect, ruthless, and believes himself superior to all others – an 'evil genius'. In other words, he is something of a sociopath/psychopath. He may react with violence, hoping to deter the detective, but there remains an element of 'whodunit' to these threats. The audience may know the identity of the perpetrator before the protagonist, or the detective, knows 'whodunit' but needs to gather evidence to prove the perpetrator's guilt. A twist on the male mastermind is the female villain. She may hide behind a domestic façade, inherit power within a criminal family, or might be a more powerful extension of the femme fatale. Secondary antagonists may be agents of the law who want the detective off the case.

Type of Plot or Story Pattern: The focus of the story is solving a mystery associated with a crime; this may be working out who the perpetrator is or the specifics of how they committed the crime. Apprehending the criminal may be handed over to the police.

- *Act I:* The inciting incident is usually the perpetration or discovery of a crime, or else the detective is approached with the details of the crime to solve. Typically it isn't clear 'whodunit' or the most obvious suspect protests his or her innocence. The point of no return or 'locking in point' is the detective's decision to take the case or to get involved if an amateur sleuth.

- *Act II:* Focuses on the investigation and intellectual exercise of ascertaining how the crime was committed, the motive, and the identity of the culprit. There may be numerous suspects. Clues are examined, evidence is gathered, and red herrings complicate the challenge. If the protagonist wins the intellectual battle against the antagonist too easily, the story will lack jeopardy. Planting clues that will pay off in the mystery's solution is key. The audience's goal is to unravel the mystery along with, or slightly before, the detective. If the clues are too opaque, or it's much too obvious who the perpetrator is, audience pleasure is undermined.

- *The Midpoint:* Something surprising may be discovered that sends the investigation in a new direction. For example, the most obvious suspect is proved innocent or becomes a victim; the evidence or events may bring a whole new layer of complication to the story.

- *End of Act II:* The identity of the perpetrator might be suspected, but his or her guilt must be proven or the perpetrator must be located. It may seem that the detective will never unravel the mystery or catch the culprit.

- *Act III:* Typically the showdown. The perpetrator is discovered and confronted. The detective pieces together the evidence and neatly explains whodunit, how, when and why, proving his or her superior intellectual skills. While it should not be obvious to the audience whodunit or, if the perpetrator's identity is known, *how* they did it, the clues that lead the detective to solve the mystery should be hidden in plain sight if the film is viewed again. The audience expects the detective to unravel the puzzle. In a twist, the perpetrator may escape capture or manage to avoid incarceration, but that tends to be an error on the part of the police or a flaw in the legal system rather than the detective's incompetence. Or sequel alert: the antagonist is shown to be a criminal mastermind who will engage in further intellectual battle with the detective.

- *Resolution:* the detective retreats back into his or her own world after the investigation.

Narrative Style: An investigation is expected, as is a battle of wits. A crime scene is established, isolated with demarcation tape, photographed, and examined for evidence (or the equivalent procedure for the historical period in which the film is set). The detective sifts through all evidence gathered, searching for clues as to the identity of the perpetrator. Tools of the trade vary, depending on the story's era and specific expertise of the detective. For example, early detectives relied on magnifying glasses whereas the modern detective will expect to dust for prints and to assist in the search for a variety of trace evidence. Interviewing witnesses and grilling suspects are expected scenes as is the final showdown when the detective confronts the perpetrator and proves his or her guilt by explaining how the detective pieced together the clues. If the detective is a hard-boiled private eye, the showdown may feature a gun fight or violent pursuit whereas the more cerebral detectives demonstrate their intellectual prowess without violence.

Timeframe/Pace: An investigation has something of a built-in ticking clock, with the timeframe often determined by the nature of the crime. It may be presumed that the perpetrator will strike again if he or she isn't caught. If the protagonist is a detective for hire, the client will be pressing for a quick resolution. Equally, the detective does not wish to be defeated by his adversary in the battle of wits. The complications of Act II may reveal that the case is more complex than originally presumed. Pressure mounts as the detective struggles to either identify the perpetrator, locate the guilty party, or prove beyond a shadow of a doubt that he or she is guilty, and the ticking clock accelerates in Act III, when nearing the 'final showdown at high noon'.

Tone: Mystery and suspense are key. The super-sleuth tends to be several steps ahead of the audience, which adds to the sense of mystery. It is important that the audience feels clever if unravelling the mystery at the same time or before the detective; if the detective seems incompetent, the audience will disconnect. Equally, if the mystery is too opaque and clues don't add up, or twists are a cheat rather than clever, the audience is either lost or made to feel stupid, which again causes a disconnection with the story. Dramatic irony might be used to raise tension if the detective is battling a criminal mastermind, particularly if he or she is manipulating the evidence or witnesses or finding ways to misdirect the detective.

Setting and Mise-en-scène: Setting and mise-en-scène are influenced by the protagonist himself. Hard-boiled detective and private-eye stories typically take place in an urban environment, if only due to the higher level of crime in cities. The focus is on the city's underbelly and the prevalence of criminal activity adds to the detective's jaded persona. Suburban or rural crime may be all the more shocking given the presumed safety of the environment, which adds tension. As noted previously, this may be where amateur detectives flourish due to the lack of professional or competent detectives. A detective, by the nature of his or her expertise, may be called to an unknown environment to solve a crime; his or her 'fish out of water' status adds complications and jeopardy. Derelict environments, concealed places, darkness, shadowy locations add to the sense of mystery and danger. The iconic accoutrements of the hard-boiled detective are belted raincoat, Fedora (or similar), gun, box of matches, cigarettes, and a bottle of the hard stuff stashed in a desk drawer or filing cabinet.

REVISIONIST DETECTIVE FILM STORIES: NEW WAYS OF SLEUTHING

'Do you doubt what's in the reports about me? What do they say when you sum them up?
They say I'm insane. No, it's okay. You can nod because it's true. I am insane.'

(Lisbeth Salander, *The Girl With the Dragon Tattoo*)

While female investigators were the protagonists of short stories and books since the early days of the detective genre, they did not take on the characteristics of more hard-boiled private eyes until much later in detection fiction. PD James created the first British female private investigator, Cordelia Gray, in 1972; Sue Grafton's Kinsey Millhone and Sara Paretsky's VI Warshawski, both introduced in 1982, are tougher types, cut from a similar cloth. Millhone lost her parents in a car crash when she was five years old; Warshawski lost both her parents to illness before she was twenty-six. Both are very independent with loner tendencies, single, without children, and sexually active on their own terms. They are physically fit, adept with a weapon, unconcerned about their looks but scrub up well, and have a penchant for junk food. Lisbeth Salander, protagonist of Stieg Larsson's *The Girl with the Dragon Tattoo*, its sequels *The Girl Who Played With Fire* and *The Girl Who Kicked the Hornet's Nest*, the Swedish film adaptations and the Hollywood remakes, has similar qualities, but is even more hard-boiled and blurs the border between private investigator and criminal. She lives by her own moral code and her character is arguably even more compelling than the mystery to be unravelled.

As previously noted, the success of serialised pulp detective stories led to their adaptation into film serials and then television detective series, featuring both private investigators such as Mike Hammer and police detectives like Sergeant Joe Friday from radio and television serial *Dragnet*. This in turn led to a new type of detective series featuring an independent specialist or expert who assists the police but is not a member of the police force, rather like C Auguste Dupin. Examples include Rick Castle, mystery writer, in *Castle*; Charlie Eppes, mathematical genius, in *Numb3rs*; Patrick Jane, fake mind-reader, in *The Mentalist*; Allison DuBois, psychic, in *Medium*; and Nicola and Charlie Buchanan, crime scene cleaners, in Australian comedy/crime series *Mr and Mrs Murder*. Lisbeth Salander, computer savant, might also be considered such an independent expert, albeit assisting a journalist rather than the police and with a thoroughly personal agenda. The independent specialist's expertise brings fresh expectations regarding narrative style – what are the tools of the expert's trade? What are his or her specific skills? And how does his or her technique, personality and approach to the mystery compare with that of the agents of the law? In other words, what makes this particular protagonist special and memorable?

Any of the other classical stage detective conventions can be experimented with to bring something unexpected to the sub-genre. Detective story conventions can also be blended with conventions from another genre to create an interesting hybrid that may eventually become another sub-genre. For example, setting a detective story in the future might require a mix of detective and science fiction or science fantasy conventions. A detective story set in the distant past will have a very specific story world and characters defined by their time period. Consider *The Name of the Rose* (1986), based on Umberto Eco's novel. A detective story mixed with a Western would need to embrace conventions from both genres. An example of a real-life cowboy detective is Charles A Siringo who worked for the Pinkerton Agency. Television series *Hec Ramsey* (1972–74) featured a detective in the Wild West at the end of the nineteenth century. Alan Parker's *Angel Heart* (1987) mixes detective story and supernatural horror, as does HBO movie *Cast a Deadly Spell* (1991) with private eye Harry P Lovecraft, whose name pays homage to horror writer HP Lovecraft; it's set in a fictional 1948 Los Angeles where everyone (except Lovecraft) uses magic. *Devil in a Blue Dress* (1995) is also set in Los Angeles in 1948 and features an African-American hard-boiled detective, bringing issues of race into a classic hard-boiled detective story. *The Singing Detective* mixes musical and detective fantasy in Dennis Potter's 1986 miniseries and the 2003 feature film adaptation.

A FARCICAL INVESTIGATION: THE PARODY STAGE

Lou Peckinpaugh: 'Your husband's dead a little over an hour and you're already dressed in black? How long you had that outfit waiting in the closet?'
Georgia Merkle: 'You're wrong. I just bought it. There's an all-night widow shop at Fifth and Geary.'

(*The Cheap Detective*, 1978)

The detective sub-genre is ripe for comic spoofing given the recognisable traits of the protagonist and the objective of solving a mystery, with a focus on motive and method; films parodying detective story conventions were being made while the genre was in its golden age. Buster Keaton's *Sherlock Jr* (1924) is one of the first detective comedies. Classic detective parodies made a few years later are Abbott and Costello's *Who Done It?* (1942); *Abbott and Costello Meet the Invisible Man* (1951); the Bowery Boys' *Hard Boiled Mahoney* (1947); and their *Private Eyes* (1953). The 1970s saw a spate of detective parodies including *The Adventure of Sherlock Holmes' Smarter Brother* (1975) with Gene Wilder and Marty Feldman and Neil Simon's *Murder by Death* (1976) and *The Cheap Detective* (1978), which spoofed Agatha Christie mysteries. Chevy Chase made three detective parodies: *Foul Play* (1978), *Fletch* (1985) and *Fletch Lives* (1989). Woody Allen hero-worships the archetypal hard-boiled detective in *Play It Again, Sam* (1972) and in his mystery-comedy *Manhattan Murder Mystery* (1993) amateur sleuths stumble across a murder with comical consequences. David O Russell's *I Heart Huckabees* (2004) features two existential detectives hired to uncover the meaning of life. Mixing the tough guy detective façade with a bumbling, inept character seems a favourite recipe for spoofing the sub-genre; the challenge for a writer is to add a new ingredient, perhaps through the dialogue, bizarre murders, or peculiar crime scenes. We might find the detective ridiculous, but invariably he takes him or herself very seriously.

......

WRITING EXERCISE: THE MAKING OF AN AMATEUR DETECTIVE

The key to any great detective film, series or novel is to create a memorable protagonist, worthy of sequels. Revisit your image kit to stretch your imagination.

Part A

- Choose a character that one would not immediately associate with being a detective. Consider why that might be: age, looks, dress sense? Give him or her a name.

- Write a short biography: where she or he grew up, where they live now, family background, education, job/former job, 'significant other' status, any pets, habitual attire, and so on.

- Consider your detective's character:
  i. Give him or her three positive and three negative traits.
  ii. What trait does she or he admire most in others?
  iii. What trait does she or he dislike most in others?
  iv. Give your detective a hobby that they are rather obsessive about; what makes them passionate about this pursuit?

- Choose a second character from your image kit. This is the murder victim who happens to be a neighbour of your detective. Give him or her a name.

- The inciting incident: your detective's neighbour is found dead. The police decide that the circumstances are not suspicious – it is not murder. Your detective knows that the police are wrong. Something about the circumstances of the death is completely out of character for the victim. (State what that is.)

- The proof: your detective will (eventually) solve the mystery of the neighbour's murder because of a vital clue, which is related to your detective's hobby. For example, if your detective is an avid gardener, the clue might have something to do with a poisonous plant mixed in with the victim's salad. Many mystery writers work out the ending for their story/investigation first, then figure out the twists and turns to get to that stage, misdirecting the audience/reader along the way.

- Pick three more characters from your image kit. These are your suspects. Give them names and write down some basic information about each such as age, job, sexual orientation, marital status, and so on. Decide why your detective initially suspects each and then give them an interesting alibi – something the suspect might not wish his or her neighbours to know about them.

Have fun with it. Think about all the eccentric, unusual, damaged amateur or private detectives in literature and film and why the best are so memorable. Experiment with tone – is it hard-boiled, whimsical, funny or serious, and how does your story change if you try a very different tone?

Part B

Write a monologue from the victim's point of view as he or she is being inspected and prodded at the crime scene and 'overhears' the conflicting theories of the investigating police team and the detective. The monologue should take into account his or her frustration with the investigation and recall precisely whodunit, how, when, where, and why (if the victim knows) as he or she contrasts the truth with the ludicrous theories. Again, consider tone. If you write the monologue in a comical tone, try rewriting it with an aggressive tone to see how it changes the characterisation.

....

TO PROTECT AND TO SERVE:
THE POLICE STORY SUB-GENRE

'On my honour, I will never betray my badge, my integrity, my character, or the public trust.
I will always have the courage to hold myself and others accountable for our actions.
I will always uphold the constitution, my community, and the agency I serve.'

(The US Law Enforcement Oath of Honor)

The Boys in Blue, law and order, cops and robbers, upholding the law, behind the badge – all phrases associated with police stories. The key focus of this sub-genre is the conflict between those who uphold the law and those who break it, and it's the cop's mission to restore the status quo of law and order, following a specific set of procedures that define 'the rules'.

Understanding the difference between private detective and police detective in a police procedural is crucial for a screenwriter in order to write a convincing police story. Just as the private or amateur detective focuses on solving the riddle of the mystery, the policeman or police detective's primary aim is to uphold the law and catch the criminal. It's their duty and also what drives them if a 'good cop'. Therefore, a screenwriter needs to be able to convincingly depict the day-to-day activities of an agent of the law, whether a policeman, forensic specialist, or other type of state-employed criminal investigator, and to understand their methodology and any rules they must follow during an investigation. Failure to do the proper research will result in work that lacks credibility and realism, which contradicts the ethos of the genre.

PRIMITIVE STAGE POLICE STORIES:
TIN STAR TO SILVER BADGE - CHASING THE BAD GUY

'Remember, we, the law, will beat them because right is on our side – and that makes a big difference.'

(Marshal Sam Hughes, *The Great Manhunt*)

Some of the earliest American films featuring police officers were made by pioneer directors Wallace McCutcheon and Edwin S Porter. Wallace McCutcheon's *How They Rob Men in Chicago* (1900) is a simple tale of thuggery and police corruption. When an elderly gentleman is robbed, the thief inadvertently leaves some of his loot behind on his victim's body; a cop comes along and takes the money, leaving the victim where he is. McCutcheon and Porter worked together to make *Desperate Encounter Between Burglar and Police* (1905) and *Police Chasing Scorching Auto* (1905), which are little more than chase sequences, early prototypes for the de rigueur pursuit scenes in police films. Their collaboration, *Life of an American Policeman* (1905), was a positive if slightly dull depiction of police officers at work being kind to street urchins and saving lives. Publicity for the film stated that all the valorous events in the film were re-enactments and two shows were held to benefit the Police Relief Fund. Porter is credited with making the first Western with his film *The Great Train Robbery* (1903), which set the basic pattern followed by subsequent 'marshal story' Westerns and police stories: a crime is committed, the perpetrator is pursued, retribution is enforced. Marshal stories deal with issues of law and order – either the lawman is sent to rid a terrorised frontier town of the bad guys, or the outlaws arrive guns ablaze and the lawman must prove he is worthy of the tin star on his chest that symbolises his authority. The same applies to the policeman patrolling his beat – his badge shows that he represents the law and has the authority to defend 'his town' from criminals. In many ways, early Westerns laid the groundwork for classic police stories. The conflict between the men-in-white and men-in-black leads up to a showdown at high noon where either law and order or chaos will prevail. And, while we must believe that evil might overwhelm good, the law must come out on top, even if the hero sacrifices himself.

The detective story also influenced the development of the police story. Unsurprisingly, some of the most popular police detective stories on screen are based on pulp fiction agents of the law whose badges gave them crucial powers not held by the amateur detectives; while the amateur detective might convincingly solve a case, he or she has no authority to make an arrest (beyond a citizen's arrest) or to shoot an armed and dangerous criminal. The police detective has this authority and can truly conclude the case. Even so, early police detective films focused on solving the crime and apprehending the criminal, rather than police procedure.

An example is police detective Charlie Chan of the Honolulu police force who first appeared in Earl Derr Biggers's 1925 novel *The Glass Key*. The focus of the Charlie Chan stories is his ability to solve mysteries rather than his work within the Honolulu police precinct; the Charlie Chan stories were ground-breaking, however, in featuring a Chinese protagonist who is a hero and an agent of the law rather than the negative stereotype of evil villain from the Orient. Police detective Chan proved to be popular with readers, prompting Fox Film Corporation's B-picture unit to make a series of 28 Charlie Chan films commencing in 1929 and Monogram Pictures to make 17 more from 1944 to 1949. Charlie Chan films were also made in Spanish and Chinese, and the American films were screened in China, apparently to great success. Charlie Chan was humble, honourable, highly logical, observant, and philosophical, with a knack for pithy aphorisms and countering racist remarks with wit, even if his command of the English language wasn't 100 per cent. He divides viewers; some believe that he is a positive character whereas others think he is an offensive stereotype. Whether ground-breaking hero or stereotype, however, the specifics of his character had an influence on future police detectives.

The police story began to move further away from the independent detective story when novels by former cops began to be published. Just as Dashiell Hammett's time working at the Pinkerton Agency was hands-on research for his hard-boiled detective stories, novels by former cops gave a new veracity to police stories. Former New York City Police Commissioner Richard Enright wrote *Vultures in the Dark* and *The Borrowed Shield*, published in 1925. Former police officer Leslie T White was author of 1937 novels *Harness Bull* and *Homicide*. *V as in Victim* (1945), written by Lawrence Treat, is an early police procedural. Even more important in the US was the popularity of semi-documentary films, which were basically re-enactments of true crime stories, made with the co-operation of the police actually involved in the case. The filmmakers behind these semi-documentaries tried to show police work authentically, rather like present day crime reconstruction shows. Examples of these films are *T-Men* (1947), *The Naked City* (1948), *The Street With No Name* (1948) and *He Walked by Night* (1948). Then Jack Webb, who had a role in *He Walked by Night*, had a brainstorm...

CLASSICAL STAGE POLICE STORIES: PULP, POLICE AND PROCEDURALS

'Ladies and gentlemen: the story you are about to see is true. Only the names have been changed to protect the innocent.'

(Opening Narration, *Dragnet*)

Jack Webb believed that the semi-documentary police film format would work on radio and his radio series *Dragnet* hit the airwaves in 1949; the successful show made the transition to television in 1951. The tone of *Dragnet* was heavily influenced by the pulp fiction of Hammett, Chandler and Cain. Los Angeles police detective Joe Friday introduced the crime and then guided the audience through the police procedure that led to the discovery and apprehension of the criminal. Each episode began with the ominous comment that the story was a true one, followed by the now iconic line: *'Only the names have been changed to protect the innocent.'* The time and place of the crime were also noted and the show always concluded with 'justice being served' by the *Dragnet* team. *The Lineup* was another police drama series focusing on procedure that began on radio in 1950 and transitioned to television in 1954, produced in co-operation with the San Francisco Police Department. The basic structure of these series has influenced many subsequent classic cop shows: a crime is committed, the police investigate, justice prevails. The format particularly suited the television episode; finding new crimes to focus on was not much of a problem, but the police detective had to be compelling enough to follow on a weekly basis. These two classic television series also had an influence on literature. When Anthony Boucher reviewed Ed McBain's *Cop Hater* in his *New York Times* column (29 April 1956), he noted that the 'police-routine novel' was patterned after semi-documentary television series such as *Dragnet*. A number of McBain's novels were adapted into feature films: *King's Ransom* (1959) relocated to Tokyo and made by Akira Kurosawa as *High and Low* (1963); *Ten Plus One* (1963) set in the French Riviera and re-titled *Without Apparent Motive* (1972); or *Blood Relatives* (1974) adapted by Claude Chabrol as *Les Liens de Sang* (1978). And so, crime literature that was influenced by television in turn re-invigorated police genre films and television series.

The 'police procedural' really came into its own in the 1970s, and the popularity of the sub-genre made it essential for writers to come up with an innovative approach to the format. An obvious way to do this was to create an unusual and intriguing protagonist. Just as Charlie Chan's ethnicity and aphorisms made him memorable, cops with specific characteristics, physical traits and verbal trademarks brought an original angle to classical stage 1970s police procedurals. A few examples are Greek-American NYC police detective Lieutenant Theo

Kojak with his trademark bald head and tootsie-pops; New York City undercover cop Tony Baretta who lived in a run-down motel room with a pet sulphur-crested cockatoo; Marshal Sam McCloud, a cowboy police detective from New Mexico on assignment in New York; and Italian-American Lieutenant Frank Columbo, with his rumpled raincoat, cheap cigar, dog and catchphrases designed to make the perpetrator underestimate him: 'Do you have a minute?'; 'Is that a fact?'; 'Isn't that something?'; and the clincher: 'Just one more thing.' Robert T Ironside was a San Francisco Police Department Chief of Detectives until paralysed by a bullet and confined to a wheelchair; he loses his job but is permitted to investigate cases as a citizen volunteer with two cops. As diverse as these police detectives are, the good guy almost always prevailed – a legacy of the Hays Code, but also an audience pleasing resolution. We might like to participate vicariously in the hunt for a criminal, but we also like to know that the hard-bitten, seen-it-all copper will not rest until law and order is restored.

....

WRITING EXERCISE:
A SURPRISING COP FROM OUT OF THE HAT

Creating memorable characters is essential no matter what type of film story you are writing, but especially important if writing a genre film for which there are certain set expectations for the protagonist – what will make your character stand out and not be deemed a stereotype? If writing a police series, what will hook us into watching this character and then make us continue to watch? You might have a great idea for a crime that your protagonist cop must solve, but what is it about your cop that will attract an actor to take on the role?

- Take a 'pick one from the hat' approach to your image kit and blindly choose the following:
  i. a character
  ii. a prop
  iii. a location

- The character will be your agent of the law; the prop will be his or her hobby, a prized object, or essential tool for daily use; the location will be where he/she lives or works OR a highly memorable place from his/her past. If the age of your selected character makes it impossible for him/her to be an official agent of the law, pick another character.

- Consider the police detectives from successful series noted earlier and any other film or television agents of the law that particularly appeal to you. What is special about their physical appearances, dress sense, mannerisms, hobbies, vices, speech patterns, pets, homes? For a further example, think about Abby Sciuto from NCIS: her goth make-up, clothing, jewellery; her hairstyle, tattoos, caffeine addiction, the hearse she initially drove (swapped for a 1932 Ford deuce coupe), the coffin she sleeps in, her Roman Catholic faith, excitable manner, habit of spontaneously hugging people, and utter expertise in ballistics, digital forensics and DNA analysis.

- Give your character a name and write them a biography that knits together your selected character, prop, location. Include key backstory to explain certain habits, likes, dislikes. Decide what specific job/area of expertise your agent of the law has. They might, for example, be an undercover cop and their image, the prop, or location might be part of that role. Develop a catchphrase for him/her.

- Write down why you think your character will interest an audience.

The goal with this exercise is to stretch your imagination without stretching credibility. Even police procedurals with a highly serious tone can have unusual characters, protagonists or secondary characters.

CLASSICAL STAGE POLICE STORY CONVENTIONS

'In the nation's war on crime, Scotland Yard is the brain of Great Britain's man-hunting machine. Routine, detailed science and tenacity; these are the weapons used by squads of highly trained men. Men like former Inspector Robert Fabian, hailed by the press as one of England's greatest detectives!'

(Narrator, *Fabian of the Yard*, 1954)

Protagonist: The main character is an agent of the law and is meant to operate within 'the system'. He or she may be a cop, police detective, FBI agent, specialist forensics officer, or any other officer of the law who operates under an official code of honour, typically only broken under duress or for the greater good. The protagonist is an active character with a sense of mission, often conservative, cynical and suspicious due to seeing the baser side of human nature on an almost daily basis. The agent of the law may be a bit of a loner, confiding little in others due to a macho nature, but equally he is loyal to his fellow cops. He may be closer to his (cop) partner than his wife or family. The protagonist is good at thinking on his feet, has a gut that tells him things, and defends the victim or the law itself. The 'blue code of silence' is the unwritten rule that police officers protect their own and don't rat on another cop's error or misconduct. At a certain stage in an investigation, a crime tends to become personal for a (movie) cop, which keeps him focused on defeating his opponent. Since the revisionist stage of the sub-genre, the protagonist often harbours a tragic past that influences his or her reactions to the crime or adversary.

Antagonist: Usually the lawbreaker is an active character and formidable adversary, due to extreme cunning, violence or power. There must be a genuine struggle between the protagonist and antagonist, raising questions as to whether the protagonist will prevail, or the conflict will not be engaging enough. The antagonist may have qualities in common with the protagonist, hence the classic villain's taunt, 'We are the same.'

Type of Plot or Story Pattern: The focus of the story is the efforts of the cop or agent of the law to apprehend the law-breaker.

- *Act I:* Many police procedural television series begin with a crime being perpetrated or showing the viewers the aftermath of a crime – normally a dead body at what will become the crime scene. We then shift to the 'ordinary world' of the agent of the law: a police precinct, in a police car, the morgue or somewhere part of the protagonist's everyday routine. A feature tends to introduce the protagonist and his or her world first, then go to the inciting incident of the crime being perpetrated or the discovery of its aftermath. The protagonist is then assigned to the case, which locks him or her into the mission to apprehend the perpetrator. No matter how dangerous the criminal or the situation, it's his or her duty to apprehend the wrongdoer. Typically, expositional dialogue is used to inform the viewer about specifics of the crime that took place and any leads.

- *Act II:* There are numerous obstacles to the protagonist achieving this goal. A police procedural focuses on the methodology and encourages the audience to unravel the crime, to participate in the drama. If the protagonist is assigned the case, there may come a point where he or she is removed for behaving recklessly, getting too emotionally involved, or due to an obstacle contrived by the antagonist; by this stage, the protagonist is so emotionally engaged in the battle with the antagonist that he or she is determined to 'win' and goes it alone. There must be a genuine struggle between 'good' and 'evil' and the stakes must be high or the story will fail to satisfy.

- *Act III:* The audience is encouraged to identify with the victim and protagonist and to hope justice will prevail. A showdown between the protagonist and antagonist is expected and while, typically, the antagonist is punished, victory should not come too easily for the protagonist. Innocent victims might get hurt or die, valuable property destroyed, and the protagonist may suffer greatly. If the protagonist is a police detective or police forensics expert, there is often a ticking clock to add tension and the potential for further victims. The classic message of a police story is that crime doesn't pay and so the law normally prevails, but one is left to wonder how the struggle has affected the cop.

Narrative Style: A classic police story deals with a crime, often involving violence, and gives a realistic portrait of the operations of a police precinct. Like the Western, it typically features gunfights and the hero might be an expert marksman. Police procedurals often include scenes of evidence gathering, interviewing witnesses, interrogating suspects and autopsies. Chase sequences are also common and there is a high ratio of objective drama, followed by a violent showdown or confrontation with the antagonist. In a whodunit police detective or forensics story, the criminal's identity is traditionally concealed until the third act. In a police procedural, the audience might be aware of the criminal's identity from the beginning of the story and the focus is on trying to catch him or her. Police series often open and sometimes close with narration that either gives introductory information about the world of the series or stresses the danger the police face in their daily activities.

Timeframe/Pace: Police stories tend to be fast-paced as there is a rush to solve the crime before the perpetrator escapes or the antagonist breaks the law again. The pace usually accelerates towards the big showdown. If the protagonist is attempting to solve one crime or capture a sole perpetrator, the timeframe tends to be shorter; if after a gang or unravelling a complex crime or series of crimes, the timeframe might be more expansive. A twist on this is the resurrection of a 'cold case', which has been unsolved for a number of years. An event tends to re-trigger the investigation, perhaps a similar murder or a perpetrator with the same modus operandi. A 'ticking clock' is used in a number of ways to increase pace and tension in police stories. For example, there might be time constraints to:

- stop a crime from happening
- catch the perpetrator

- conclude the case as demanded by the powers above
- meet or thwart a criminal's demands

Tone: Realistic, typically gritty and suspenseful. Mystery, dramatic irony and suspense are heavily employed to immerse the audience in the investigation and pursuit of the perpetrator.

Setting and Mise-en-scène: Many police stories take place in urban settings where there tends to be more crime and cops deal with infractions on their beat. A federal agent or specialist expert may be required to investigate a crime in an environment that is very alien to him or her, thus adding more tension and complications. More rural or suburban settings for a murder case can bring an additional layer of horror as 'things like that don't happen around here'.

REVISIONIST STAGE POLICE STORIES: GOOD COP, BAD COP, FEMALE COP

'What's this for? For being an honest cop? Or for being stupid enough to get shot in the face? You tell them that they can shove it.'

(Frank Serpico, on being honoured with a gold badge, *Serpico*)

'It's the law? Then the law is crazy.'

(Harry Callahan, *Dirty Harry*)

The late 1960s and early 1970s saw something of a boom in Hollywood police story feature films such as *Bullitt* (1968), *Madigan* (1968), *Klute* (1971), *The French Connection* (1971), *Dirty Harry* (1971), *Electra Glide in Blue* (1973) and *Serpico* (1973). In America, this was the time of Vietnam War protests, the counter-culture, the civil rights movement, and questioning all authority and systems of control. With the repeal of the Motion Picture Production Code, gone were stipulations against showing representatives of the law in a negative light and criminals in a positive one. Graphic violence, vengeful behaviour, illegal drug trafficking, prostitution, nudity and profanity were no longer banned outright and filmmakers wasted little time in bringing a lot more 'dirty realism' to their stories. Police stories were gritty, but the cops were grittier. Even if their goal was still to uphold the law and apprehend the criminal, their methods might be outside normal police protocol with a focus on getting 'justice' by any means necessary. Or the tales might focus on police corruption – dirty cops, cops on the make. For example, the tagline for *Dirty Harry* was: *'Dirty Harry and the homicidal maniac. Harry's the one with the badge.'* The confrontation scene between 'Dirty Harry' Callahan and the killer includes the now classic dialogue that sums up Harry's unorthodox approach to law enforcement: 'I know what you're thinking. "Did he fire six shots or only five?" Well, to tell you the truth, in all this excitement I kind of lost track myself. But being as this is a .44 Magnum, the most powerful handgun in the world, and would blow your head clean off, you've got to ask yourself one question: Do I feel lucky? Well, do ya, punk?' If Harry's verbal threat doesn't work, there is little doubt that he will pull the trigger. Films like the *Lethal Weapon* and *Die Hard* franchises have a law enforcement agent as protagonist, but take Dirty Harry's methodology much further so that the focus is far more on the testosterone-fuelled chase and combat scenes of the action heroes rather than a police story. More recent police features such as *The Untouchables* (1987), *Internal Affairs* (1990), *LA Confidential* (1997), *The Departed* (2006) and *Brooklyn's Finest* (2009) also deal with police corruption and cops administering their own brand of justice.

While the plethora of TV cop shows still tend to finish with justice being served, they also took a more realistic turn in the 1970s, pre-empted by ground-breaking American television series, *M Squad* (1957–60), which was strongly influenced by the duplicitous characters and mean streets of film noir. The main protagonist was a plain-clothes cop (played by the magnificent Lee Marvin) who worked with a special unit to investigate organised crime; the show paved the way for more realistic police dramas with less-than-perfect cops and stories dealing with social issues, corruption and cops going under cover. *The Mod Squad* (1968–73) aimed to appeal to a younger audience with three twenty-something counter-culture delinquents (tagline: one white, one black, one blonde) who were coerced into going undercover. The undercover cop must blend in with the criminal underworld, which often causes him or her much internal conflict with respect to loyalty, following the rules, and the temptation towards corruption or 'the dark side' while they are trying not to be found out by the people they are investigating. Features such as *Rush* (1991), *Donnie Brasco* (1997), *Point Break* (1991), *Narc* (2002) and *The Departed* (2006) deal with these difficulties. Revisionist series *Hill Street Blues* (1981–87), *Law and Order* (1990–2010), *NYPD Blue* (1993–2005), *Homicide: Life on the Street* (1993–99), *Law and Order Special Victims Unit* (1999–), *The Shield* (2002–08) and *The Wire* (2002–08) take the relative realism of *M Squad* several strides further, exploring a variety of social and police issues and giving the audience much more information about the cops' personal life and struggles with everything from alcoholism, addiction, family issues, debt and sexual orientation, making it clear that the stress of dealing with the darker side of humanity and 'life on the streets' comes with a price. *NYPD Blue* and *Homicide: Life on the Street* had dry, wise-cracking dialogue reminiscent of film noir, a twist on the usual minimalist, realist dialogue typical of police procedurals.

Initially law enforcement was a man's game in film and television, despite the fact that women have been on the police force (albeit in small numbers) since the early twentieth century. Revisionist police series started to include female law enforcement officers; US shows like *Policewoman* (1974–78) and *Cagney and Lacey* (1982–88) feature female cops, as do *The Closer* (2005–), *The Mentalist* (2008–) and *Saving Grace* (2007–10). The British series *Prime Suspect* features Inspector Jane Tennison, a hard drinking, troubled character who not only has to deal with appalling crimes, but also sexism from her male subordinates. Sarah Lund of *The Killing* (*Forbrydelsen*) (Denmark, 2007–12) struggles to maintain a personal life due to her dedication to her job.

An offshoot of the police procedural is the forensic investigator, pathologist or criminalist show in which experts employed by the state work to solve crimes, using their specialist skills. *Quincy ME* (1976–83) is one of the earlier examples; protagonist Dr Quincy, a medical examiner working for the Los Angeles County Coroner's Office, investigates suspicious deaths forensically, with what were cutting edge methods at the time. It was a predecessor of the *CSI: Crime Scene Investigation* (2000–) franchise, which focuses on police forensic evidence investigation experts in Las Vegas, New York and Miami; each show has a slightly different 'flavour' in keeping with its location. Arguably, the team with the most memorable characters and 'morgue humour' is the one in the original Las Vegas series. *Body of Proof* (2011–) is an updated take on *Quincy* with a female medical examiner working for the Philadelphia Medical Examiner Office. *Bones* (2005–) features a female forensic anthropologist collaborating with an FBI agent, and *Criminal Minds* (2005–) explores the investigations of the Behavioural Analysis Unit of the FBI, based in Quantico, Virginia – expert profilers who specialise in serial killers and are called in by local police departments. These specialists might be scientists or psychologists, but they are either agents of the law or work in tandem with the police and therefore must follow police procedure – at least with respect to dealing with evidence – or the perpetrator might walk free.

Again, the specifics of the protagonist's job – the day-to-day procedures when dealing with a crime scene or victim – should be accurate. Some shows take artistic licence with procedure and a general audience might go with such lapses, but viewers with more specific knowledge will not. An expert may be hired as a consultant to fact check, but having a good knowledge of profiling, gathering forensic evidence, or unusual jobs linked to solving crimes can lead to interesting ideas for characters or stories, whether for television series or feature films.

ANOTHER TIME, ANOTHER PLACE

Transposing a police procedural or police detective story to another time period can bring a fresh angle to a classic crime story, but changing circa isn't simply changing mise-en-scène and tweaking dialogue. If setting a crime story in the past, the writer must research how agents of the law operated during that time period, in that specific place. What was the usual procedure when dealing with a crime scene, a mystery, a criminal? Potential viewers with an interest in the specific era are likely to know such details and will be unforgiving if there are anachronisms. A number of fairly recent Hollywood police films have been set back in the 1940s and 1950s – some revisionist in content and some revisiting classical stage conventions. *The Black Dahlia* (2006) and *Hollywoodland* (2006) are both based on real characters – the first on an unsolved murder of a woman in 1947 and the second on George Reeves' death. *LA Confidential* (1997), based on James Ellroy's novel, is set in 1953 and deals with police corruption. All three films explore the underbelly of Hollywood and give a convincing depiction of the time, place and police procedure.

Setting a police investigation in the future has its own rules. Using a recognisable approach to apprehending a criminal or investigating a crime scene but with new 'tools of the trade' is common and part of the necessary world building. Mixing science fiction and police stories also gives the writer an opportunity to comment on systems of control and agents of the law in a potentially original way. Films such as *Minority Report* (2002) and *I, Robot* (2004), both based on science fiction stories, focus on police detectives trying to solve a murder in a future society who stumble across more than they bargained for; the investigation gives the viewer a sense of grounding in these strange new worlds.

Location is another key element to consider when devising either a police series or film – this is your cop's 'beat' and the more you know about it the better. Conventionally, police series are set in urban environments as a new crime is needed for every episode and city life tends to provide ample material. Specifics of the place can also trigger story ideas. Las Vegas evokes casinos, show girls and an oasis of neon surrounded by desert whereas New York City has its famous monuments, high-rises, subway and specific boroughs – any of these elements could provide inspiration for a story. The *Criminal Minds* team is based in Quantico, but may be called to a variety of locations, including rural and suburban settings. As Truman Capote's best-selling true-crime non-fiction novel *In Cold Blood* (1966) demonstrated, a brutal murder in a non-urban setting can be even more disturbing, rocking a small town or rural community to its very foundations. There is an expectation that knowing your neighbours makes them incapable of violence and that the picket fences of small towns keep their inhabitants safe. John Wayne Gacy proves that theory wrong. David Lynch's weird and wonderful series *Twin Peaks* (1990–91) brought straight-laced Special Agent Dale Cooper to the small Washington state town of Twin Peaks to solve the brutal murder of a teenage girl and, of course, he proceeded to uncover the dark underbelly of the American dream. Rather than having a gritty realist tone, *Twin Peaks* is typically 'Lynchian': odd, off-kilter and, at times, nightmarish.

THE PARODY STAGE: BUMBLING COPS, CLUELESS POLICE DETECTIVES

'Facts, Hercule, facts! Nothing matters but the facts. Without them the science of criminal investigation is nothing more than a guessing game.'

(Inspector Jacques Clouseau, *A Shot in the Dark*, 1964)

Police story parodies allow comedy writers to poke fun at authority figures, rules and regulations in general, police ineptitude and corruption, and a cop's specific 'tools of trade' using either a light, goofy touch or more pointed satire. *The Pink Panther* film series, beginning in 1964, features the trench coat wearing, self-regarding French Inspector Clouseau, brilliantly portrayed by Peter Sellers, who was all attitude with little sleuthing talent. 1982 television parody *Police Squad!* spoofs classic police series like *Dragnet* and evolved into the *Naked Gun* (1988) film franchise, starring Leslie Nielsen as an incompetent police lieutenant.

The Coen Brothers' *Fargo* isn't an out and out parody, but they use police procedural genre tropes to mine (black) comedy from a murder investigation conducted by the very competent and very pregnant female police chief as she investigates a crime scene with her less than savvy sidekick, interviews clueless witnesses, and tries to apprehend the simultaneously psychotic and incompetent criminals. Genre tropes can be used for comic effect no matter what the 'flavour' of the comedy.

....

WRITING EXERCISE:
UPHOLDING THE LAW OR SUPPORTING THE FAMILY?

Police stories focus on upholding the law, following procedure, and getting justice for a criminal's victims, but what might compromise a dedicated police officer's commitment to the oath of honour? Difficult dilemmas lead to big choices for protagonists, which makes for compelling drama. Experiment with putting your protagonist under pressure through the following scenario:

Part A: Setting Up the Dilemma
Outline the following scenario:

- The protagonist: a small town cop. His or her father is a cop. So are his brother and grandfather. Think of a location and write a short description of the place. Name your characters. Your protagonist is an idealist who is intensely loyal to his or her family, home town, and fellow officers. He or she has always wanted to be a cop and is extremely good at it.

- The main antagonist: the older brother. The two get along, but are opposites. He is charming and charismatic, whereas the protagonist is earnest and sometimes a little too good; the protagonist looks up to his or her older brother. Flesh out the specifics of both characters.

- The inciting incident: A very serious crime is committed, which rocks the small town. Decide what the crime is. The brother has committed the crime but, in his role of cop, casts suspicion on an innocent party. Decide who that 'suspect' is and why he or she is blamed. The brother does not confide in the protagonist.

- The investigation: Think of two clues that make your protagonist suspect his or her brother. How does he or she manage to justify these clues or the brother's excuses? The brother tries harder to blame someone else and everyone else on the (small) force believes him, including their cop father. The accused is arrested and it looks like an innocent person will go to prison.

- Your protagonist finds evidence that makes it absolutely clear his/her brother is guilty – it may be an object; a witness; new evidence; an exposed lie; an alibi for the accused that has surfaced. Decide what the irrefutable evidence is.

Part B: Confrontation Between Protagonist and Antagonist
Script the confrontation scene between your protagonist and his/her brother:

- Think about character strategy. What is his/her frame of mind? What location does your protagonist choose to broach the subject? Is he or she direct or indirect? What is their activity? Consider props and atmosphere and how mood might change from the scene opening. The chosen location and activity should reveal something about the protagonist and antagonist.

- How does his/her brother react? Think about progression from denial to admission, bargaining to threats. What does your protagonist stand to lose if he/she upholds the law? End the scene with the brother walking away. Your protagonist is left alone to come to a decision.

Part C: Scene of Decision and Aftermath
Outline the following scenes of decision and aftermath:

- What decision has your protagonist arrived at? Will he or she reveal the truth about the brother, OR lie to protect the brother, OR choose not to intervene to save the wrongfully accused party?

- Your protagonist must make a public declaration of some kind about the crime committed. What is the location of this declaration? Activity? Who is there?

- Write a monologue (first person present tense) from your protagonist's point of view as he or she acts on their decision. Your protagonist should feel under enormous pressure and the monologue should reveal this tension. Consider how this difficult decision will change your character.

- Scene of aftermath: Outline a short scene that shows your character in an activity or situation some time in the near future. The scene should reveal how your protagonist's decision regarding his/her brother has affected their life and how the people in the small town who know your protagonist feel about him or her. For example, is he or she still a cop? Has your protagonist moved somewhere else? Is guilt destroying them? Be succinct with the scene and focus on a visual reveal rather than dialogue.

....

WISE GUYS AND TOMMY GUNS:
THE GANGSTER SUB-GENRE

'For us to live any other way was nuts. To us, those goody-good people who worked shitty jobs for bum pay-checks and took the subway to work every day and worried about their bills were dead. I mean, they were suckers. They had no balls. If we wanted something, we just took it. If anyone complained twice they got hit so bad, believe me, they never complained again.'

(Henry Hill, *Goodfellas*)

Cody Jarret, Little Caesar, Scarface, Don Vito Corleone, Henry Hill, Frank Lucas and law breaking lovers, Bonnie and Clyde – some memorable characters brought to life in gangster films. It isn't so much the crimes the gangster commits that fascinate us as much as the gangster himself. What drove him (for classically the gangster is a male) to become a gangster; what qualities did he have that enabled him to rise to the top; and what brought about his inevitable fall? This is the focus of the gangster sub-genre. A screenwriter who wants to write a compelling gangster film has to create a villain-protagonist so memorable, the audience wants to join his or her gang for the duration of the film. Extreme violence, tough guy talk, and breaking the law does not a compelling gangster make – he needs some quality that surprises, engages, hooks us, be it extreme audacity, cunning, charisma, or love of family, combined with leadership, self-confidence and the will to succeed at any cost.

PRIMITIVE STAGE GANGSTER FILMS: TRUE CRIMES AND FOLK HEROES

'...Some day they'll go down together
they'll bury them side by side.
To few it'll be grief, to the law a relief,
but it's death for Bonnie and Clyde.'

('The Trail's End', extract of poem by Bonnie Parker)

Pulp fiction featuring gangster protagonists found an eager audience in Europe, particularly in France, and these exciting, villainous characters were quickly recruited for screen adventures. Victorin-Hippolyte Jasset followed his Nick Carter detective film serials with some of the earliest films featuring a master criminal – Zigomar – as protagonist: *Zigomar, Roi de Voleurs* (1911); *Zigomar the Eelskin* (1911); *Zigomar Contre Nick Carter* (1912); and three episodes of *Zigomar the Black Scourge* (1913). These French silent short films were based on the inexpensive and hugely popular pulp fiction tales of Léon Sazie.

French director Louis Feuillade also made a film serial with a super-villain as its protagonist. *Fantômas* (1913–14) was based on the hugely popular pulp fiction, 32-volume serial created in 1911 by co-writers Marcel Allain and Pierre Souvestre, with 11 further volumes written by Allain alone. The novels and films follow the exploits of the 'Genius of Crime', who commits audacious, creative and gruesome crimes in Paris, yet always manages to evade capture by his nemesis Inspector Juve. Fantômas is a master of disguise and confident leader of a force of 'apaches'; he would also seem to be highly seductive as his long-term lover is Lady Beltham, the widow of a man he murdered. Fantômas is so compelling that the novels have been adapted into films, television and comic books – and he was referenced in silent film homage *The Artist* (2011). Feuillade also made *Les Vampires* (1915), a film series about an apache gang headed by a female criminal, the vampish Irma Vep. He followed these with crime serials *Judex* (1916), *Tih Minh* (1918) and *Barrabas* (1919).

Italian actor, writer, and director Emilio Ghione created the underworld apache Za La Mort, playing the villainous lead himself in his first film *Nelly la Gigolette* (1914). The success of the film encouraged Ghione to make a further 12 Za La Mort films, giving his protagonist a companion: Za La Vie. Za La Mort's character was somewhat inconsistent in the series, ranging from ruthless, murderous villain to romantic avenger, but he had a 'code'. Ghione went on to write several novels based on the Za La Mort character.

Early American films also focused on the activities of criminals and the rise of organised crime. Wallace McCutcheon's one-reelers *The Moonshiners* (1904) and *The Black Hand* (1906) are simple precursors to the gangster film in that the first deals with bootlegging and the second with a Mafioso-like protection racket that leads to a kidnapping. DW Griffith's *The Musketeers of Pig Alley* (1912) also deals with organised crime and *The Regeneration* (1915), Raoul Walsh's first feature, focuses on the rise of an Irish-American 'Bowery-boy' to gangster in the Lower East Side slums of New York City. *Gentleman-cambrioleur* Arsène Lupin first appeared in Vitagraph's 1917 film, played by silent film star Earle Williams, and has been the protagonist of a number of films and television series thereafter, most recently in 2004. Josef von Sternberg's *Underworld* (1927) is a gangland story, shot from the gangster's point of view. Paramount Pictures predicted that *Underworld* would be a flop but, despite its release in only one theatre, strong word-of-mouth from audiences turned the film into a hit and screenwriter Ben Hecht won an Academy Award for best original screenplay. Lewis Milestone's *The Racket* (1928) was concerned with corruption and a city being controlled by the mob. *The Lights of New York* (1928) is considered the first 'talkie' gangster film, the sound allowing for snappy dialogue and increased tension through gun shots, and 'getaway' car sound effects.

The success of the early Hollywood gangster films was based in part on their biographical aspects; main characters were inspired by gangsters such as Al Capone, John Dillinger, Pretty Boy Floyd, and Bonnie Parker and Clyde Barrow, all of whom became folk legends. Two phases in American history contributed to this: Prohibition and the Great Depression. From 1920 to 1933, the manufacture, sale and transportation of liquor (but not the drinking of it) was outlawed under Prohibition. Bootleggers and speakeasy owners were breaking the law, but that certainly didn't make them unpopular with the public. The Great Depression was triggered by the stock market crash of 1929, which resulted in record unemployment and homelessness. Bankers plummeted to an all time low in popularity as banks had invested their customers' savings in the stock market and, when the banks collapsed, ordinary people were left bankrupt. The dust bowl hit the Midwest compounding the economic crisis and banks foreclosed on mortgages, driving 38 per cent of farmers from their land. It's not difficult to see why bank robbers became folk heroes when the general public felt victimised by bankers. Most of these gangsters grew up poor in rough urban neighbourhoods – like Al Capone – or came from impoverished farming areas like Clyde Barrow, and their 'grab it' attitude chimed with people who felt the system had let them down. In April 1930, Frank J Loesch, Chairman of the Chicago Crime Commission, used the term 'public enemy' to denounce Chicago's most notorious gangsters and make their criminal status clear to the public, but this did not stop the public from flocking to see gangster films.

FIGURE 6: **GANGSTERS WHO INSPIRED HOLLYWOOD**

Al 'Scarface' Capone (1899–1947): 'Scarface' was probably America's best-known gangster. Born Alphonso Caponi to Italian immigrant parents in a rough neighbourhood in Brooklyn, New York, he was a member of the Brooklyn Rippers and the Forty Thieves Juniors as a kid before graduating to the Five Points gang in Manhattan. After moving to Chicago, he became an organised crime mastermind, running every illegal racket (bootlegging, gambling, brothels) and building an illicit empire before his 1931 arrest for failing to file an income tax return.

He served eight years then lived quietly in Florida until he died of ill-health exacerbated by long-term syphilis.

John Herbert Dillinger, Jr (1903–34): Dillinger grew up in rural Indiana and was involved in petty crime as a teenager. He was dishonourably discharged from the Navy for going AWOL, then served nine and a half years in prison after robbing a grocery store of $50. Dillinger was released at the height of the Depression in 1933. He returned to crime, robbing two dozen banks and four police stations with his gang. He escaped from jail twice and was the newly formed FBI's first Public Enemy Number One. Unlike many of his gangster contemporaries, he was accused of only one murder, which occurred during a Chicago shoot-out. It is unlikely that he was actually the perpetrator, and he was never convicted. Dillinger was shot by FBI agents as he attempted to flee the Biograph theatre in Chicago; some believe that a 'double' was killed in Dillinger's place, and he took an assumed identity.

Lester Joseph Gillis (1908–34): Gillis, better known as Baby Face Nelson, was sent to a Chicago reformatory aged 12 after accidentally shooting another child with a found pistol. Upon his release he continued with petty crime and was hired to drive bootleg alcohol through the Chicago suburbs. He took to targeting the wealthy in home invasions and robbing banks in 1930. Baby Face partnered with Dillinger and engineered the Crown Point Indiana Jail escape. He was a devoted family man, but did not enjoy the public popularity of other gangsters as he was known for firing indiscriminately and hitting both lawmen and civilians. Baby Face Nelson murdered more FBI agents than any other person and was fatally wounded in Indiana during a shoot-out with the FBI in the so-called Battle of Barrington.

Charles Arthur Floyd (1904–34): 'Pretty Boy' Floyd grew up in Oklahoma and served three and a half years in prison after committing a payroll robbery in 1925. He returned to robbing banks in the Midwest and West South Central states after his release, but gained a reputation for being generous to the poor. Floyd was romanticised by the press and in a song by folk singer Woody Guthrie. He was gunned down in revenge for killing a policeman in the Kansas City massacre, a murder he denied.

Bonnie Parker (1910–34) and Clyde Barrow (1909–34): Probably the most famous gangster lovers of their era, Bonnie and Clyde were Texas natives. Bonnie's mother was a struggling widow and Clyde came from a dispossessed farming family that moved to the slums of Dallas, initially living under their wagon and (when circumstances improved) in a tent. Clyde was involved in petty crime as a teenager and Bonnie married (and never divorced) petty criminal Roy Thornton before she turned 16. Bonnie and Clyde met and fell in love in January 1930; she joined his gang, although it is debatable whether she ever shot anyone. Their two-year crime spree began in 1932 and famously came to an end in a hail of bullets in Louisiana. Despite the murders committed by the Barrow gang, the public was sympathetic towards them as robbing banks was considered hitting back at the system. The couple's good looks, and the photographs of them posing 'gangster style', contributed to their iconic status as did Bonnie's poetry. 'The Trail's End' was her prediction in verse of their inevitable demise. Bonnie and Clyde still capture the public imagination; in 2012, two of their guns fetched $500,000 at auction and Barrow's pocket watch and a 1921 Morgan silver dollar that was in his pocket when he was killed were sold at auction for $1.1 million.

Alvin Karpis (1907–79): Karpis was born to Lithuanian immigrants in Montreal, raised in Kansas, and began working for racketeers when he was ten years old. He was sentenced to ten years for attempted burglary in 1926, but escaped prison. During a second prison stint, Karpis met Fred Barker, a member of the Bloody Barkers, a family of impoverished sharecroppers turned to crime. They joined forces and started a crime spree of holding the wealthy to ransom and robbing banks. The FBI reinvented 62-year-old Ma Barker as a criminal mastermind, probably to justify shooting the matriarch. Karpis was the last 'public enemy' captured by FBI agents and served a 26-year sentence in Alcatraz and seven years in McNeil Island Penitentiary when Alcatraz was closed. He was paroled in 1969 and deported to Canada where he wrote two sets of memoirs, before moving to Spain in 1973 where he died six years later.

These micro-biographies indicate how a number of gangster genre conventions originated in reality, which is hardly surprising given the number of gangster films loosely based on real people. Two of three seminal gangster films that launched the genre's classical stage are based on Al Capone.

WRITING EXERCISE: INSPIRED BY...

Part A

As we have seen (and will continue to see), many films are based on literary works or inspired by real events or characters. Some are direct adaptations – 'based on a true story' – and some are very loosely 'inspired by' reality. The series *Castle* (2009–) plays with this idea; best-selling mystery writer Rick Castle gets permission to shadow NYPD homicide detective Kate Beckett and team after a serial killer imitates the plots of his novels. His skills for creating credible murders and investigations in literature make him a naturally gifted detective and Beckett inspires Castle to create a protagonist for a new crime series: 'Nikki Heat'. Complicating matters further, publisher Hyperion has released four Nikki Heat crime novels written by... 'Richard Castle'. The author's true identity has not been officially revealed.

- Choose one of the short gangster biographies from Figure 6.

- Rename the character(s) and set the story somewhere completely different in location and time: a foreign city, a small town, even another planet; present day, far in the past, in the future.

- Write a revised character biography, taking into account the new setting and circa. The most basic information should stay the same (example: sent to a reformatory aged 12 after accidentally shooting another child with a found pistol) but the specifics of revised place/time must be brought into the biography. For example, what kind of gun? How is that gun relevant to that specific world and your protagonist's family or acquaintances? Some producers mistakenly think that it's quite simple for a writer to relocate a story from London to Edinburgh – or Paris or Istanbul in a 'search and replace' kind of way. It's not just the visual aspects that must change in an adaptation that relocates a film in place or time; the writer must consider how specifics of time and place impact on characterisation, dialogue and plot.

....

CLASSICAL STAGE GANGSTER FILMS: PUBLIC ENEMY NUMBER 1

'Made it, Ma! Top of the world!'

(Cody Jarrett, *White Heat*)

'Mother of mercy, is this the end of Rico?'

(Rico Bandello, *Little Caesar*)

The Public Enemy (1931), *Little Caesar* (1931) and *Scarface: The Shame of a Nation* (1932) are three of the best-known and earliest classical stage gangster films, which gave career defining starring roles to James Cagney, Edward G Robinson and Paul Muni. *The Public Enemy* features small-time gangster Tommy Powers (played by James

Cagney), who differs from more 'classic' gangsters in that he lacks overwhelming ambition – he is not driven to rise to the top of the bootlegging hierarchy, to be top dog, or to escape his neighbourhood. Rico Bandello and Tony Camonte are another story; these violent villain-protagonists, both based in part on Al Capone, influenced the rise (and fall) of the power-driven, money-hungry gangster who will stop at nothing, including murder, to get what he wants. Edward G Robinson as Rico in *Little Caesar* gains control of Chicago's north side through his drive and ruthlessness, but discovers few can be trusted after reaching the top of the criminal heap. He shows some humanity when he finds he cannot murder his friend, but his worst traits prevail. Rico succumbs to his pride and anger after reading in the newspaper that a cop called him a coward and makes a fatal error. He threatens to murder the cop, but is shot down in a hail of bullets from a tommy gun. Tony Camonte, protagonist of *Scarface* and played by Paul Muni, is also highly ambitious and violent; as a subordinate, he starts a war with the North Side gang, which allows him to take control of his boss's gang and girlfriend. Camonte is highly protective of his sister but, when he finds her in a hotel room with his best friend, he presumes the worst and, in a classic case of shoot first, ask questions later, kills him. He feels remorse when he discovers that the two had secretly married and were planning to surprise him. His guilt is compounded when his sister is killed by a ricocheting bullet before he himself is gunned down by police. Both 'Little Caesar' and Tony Camonte want the American dream and will work hard (albeit illegally) to get it, but their positive qualities cannot compensate for their fatal flaws.

These three films are considered pre-Hays Code films as the Motion Picture Code of 1930 was not being very stringently enforced. The Hays Office did, however, warn producer Howard Hughes not to make *Scarface*, primarily due to its violence; it featured the first machine gun toting gangsters and 28 characters died in the film. Hughes responded with the claim that the film was made to fight the 'gangster menace'. The film was initially completed in 1931, but was not released until 1932 after scenes were edited to cut violence and 'The Shame of a Nation' was added to the title.

The Hays Office's objections to gangster film violence were not echoed by the public who were considerably less squeamish and seemed to take vicarious pleasure in watching swaggering tough guys flaunting the system. The FBI under J Edgar Hoover tried to counter this attitude by labelling the gangsters they were pursuing 'Public Enemy Number 1' whereas the studios responded to the fascination with an explosion in gangster film productions: nine were released in 1930, 26 in 1931, 28 in 1932, and 15 in 1933. The sheer output of gangster films during these years helped shape genre conventions, as did the strictures imposed by the Hays Office.

The Hays Office became much more vigilant about enforcing the Code after the release of *The Public Enemy*, *Little Caesar* and *Scarface*. In a nutshell, films were prohibited from influencing young people from taking up the life of crime by showing gangsters in a romantic light or 'getting away with it'. The Hays Office was determined to save an unsophisticated audience from its love of gangster films – and itself. Filmmakers were strongly encouraged to present criminals as sociopaths, to minimise the violence, and to emphasise that crime doesn't pay. The appeal of the 'classic' gangster film began to wane after 1934 and consequently studios stopped producing so many. Raoul Walsh's *The Roaring Twenties* (1939) is often seen as one of the last great classical stage Hollywood gangster films.

CLASSICAL STAGE GANGSTER SUB-GENRE CONVENTIONS

'A lot of holes in the desert, and a lot of problems are buried in those holes. But you gotta do it right. I mean, you gotta have the hole already dug before you show up with a package in the trunk. Otherwise, you're talking about a half-hour to 45 minutes worth of digging. And who knows who's gonna come along in that time? Pretty soon, you gotta dig a few more holes. You could be there all fuckin' night.'

(**Nicky Santoro**, *Casino*)

Protagonist: The man who would be king. The gangster is normally from an impoverished background and is often a first or second generation immigrant. He – for, classically, the gangster is a 'he' – is full of ambition and determined to enjoy material success, prestige and power, but has observed that following the rules does not guarantee success for those from his background. He is often entrepreneurial and aggressive in business; he will attempt to crush any rivals and is happy to break the law in his aspirational quest. The gangster has courage, street smarts, bravado, and is often cocky, self-assured, charismatic, violent and vengeful. He also tends to be self-destructive with some kind of fatal flaw such as a hair-trigger temper. If offended, he may over-retaliate and his need for revenge may cause his own self-destruction. The gangster may also have a personal code of conduct; he may be loyal to his family and friends, his people, his roots. This code is much more formalised when a gangster is part of a gang or organised crime group that may also have initiation rites. The Italian-American Mafia, for example, has strict rules: the code of silence (never talk to agents of the law); only Italian males may be full members; the boss gets a monthly tribute and cut of any extra business; no talk of family business to non-members; no infighting; no blood revenge within the group except if approved by the boss; no adultery with another family member's wife. These rules were clearly developed to prevent the organisation from imploding and to support the hierarchy the ambitious gangster wishes to ascend. Gangsters may have a particular sense of style and way of speaking with jargon that outsiders are less likely to understand. All in all, the ends justify the means in the gangster's eyes. As the gangster ascends in power, his morality is increasingly compromised and his character flaws tend to inflate, accelerating his fall towards destruction.

Antagonist: Agents of the law or another gangster. The gangster encounters much conflict in his quest for power and material success and he may have a number of antagonists rather than one main foe. As he rises to power, he may take the territory of another gangster, one who may previously have been his mentor. Any agent of the law is an antagonist unless 'in his pocket'; there is often one agent of the law who has made it his special mission to bring down the gangster. There may almost be a sense that jealousy drives the agent of the law and the gangster may sense this and use it to his advantage. Ultimately, the gangster is also his own antagonist – hubris or any other fatal flaw contributing to his inevitable downfall.

Type of Plot or Story Pattern: The rise and fall of the gangster. The classic gangster tale is a rags to riches story with an unhappy ending. The protagonist will stop at nothing to prevail in life but, because the gangster's riches are ill-gotten, he typically pays the price for them with his life after a final, desperate fight. His downfall tends to be caused by hubris or betrayal by another aspirational gangster.

- *Act I:* An introduction to the gangster's world, often beginning with a scene of youthful deprivation. Or, the protagonist may already be a gangster, albeit an underling who wants to rise to the top. The inciting incident may be an introduction to 'the life', a chance to join a gang, or an opportunity to make a tempting amount of money doing something illegal. It is clear that the protagonist is seduced by the gangster lifestyle and wants all the gangster accoutrements. The 'godfather' or gang leader sees the protagonist's potential and becomes a kind of mentor figure. The point of no return or locking in point is either the gangster's decision to get involved with the gang, do a job, make a bid for power, or break the law in some way. Once in 'the life' it's very difficult to get out of it.

- *Act II:* Initially focuses on the gangster's struggle to reach the top and what he does to get there, which involves violence and murder. We typically also get to know something positive about him, be it loyalty to family and friends, generosity, or some other good trait. Once the top is reached, the gangster must retain his power and position. He may be under police surveillance, have jealous rivals, or start to unravel due to paranoia or personal vices.

- *End of Act II:* The gangster may have everything he has dreamed of, all the accoutrements of wealth and prestige; his power is at its greatest, but we are aware that the forces of antagonism are closing in.

- *Act III:* Typically the fall and the gangster's final fight. The law or rival gangster starts to close in; someone betrays the gangster protagonist. This all escalates to the final showdown with the gangster doing everything possible to retain his position.

- *Resolution:* The gangster is typically dramatically shot down in a hail of bullets, unwilling to relinquish his power or go to prison. From the gangster's point of view, it's better to die than be a loser or an ordinary schmuck. The message delivered is that lusting for power and success by any means necessary is bad – crime doesn't pay in the long run. The law of the jungle prevails again.

Narrative Style: A battle of wits and physical power is expected as the gangster aims for the top – conflicts with police and other gangsters who must be conquered/killed. Tools of the trade include guns, and symbols of material success such as sharp clothes, expensive material goods, jewels, good food and drink, illegal substances, enterprises, activities. The sub-genre tends to be male dominated with little scope for male-female relationships – women as 'arm candy' and symbols of the gangster's success.

Timeframe/Pace: The timeframe tends to be expansive in order to show the gangster's rise and fall.

Tone: Violent, aggressive, action-oriented; a tense, suspenseful struggle. The gangster is someone who wants something badly and will stop at nothing to get it.

Setting and Mise-en-scène: The city is normally the gangster's home and place of business, although he may move his family home to the suburbs or an easily defended estate for safety. The appearance of his home, possessions and clothing changes to reflect his ascent, shifting from images of deprivation to ostentation.

··

WRITING EXERCISE: A GANGSTER'S UPS AND DOWNS

The gangster typically changes enormously from the start of the film to its end, beginning as an ambitious and power hungry 'have not' and transforming into a 'have' with power and all the trappings of material success. Part of the pleasure of the gangster film is to witness how far the protagonist has risen and what might provoke his fall. Knowing where a character begins and where he or she will end up can help you to create a credible character arc. First, revisit the character you created in Part A (Inspired by…), and then try the exercise again with a new character.

Part B
Prelude to the Rise: An ambitious youngster.
Give your fledgling gangster a name and decide his age. Where does he live and where did his parents emigrate from? Why did they emigrate? What do his parents do for a living and what is their home like? Or does he live with relatives if his parents are no longer alive? Your main character is dissatisfied with his or her life. Briefly summarise why, writing it in the first person.

- Inciting incident: Your protagonist comes in contact with a local gangster, Mafia character, or gang member. Something in this scene gives your protagonist the idea to be a gangster too. Describe what happens from the protagonist's point of view, in the first person. Make the scene vivid.

- An event occurs that locks your protagonist into moving forward with his rebellion – there's no turning back. It could be a job, or something he does, or something done to him. Again, describe this event in the first person. End the monologue with a declaration from your protagonist as to where he will end up in life.

The Fall: Hubris conquers all – teetering at the top.
Your protagonist years later. Decide how much time has passed. He is top dog in the criminal world. What does he specifically

do? What illegal activity has made him all his money? Has he committed murder and how does he feel about any violent acts he has committed? Is he in a relationship, does he have a family? What is his main flaw and how will it get him in trouble? Is there anyone he trusts... and is he right to trust them? Who is plotting against him? Sketch out the circumstances of the final scene when he loses his empire, someone he loves, or his own life. Again, write the scene outline in the first person, present tense.

....

REVISIONIST GANGSTER FILMS: FAMILY BUSINESSES, ORGANISED CRIME

'It's a Sicilian message. It means Luca Brasi sleeps with the fishes.'

(Clemenza, *The Godfather*, 1972)

Francis Ford Coppola and Martin Scorsese in particular revitalised the Hollywood gangster film in the early 1970s, reworking classical stage tropes and making films that remain touchstones for the genre. With the strictures of the Motion Picture Code abolished, filmmakers were no longer obliged to adhere to the theme 'crime doesn't pay'. Gangsters could be depicted as they wished and violence and profanity weren't such issues. Depression era gangsters were replaced by a criminal element that had been operating for years, but was only made known in detail to the general public in 1963 when former Cosa Nostra member Joe Valachi was recruited by the FBI. He broke 'the code' and divulged the structure, internal workings and rituals of the Mafia while exposing its members to a special US Senate committee. Of course, these revelations resulted in books on the subject of organised crime published from the late 1960s onwards and, just as pulp fiction had influenced the development of the detective and police genres, books about organised crime mobsters such as Mario Puzo's *The Godfather* (1969) provided material for some groundbreaking revisionist gangster films.

Francis Ford Coppola's *Godfather* trilogy is hugely responsible for shaping the general public's knowledge of the Italian-American Mafia through the depiction of Don Corleone's family and organised crime dynasty. Dialogue from the *Godfather* films has seeped into common parlance, most particularly 'Godfather' Vito Corleone's 'I'm gonna make him an offer he can't refuse', which has been quoted and parodied endlessly. ('Leave the gun, take the cannoli' is a distant but brilliant second.) Coppola made *The Godfather* in 1972 and *The Godfather, Part II* in 1974, co-writing the scripts with author Mario Puzo. Coppola completed the trilogy in 1990. Paramount Pictures had optioned Puzo's novel, and Coppola was not their first choice of director, but his Italian heritage eventually sold him to studio head Robert Evans. The studio was cash-strapped at the time and needed a hit so, in a complete reversal of Hays Code dictums, Paramount kept pushing Coppola to add violence to make the film more exciting. Despite a troubled shoot, the film was a huge hit both critically and at the box office; it was nominated for numerous awards and won three Oscars: best picture, best actor in a leading role, and best adapted screenplay for Mario Puzo and Coppola.

The Corleone family are not folk hero gangsters out to steal from bankers who destroyed 'the little guy', but are depicted sympathetically, with psychological depth, which was an innovative approach to a gangster picture. *The Godfather* trilogy is as much a family saga as a story of organised crime gangsters. Many classic gangster conventions are utilised, but the scope of the story and its structure allow for more focus on character motivation. Don Corleone is a complex character, not just a hard man out to grab material success and power. In *The Godfather, Part I*, we see that he commands both respect and fear; he collects tributes from his 'subjects', but also protects the weak and administers justice. He is deceptively cordial and diplomatic when doing business, but there are violent repercussions for those who disrespect him or go against his wishes. He and the government officials in his pocket consider gambling a harmless vice, but he balks at getting involved in heroin distribution as he believes drug addiction destroys families and children. Don

Corleone has his own moral code with a focus on loyalty to friends and, most importantly, his family. Scenes of extreme violence are countered by genuinely tender family scenes that leave the viewer in no doubt that the Corleones truly love each other, which again makes them much more empathetic characters. 'A man who doesn't spend time with his family can never be a real man,' he tells Johnny Fontane. The importance of family is a key theme for the trilogy and does much to make us empathise with the Corleones, despite their ruthlessness and violence. In *The Godfather, Part I* we witness Don Corleone's affection for his family and his insistence that only family is to be trusted. We also learn that he has unofficially adopted Tom Hagen, his *consigliere*, who was orphaned as a child. This is a kind thing to do, which takes on deeper meaning when we learn about Vito Corleone's childhood in *The Godfather, Part II*; this backstory goes some way to explain why family is so important to him and makes us much more sympathetic towards him. It turns out that the Godfather was born Vito Andolini in Corleone, Sicily; his father was killed for insulting the local Mafia boss Don Ciccio who then murders his elder brother Paolo. His mother pleads with the Don to spare her remaining child, but he refuses, claiming that the boy will seek revenge as an adult. In desperation, she holds Don Ciccio at knifepoint, allowing her son to escape as she too is murdered. He is somehow smuggled away from Sicily onto an immigrant ship to America, is renamed 'Corleone' at Ellis Island, and is adopted by the Abbandando family. We meet Vito again when he is married with an infant son and working in the Abbandando grocery store. He loses his job thanks to Don Fanucci, the neighbourhood *padrone* who wants his nephew hired instead. Don Fanucci later tries to extort protection money from Vito, but he decides to fight back and shoots Don Fanucci, then steps into his shoes as the new, much more reasonable local *padrone*. Five years later, successful in both his olive oil import business and his illegal activities, Vito Corleone returns to Sicily and brutally murders Don Ciccio, taking the revenge Ciccio himself predicted. Don Corleone is a killer, but the backstory provides 'cause', particularly as it's clear no agent of the law will help him. Vito can choose to be a victim or to retaliate; fighting back makes him seem rather heroic as his oppressors are presented in such a negative light.

This strategy is used throughout the *Godfather* trilogy. Most of the violence we witness from the Corleone family is in retaliation to violence visited upon them. This is not to say that unprovoked violence doesn't take place. When Don Corleone makes an offer that can't be refused, it is a veiled threat of murder, as when movie mogul Jack Woltz wakes to find the head of his champion racehorse in his bed. But, in contrast to this brutal and horrifying threat, both Vito and Sonny Corleone go down in the proverbial hail of bullets after Don Corleone refuses – very politely and logically – to financially support Virgil Sollozzo's heroin distribution enterprise. Sollozzo instigates war; Don Vito survives two attempted hits, but Sonny is gunned down. This attack on his family leads to 'civilian' Michael taking revenge and killing corrupt cop Mark McCluskey and perpetrator Virgil Sollozzo. Michael is sent to Sicily to avoid retaliation where he falls in love with local beauty Apollonia, but she is blown up by a car bomb meant for him. Here too is a man who has witnessed the murder of those he loves – should he be a victim (knowing the police are supporting Sollozzo) or retaliate? As much as Michael Corleone may have wished to avoid participating in the 'family business', he is dragged in because of his love for his family and, despite his attempts to go legitimate and get out, fate seems to conspire against him: 'Just when I thought I was out, they pull me back in.' The epic timescale of the trilogy presents the rise and fall of a gangster family rather than one gangster, beginning with a boy who loses his family, but makes his mark as an immigrant criminal who rises to the top as a 'businessman' and dies an old man, loved by his family. His son Michael does not wish to join the family business, but love for his family pulls him in. He is fantastically successful with the business and close to achieving his goal to go completely legitimate but, like a feudal chieftain, is constantly under threat from his rivals. We see him survive two assassination attempts and, while he survives the second 'hail of bullets' at the opera house in *The Godfather, Part III*, his daughter does not. Don Michael Corleone dies at home in the garden as did his father, but alone and lonely, a terrible fate given the Corleone focus on family.

Coppola's most iconic works are, arguably, the films of the *Godfather* trilogy; he revisited the gangster genre with jazz age film *The Cotton Club* (1984), which deals with the famed Harlem club and Prohibition era gangsters. *The Outsiders* (1983) and *Rumblefish* (1983) are teen gang stories based on SE Hinton's best-selling novels and, like the *Godfather* films, paint emotionally rich, sympathetic portraits of their subjects and deal with the importance of friendship and family. Both films are set in Tulsa, a post-industrial, mid-western town, which offers little to boys from the wrong side of the tracks. In a sense, the teens are wannabe gangsters with nowhere to rise, doomed to battle out their petty rivalries on the mean streets of Tulsa.

Martin Scorsese made *Mean Streets* in 1972, an equally ground-breaking film based in part on his own experiences growing up in Little Italy, New York City. Its focus is primarily on the friendship between aspirational Mafia underling Charlie and his self-destructive friend Johnny Boy. Scorsese followed *Mean Streets* with other crime films, most notably *Taxi Driver* (1976), the portrait of a loner vigilante Vietnam vet and of New York City itself in the early 1970s. He returned to gangster films with *Goodfellas* (1990), which is adapted from Nicholas Pileggi's novel *Wiseguy: Life in a Mafia Family*, based on the life of former mobster Henry Hill. *Goodfellas* uses voiceover extensively – quite a common film noir device – which has the effect of making us empathise more with charismatic gangster Henry Hill as we get inside his head. Further, we are presented with two voices: Henry Hill's and his wife Karen's, an innovative strategy that provides a contrasting male and female point of view rather than the more macho focus of classic gangster films. Both characters guide us through the rise and fall of the gangster and, while Henry avoids going down in a hail of bullets, his 'revisionist' resolution – entering the witness protection plan and ratting on former associates – is still a fall from Henry's perspective and in some ways harder for him to take. 'I get to live the rest of my life a schnook,' he tells us at the film's end, which is in bitter contrast to his opening line: 'As far back as I can remember, I always wanted to be a gangster.'

Nicholas Pileggi co-wrote both *Goodfellas* and *Casino* (1995) with Scorsese; the latter is based on his book *Casino: Love and Honor in Las Vegas*. Rather than the rise of the gangster, Casino begins with his apparent fall as we see protagonist Ace Rothstein blown up with a bomb planted in his car. Again, Scorsese uses voiceover with two points of view: Ace's and his friend Nicky Santoro's. The rise and fall of Ace, Nicky, and Ace's wayward wife, Ginger, mirrors the rise and fall of the mob in Las Vegas. Ace survives the explosion and at the film's end tells us: 'But, in the end, I wound up right back where I started.' For a *real* gangster, this is a resolution worse than death.

Family is an important element of Scorsese's *Gangs of New York* (2002), set in the Five Points area of New York City in the mid-nineteenth century. Protagonist Amsterdam Vallon wants to avenge his father's death at the hands of Bill the Butcher, notorious gang leader of 'native' New Yorkers who tries to keep out the new, primarily Irish, immigrants. Scorsese's *The Departed* (2006) is a remake of Wai-keung Lau and Siu Fai Mak's successful Hong Kong crime film *Infernal Affairs* (2002), relocated to Boston, with an Irish-American gangster antagonist, crooked cop/gangster informant, and undercover cop who has infiltrated the gangster's gang. In this complex story of corruption, no one gets out alive but the embittered Detective Sergeant Dignam who takes Mafia-style revenge on the corrupt cop.

Scorsese is also executive producer of television series *Boardwalk Empire* (2010–), set in Prohibition era Atlantic City, where fictional character 'Nucky' Thompson's real-life inspiration, the politician and racketeer Enoch Johnson, allowed vice in exchange for a kickback, and in 1929 hosted a meeting of organised crime leaders. Johnson's obituary in the *Atlantic City Press* (10 December 1968) makes him sound like a classic gangster: 'He had flair, flamboyance, was politically amoral and ruthless, and had an eidetic memory for faces and names, and a natural gift of command... [Johnson] had the reputation of being a trencherman, a hard drinker, a Herculean lover, an epicure, a sybaritic fancier of luxuries and all the good things in life.' He was even sent to prison for income tax evasion like Al Capone.

Other key revisionist gangster films experimented with story structure, timescale and the gangster's journey. Louis Malle's *Atlantic City* (1980) shows the city well past its *Boardwalk Empire* heyday and the film's characters mirror this: Lou, an ageing small time gangster; Sally, who has been in the city for ten years, still nursing her dream of being a croupier in glamorous Monte Carlo; and Grace, who entered a Betty Grable lookalike contest and ended up marrying a mobster. Sally's past comes back to haunt her in the form of her estranged husband and pregnant sister who are trying to sell cocaine that belongs to the Philadelphia mob. Malle twists the gangster conventions by having the never-made-it-big gangster Lou shoot their would-be killers and free Sally to leave Atlantic City to pursue her dreams, all of which revitalises Lou's existence, even as he fades back into obscurity with Grace.

Arthur Penn's *Bonnie and Clyde* (1967) was innovative in its focus on the love story between Bonnie and Clyde, which brought a likeability to the characters and mixed tender romance with extreme violence. Such an approach would not have been possible under the Motion Picture Code.

Filmmakers also examined gangsters of various ethnicities in different American cities. Sergio Leone's *Once Upon a Time in America* (1984) is an epic tale of Jewish-American gangsters set in New York, based on *The Hoods* by Harry Grey. Brian De Palma's remake of *Scarface* (1983), written by Oliver Stone, contemporises the original by making the gangster protagonist, Tony Montana, a Cuban refugee determined to succeed by any means necessary in Miami. De Palma's film *Carlito's Way* (1993) focuses on a Puerto Rican gangster just released from prison who wants to go straight, but who can't seem to escape his old life and is gunned down. A prequel to Carlito's story focuses on his rise to power – *Carlito's Way: Rise to Power* (2005). *American Gangster* (2007), directed by Ridley Scott, is based on a true rise and fall story of 1970s Harlem gangster and heroin smuggling kingpin Frank Lucas. All of these films indicate ways in which a writer may be creative with gangster genre conventions.

....

WRITING EXERCISE:
TAKING REVENGE AS A PRELUDE TO POWER

Turning the other cheek is not something the aspirational or established gangster enjoys – revenge is. But the gangster who will rise the furthest to the top is likely to strategise before retaliating. The gangster's quest for revenge may be the focus of just a few scenes, a subplot, or the film's entire plot. In this scenario, your gangster plans revenge in order to seize power. Outline the following scenario based on specific characters, their operation and location. The actions of the characters should give a good sense of their personality and values.

Act 1/Part 1: Your gangster protagonist is part of a gang, but is not content with his position in the hierarchy. A rival continually belittles him, taking every opportunity to make him look bad in front of the gang leader. Your protagonist has been strategically working to gain the trust of the head honcho and to advance, but his rival somehow frames him for a job that goes wrong. Excuses will not placate the big boss. Your protagonist decides to take revenge on his rival and take him out of the equation.

Act 2/Part 2: Your protagonist prepares for his revenge, an event that will destroy his rival. This might be as basic as permanently undermining the rival's credibility, ousting him from the gang, or outright murder that is untraceable to the protagonist. Know the plan, but do not reveal it yet. Instead, show step by step how the protagonist is setting up his revenge. Who is he involving in the plan? Do they know what his objective is? What is their relationship to the rival? Consider props and location. What items does he buy or gather to facilitate his plan? (Guns, duct tape, masks, disguises...) Does he scout out locations (a bridge, tall building, remote location...) When the plan is ready to go, a phone call is made...

Act 3/Part 3: The plan for revenge is put into action. The associates perform their tasks, the props and locations should be used in an interesting or surprising way. Decide if your protagonist is successful in his bid for revenge or if a twist makes it all go wrong. Did the rival anticipate the revenge plot? Or did the Big Boss? Or was the protagonist betrayed? Or does everything go smoothly, with the protagonist rising further in the hierarchy, with perhaps a hint that there is another rival waiting in the wings?

....

THE UNMAKING OF TWO YOUNG GANGSTERS: *FRESH* AND *TSOTSI*

Two revisionist gangster films with young protagonists and a redemptive character arc are Boaz Yakin's *Fresh* (1994) – his first feature as both writer and director – and Gavin Hood's *Tsotsi* (2005), based on the novel by Athol Fugard. This major twist on the classic gangster film resolution brings a sense of hope without compromising the genre's inherent realism. Like *The Godfather*, both films deal with family as a key theme; how loss of a caring family can lead to a loss of humanity, but how familial love can also redeem.

Fresh introduces a number of gangster tropes, then twists them for a new take on the genre. Protagonist Michael, known as 'Fresh', is a Brooklyn-based, 12-year-old gangster in the making who works for local drug dealer Esteban as a drug pusher and courier. He is serious, tough, hardworking, and disdainful of the drug addicts he deals with. Fresh watches everything that goes on, but reveals little about himself and saves the money he earns. He continues to attend school, trying to balance his job and education. Initially it seems that his plan is to work his way up the 'gangster ladder', which is encouraged by Esteban.

Family is important to Fresh but, unlike the close-knit unit of *The Godfather*, Fresh's family is fractured. He lives with an aunt and numerous cousins in public housing, but isn't particularly close to them. His mother is dead and his sister – whom he does care about – lives with a man because he provides her with drugs. Fresh's only contact with his father, an alcoholic speed chess hustler who lives in a caravan, is when they meet to play speed chess in the park. These chess lessons serve as metaphors for life, particularly when his father tells him, 'You're playing each piece like losing it hurts. This ain't checkers. You want my king, you got to come get my king. All these other pieces are just the means to do it.' After Fresh witnesses the death of a girl he likes from a stray bullet, he decides to get his sister and himself out of a world that will undoubtedly destroy them. He puts his father's advice into action and comes up with a plan that pits drug dealer against drug dealer and requires Fresh to act fearlessly and ruthlessly, pursuing his goal by any means necessary – like a gangster – but he is also objective and strategic, skills learned by playing chess with his father. Fresh manages to escape being gunned down and his plan succeeds. This positive resolution is a major twist of gangster genre conventions; the protagonist is no innocent and perhaps he will continue along a criminal path in future, but we are left with a sense of his redemption.

The teenage protagonist of *Tsotsi* goes by that name as it means 'thug'; he is a brutal, hardened gang leader who lives in the townships of Johannesburg and exists by robbing people and stealing cars to sell. He is intense, fearless, and ruthless, with little apparent respect for other human beings, except for his gang – Butcher, Aap and Boston – who are his surrogate and utterly dysfunctional family. After Butcher murders a man they are mugging, Boston is traumatised and Tsotsi is visibly affected. This is amplified when Boston drunkenly harangues them about their lack of humanity and decency, prompting Tsotsi to brutally beat him. Tsotsi then hijacks a car, shooting the female owner in the stomach. After driving away, he discovers a baby in the back. It's never clear why Tsotsi doesn't abandon the baby somewhere, but it seems that he now considers the child his and tries ineffectually to care for it. We then learn through short flashbacks that his beloved mother, dying from a terminal illness, left him in the control of his embittered alcoholic father who brutally killed Tsotsi's dog without provocation. This prompted Tsotsi to leave home for life on the streets when still a child and this is how the gang came together.

Struggling to care for the infant begins to humanise Tsotsi. He soon understands that he can't cope with the baby on his own, so he forces Miriam, a local girl with a young child, to feed the infant. His interaction with this new surrogate family humanises him further, and he attempts to make amends to some of the people he has brutalised, giving money to a beggar he previously threatened and moving Boston into his shack to recuperate. He then promises to finance Boston's examination to become a teacher and decides to rob the wealthy parents of the infant to achieve this, while simultaneously stealing things for the baby. But the robbery goes wrong when John, the baby's father, triggers an alarm. Butcher readies to murder John, but Tsotsi shoots Butcher first, shocking both Aap and John. Soon after, Miriam discovers that Tsotsi abducted the infant and persuades him to return the child. He finally capitulates and tells John over the house intercom that he will hand over the baby. But the police arrive and it looks like Tsotsi will be gunned down. John takes the baby and tries to persuade the police not to kill the emotional Tsotsi. The film ends with Tsotsi facing the police, hands in the air.

Two alternative endings were shot, but director Gavin Hood went with the ambiguous ending after audience testing. In one, Tsotsi is shot in the shoulder, but escapes. By the end of the film we should be hoping that Tsotsi survives, but it's also rather too 'feel good' as an option. In the other alternative version, Tsotsi is gunned down after reaching for the baby's milk, which of course the police presume is a gun. This is more in keeping with the classic gangster demise, but would feel rather predictable when the basic premise has more originality. It would also focus on futility as a key theme – Tsotsi might have regained some humanity, but he has died nevertheless, which undercuts a sense of hope.

WORLD DOMINATION:
EUROPEAN, JAPANESE AND OTHER GANGSTER FILMS

Casino Manager: 'It was a good night. Nothing unusual.'
Harold: 'Nothing unusual, he says! Eric's been blown to smithereens,
Colin's been carved up, and I've got a bomb in me casino, and you
say nothing unusual?'

(*The Long Good Friday*, 1980)

Gangster films are obviously not just 'Hollywood'; European films about gangsters and the criminal underworld evolved from early pulp fiction criminal mastermind films, sometimes with an added twist of Hollywood gangster and a dash of noir.

There were few gangster films made in Great Britain prior to the late 1940s, in part due to restrictions set by the British Board of Censors. Murder mysteries or lone perpetrators were more acceptable than criminal gangs taking on the systems of control. When censorship policies were relaxed after the Second World War, British gangsters began to appear on screen. *Brighton Rock* (1947), adapted from Graham Greene's novel, is one of the most acclaimed classical stage British gangster films, charting the rise and fall of gangster sociopath Pinkie. This was followed by a flurry of dark, more realist gangster films in the early 1960s such as *The Criminal* (1960) and *The Frightened City* (1961). Two more acclaimed British films that feature gangsters are *Get Carter* (1971) and *The Long Good Friday* (1980); the protagonists of these two films, Jack Carter and Harold Shand, are both established gangsters who have already risen to the top of the London underworld. Both have a problem that they approach like the hardened gangsters they are. Carter returns to his home town of Newcastle to take vengeance on whoever killed his brother. Harold Shand is out to destroy an unknown antagonist that is sabotaging his plans to go legitimate. These quests both lead to their fall/execution, but within a tighter timeframe to increase tension and heighten the thriller aspects.

Gangster No 1 (2000) is a more recent, well-received film that chronicles the rise and fall of a British gangster. While there is no shortage of British crime films involving gangsters, many are heist films, which have a different structure and focus. Some urban gang films such as *Bullet Boy* (2004) feature characters who want to be gangsters or are trying to escape that life, but 'fall' before reaching the top of the heap or are killed despite their efforts to get out of the life.

There is a strong tradition of French crime films with gangster protagonists, but classic works by Jean-Pierre Melville are arguably more film noir, due to their more jaded protagonists and story, or heist pictures. There has been a recent resurgence of acclaimed gangster films in Europe, such as Jean-François Richet's two-part film about the rise and fall of France's most notorious gangster: *Mesrine: L'instinct de Mort* (2008) and *Mesrine: L'ennemi Public N° 1* (2008). Italian film *Romanzo Criminale* (2005), based on Giancarlo De Cataldo's novel, is an epic rise and fall tale of a criminal gang in Rome, dealing with issues of loyalty and vengeance. *Gomorrah* (2008) focuses on the feuding and vengeance within the Casalesi clan, based in Campania, Italy, and characters affected by the gangsters' actions. *City of God* (2002) follows the rise of young gangsters, led by the ruthless Li'l Zé, in the barrios of Rio de Janeiro, all documented by their friend and photographer Rocket – until the gang's inevitable fall.

The Japanese gangster or Yakuza film sub-genre evolved from Ninkyo eiga films, primarily produced in the 1960s, in which the Yakuza protagonist is an honourable outlaw, torn between duty and personal desires. Many of these films were influenced by American film noir. Akira Kurosawa's *Drunken Angel* (1948) features a gangster torn between loyalty to his old boss and going straight; it was made in post-war, American-occupied Japan and subject to American censorship. Kurosawa stated that his film *Yojimbo* (1961) was inspired by Dashiell Hammett's *The Glass Key*. *Pale Flower* (1964), *Tattooed Life* (1965), *Abashiri Bangaichi* (1965), *Tokyo Drifter* (1966), *Branded to Kill* (1967) are other early Yakuza films. Yakuza films in Japan declined in the 1990s, with the exception of Takeshi Kitano's films, which introduced the sub-genre to new audiences. A number of his films, such as *Sonatine* (1993), *Hana-bi* (1997) and *Ichi the Killer* (2001), are known internationally.

Different types of crime films feature aspirational gangsters, but what differentiates the gangster sub-genre from a heist, social drama, or crime thriller is the focus on gangster as protagonist, his complex character, and his rise and fall. Key themes addressed in gangster films tend to be loyalty, family, ambition, and the notion that crime doesn't pay. Experimenting with any of the classical stage tropes may result in a script of a different sub-genre, but that's fine if the material is exciting and has some originality.

An obvious element to experiment with is gender; gangster films invariably explore the rise and fall of the male gangster. There are heist films with female protagonists and girl gang movies, but the female gangster is a rarity in films. This is less the case in literature. Author Martina Cole writes about female gangsters and her novel *Dangerous Lady*, which focused on a London West End gangster of Irish descent, was adapted for television in 1995; Lynda La Plante's television film *Bella Mafia* (1997) was about Mafia wives out for revenge. When pampered wife Helena Ayala takes over her husband's drug smuggling operation out of sheer necessity in *Traffic* (2000), her transition to ruthless drug lord is surprising and exciting – if anything she is far more ruthless than her husband. ('Get out of the car and shoot him in the head!') It is equally satisfying and not a little frightening when Livia Soprano tries to get her own son Tony whacked in *The Sopranos*.

YOU LAUGHIN' AT ME?: THE PARODY STAGE

'Thank you, fellow opera-lovers. It's been ten years since I elected myself president of this organisation and if I say so myself, you made the right choice. Let's look at the record – in the last fiscal year we made a hundred and twelve million dollars before taxes... only we didn't pay no taxes!'

(Little Bonaparte, *Some Like it Hot*)

Given that many gangster films focus on the rise and fall of the gangster himself rather than one specific investigation or heist, gangster parodies tend to focus on parodying a tough guy, perhaps in an unusual situation and poking fun at audience expectations for such a character, but there are a few notable exceptions. *Bugsy Malone* (1976) is a rise and fall of the gangster Bugsy, with all the roles played by children and music thrown in. The tagline for *Johnny Dangerously* (1984) was 'Organised crime has never been so disorganised!' Michael Keaton parodies 'classic' gangster James Cagney when playing Johnny Dangerously. In *The Freshman* (1990) Marlon Brando plays Carmine Sabatini, spoofing his iconic performance as Don Corleone. In *Home Alone* (1990), the video Kevin McCallister plays over and over to scare off the thugs is *Angels with Filthy Souls*, a film-within-a-film parody of *Angels with Dirty Faces* (1938); it was followed up by *Angels with Filthier Souls* in *Home Alone II*. *Get Shorty* (1995) is based on the comic gangster novel by Elmore Leonard, which places wise-guy Chili Palmer in Hollywood trying to get into the film business. This fish-out-of-water concept offers plenty of material for comedy as the taglines indicate: 'Drug smuggling. Racketeering. Loan sharking. Welcome to Hollywood!' or 'The Mob Is Tough. But It's Nothing Like Show Business.' In the follow up novel and adaptation, *Be Cool* (2005), Chili tries the music business. The novels and films poke fun at both gangster movies and the film and music industries. *Jane Austen's Mafia!* (1998) – 'the comedy you can't refuse' – is a parody of *The Godfather*. Billy Crystal's *Analyse This* (1999) and *Analyse That* (2002) put the archetypal tough guy mobster Paul Vitti in a 'fish out of water' situation when he is released into psychologist Dr Ben Sobel's care. Again, the tagline is revealing: 'New York's most powerful gangster is about to get in touch with his feelings. YOU try telling him his 50 minutes are up.' *Analyse This* makes numerous references to *The Godfather* and part of the conceit was in casting Robert De Niro, who has brilliantly portrayed a number of gangsters, including a young Vito Corleone.

Gangsters were parodied even earlier in cartoon animations. In *Racketeer Rabbit* (1946) Bugs Bunny tangled with gangsters Rocky and Mugsy in a spoof of *Little Caesar*. *Bugs and Thugs* (1954), *Bugsy and Mugsy* (1957) and *The Unmentionables* (1963) are other Bugs

Bunny animated episodes that spoofed gangster films, as did *Catty Cornered* (1953) with Tweety Bird and Sylvester. Edward G Robinson's iconic performance was also parodied by a frog in *Courageous Cat and Minute Mouse*. Animations in particular emphasise a genre's classic tropes as they are parodied with an exaggerated visual style.

....

WRITING EXERCISE:
THE UNEXPECTED RISE OF AN UNEXPECTED GANGSTER

Either randomly select a character from your image kit or think of a very unlikely character for a mobster. His or her apparent unsuitability might be due to age, gender, occupation, where they live, their level of intelligence, personality, or any other factor. Think of a situation where the rise and fall of an unusual gangster might play out, such as in a retirement village or a gardening club. Outline the rise and fall of your gangster, satirising key tropes. Consider what truths you might expose about that specific world or its characters through a gangster parody.

....

THE SHADOWY ART OF DECEPTION:
FILM NOIR

'I didn't know I was doing film noir, I thought they were detective stories with low lighting!'

(Marie Windsor)

Neon sizzles through the black, bounces off gloomy, rain-slicked city streets, spelling out: O'Flanagan's Bar. Above the bar, a window. Inside, a dingy room. Light seeps through the slates of Venetian blinds, glinting off an empty bourbon bottle. A man sits in the shadows, feet up on his desk, Fedora pulled down over his eyes, nursing the last of the bourbon. The sound of high heels echo in the hallway – approaching. He stirs, then sits up when a woman walks through the door. She's beautiful, she's in trouble, and she thinks the down-at-heel detective can help her. He figures she's bad news and her story is a little crooked, but he doesn't turn her down.

Most would figure this for a film noir sequence. It has a recognisable style and tone, but is it a genre? Paul Schrader, for one, says no. 'Film noir is not a genre. It is not defined, as are the western and gangster genres, by conventions of setting and conflict, but rather by the more subtle qualities of tone and mood. It is a film 'noir', as opposed to the possible variants of film gray or film off-white' (Paul Schrader, 'Notes on Film Noir', *Film Comment*, 1972).

A number of film theorists agree with him. Film noir certainly has an expected visual style, but the stories themselves can be associated with other sub-genres such as gangster, social realism, political thrillers and love stories, so it's easy to argue that film noir is the style but not the substance. Film noirs were primarily labelled melodramas by Hollywood studios when released. The term originated in France and was applied to European films well before Hollywood 'noirs'. It would seem that French noir films of the 1930s were predecessors of 1940s American noir, which in turn inspired filmmakers who launched the French New Wave, a movement that influenced revisionist filmmakers in America to create films that might be termed 'neo-noir'. Whether or not film critics and academics believe that film noir is truly a genre, films labelled as 'noir' do have specific conventions. The noir protagonist is the most particular: the hero on a downward spiral. This jaded, cynical character is very different to the aspirational gangster, the duty-driven police man or woman, or the inquiring sleuth. Deception is also a key part of film noir, typically in the shape of the antagonist, often a femme fatale. Perhaps when trying to define if a picture is truly 'noir' or merely copying the stylistics of film noir, the key is to examine the nature of the protagonist, antagonist and theme. Certainly a screenwriter who wishes to write a film noir or neo-noir piece must be able to capture the jaded, bitter realism of the noir world, where trust leads to deception and, usually, murder. Rarely is there redemption unless found in death itself.

PRIMITIVE STAGE FILM NOIR: OUT OF THE SHADOWS

'Stories about life on the streets. Shady characters, crooked cops, twisted love and bad luck. The French invented the name for these pictures: "film noir" – black film, that's what they called them. About a darker side of human nature, about the world as it really was.'

(Richard Widmark)

One of the arguments made against film noir being a genre is that it had a limited period of few films, beginning in 1940 with RKO's

Stranger on the Third Floor (or, some say, in 1941 with *The Maltese Falcon* as the first detective noir) and ending in 1959. This would suggest that there is no real primitive stage to film noir or that there is little differentiation between primitive stage and classical stage noirs. The style of film noir had precursors in Europe, however. The high contrast lighting and unusual camera angles of early 1920s German expressionist cinema that included films such as *The Cabinet of Dr Caligari* (1920) and FW Murnau's *Nosferatu* (1922) were an inspiration for the visual style of Hollywood film noir, while the Neue Sachlichkeit movement with its objective, realist content seems an appropriate predecessor. *Die Freudlose Gasse* (1925) by Georg Wilhelm Pabst focused on poverty in post-war Vienna and is a story of corruption, prostitution and murder. It was heavily edited by censors. Equally dark tales by Pabst include *Diary of a Lost Girl* (1929), which deals with suicide, illegitimacy and prostitution, and *Pandora's Box* (1929), with proto-femme fatale Lulu. Murnau's Hollywood film *Sunrise* (1927) also features a proto-femme fatale who meets her comeuppance after urging a married man to murder his wife; his final film *Tabu* (1931) influenced filmmakers such as Jean Renoir and Renoir's assistant at the time, Luchino Visconti.

Renoir is considered a leading filmmaker of the French Poetic Realism movement, which recreated 'realism' in a stylised manner, influenced by realist literary and pre-war French society. The films depicted working class or criminal characters sympathetically but also fatalistically in that the resolution was typically the disillusionment or death of the protagonist. The lighting and art direction was influenced by German expressionism. The overall tone of these films is bitter – not dissimilar to a film noir – and all were adapted from preexisting texts. Renoir's films *Les Bas-fonds* (1936) and *La Bête Humaine* (1938) are considered key poetic realist films. Other influential films of the movement are Julien Duvivier's *Pépé le Moko* (1937) and Marcel Carné's *Le Quai des Brumes*, which won the *Grand Prix National du Cinéma Français* in July 1938; a review in the 8 July 1938 edition of *Le Petit-journal* noted that the film was 'full of artistic merits but of a highly peculiar kind. A *film noir*, an immoral, demoralising film whose effects on the public can be nothing but harmful.' The Motion Picture Code of 1930 could not have put it better, and this comment is a foretaste of the reactions to American film noirs such as *Murder My Sweet* (1944), *Double Indemnity* (1944) and *The Lost Weekend* (1945), three films French critic Jean-Pierre Chartier labelled as 'noir' in his article 'Americans Also Make Noir Films' published in *La Revue du Cinéma* (November 1946). Film noir also has something of a link with Italian neorealism. Not only did Luchino Visconti work with Jean Renoir, but Renoir gave Visconti his copy of James M Cain's 1934 novel *The Postman Always Rings Twice*. The novel was the basis for Visconti's film *Ossessione* (1943), often considered the first Italian neorealist film, a movement that had similar characteristics to poetic realism.

CLASSICAL STAGE FILM NOIR: FEMMES FATALES AND DOWNWARD SPIRALS

'Yes, I killed him. I killed him for money and for a woman. I didn't get the money and I didn't get the woman. Pretty, isn't it?'

(Walter Neff, Double Indemnity)

Raoul Walsh's *The Roaring Twenties* (1939) is frequently considered the last great gangster film, which was followed by the advent of film noir; émigré German and Austrian directors, writers and cinematographers are credited with introducing many of the elements of noir to Hollywood. Whether the cycle of Hollywood melodramas rebranded as film noirs began in 1940 or 1941, these cynical tales were first produced during the Second World War and continued after the war concluded, introducing post-war elements to the stories. The titles of classic film noirs suggest that these 'hard-boiled melodramas' did not have the content of happy-go-lucky musicals: *This Gun For Hire* (1942), *Double Indemnity* (1944), *The Lost Weekend* (1945), *Detour* (1945), *The Postman Always Rings Twice* (1946), *The Killers* (1946), *The Big Sleep* (1946), *Brute Force*

(1947), *The Big Steal* (1949), *Night and the City* (1950), *The Asphalt Jungle* (1950), *Sunset Boulevard* (1950), *In a Lonely Place* (1950), *Kiss Me Deadly* (1955) and *Touch of Evil* (1958) to name a few. Famously jaded protagonists include characters played by Humphrey Bogart and Alan Ladd in doomed relationships with femme fatales performed by actresses such as Barbara Stanwick, Ava Gardner, Gloria Grahame and Lana Turner.

The French critic Jean-Pierre Chartier summed up Hollywood film noirs with the following in his article 'Les Américains aussi font des films "noirs"' for *La Revue du Cinéma* (November, 1946): 'Women as insatiable as Empress Messalina, animalistic or senile husbands, young guys ready to kill for the sexual favours of a femme fatale, unrepentant alcoholics – these are the charming types from the films we've discussed. There's been talk of a French school of "film noir," but *"Le Quai des Brumes"* and *"L'Hotel du Nord"* contain some glimmer of resistance to the dark side, where love provides at least the mirage of a better world, where some revindication of society opens the door for hope, and even though the characters may despair they retain our pity and our sympathy. There is none of that in the films before us now: these are monsters, criminals and psychopaths without redemptive qualities who behave according to the preordained disposition to evil within themselves.' Chartier also observed that: 'The result is that the actions of all these figures seem conditioned by an obsessive and fatal attraction to the crime itself.'

Some French poetic realist films were remade in Hollywood such as Jean Renoir's *La Chienne* (aka *Isn't Life a Bitch?*) (1931), retitled *Scarlet Street* and directed by Fritz Lang in 1945. *Scarlet Street* was banned in a number of US states as its content was deemed potentially corruptive with an illicit love affair, deception, theft, a corrupt policeman and, most importantly, protagonist 'Chris Cross' getting away with murder.

CLASSIC FILM NOIR CONVENTIONS

'You're like a leaf that the wind blows – from one gutter to another.'
(Jeff Bailey to Kathie Moffat, *Out of the Past*, 1947)

Film noir is a cynical take on melodrama with a focus on deception to achieve a goal and finding a fall guy to take the rap. It's not about the characters' dreams, but their nightmares. A sense of underlying desperation permeates film noirs – desperate men and women will go to unpleasant extremes to get what they want if they see no other way out.

Protagonist: The Hero on a Downward Spiral

'It was the bottom of the barrel, and I was scraping it.'
(Jeff Bailey, *Out of the Past*)

'What I like about you is you're rock bottom. I wouldn't expect you to understand this, but it's a great comfort for a girl to know she could not possibly sink any lower.'
(Joan to Halliday, *The Big Steal*)

The film noir protagonist is typically a male anti-hero – a jaded, cynical and pessimistic loner who doesn't like to get involved with anything or anyone. It is hinted that an event in his past has made him this way, but the specifics usually aren't revealed. He is on a downward spiral and tries to hide an acute sense of loneliness that makes him ripe for seduction (and, with that, deception). There is no rise and fall – his journey is just down, down, down… a descent temporarily stalled by his mistaken impression that a woman might be his salvation. But, instead, as he dangles from a window ledge high above his own destruction, the femme fatale grinds her high heels into his fingers until his final grip loosens, and he plunges to his metaphorical death – if not his literal one. The relationship between the protagonist and his (perceived) female saviour is highly charged, sexual, and often leads to violence, either to a third party, the protagonist, or both. The protagonist is typically required to make morally ambiguous decisions, is lured into committing a crime – typically murder – and the loved one usually betrays him, reinforcing his negative world view or resulting in his destruction.

Antagonist: The Deceiver, the Femme Fatale

Ann Miller: 'She can't be all bad. No one is.'
Jeff Bailey: 'Well, she comes the closest.'

(***Out of the Past***)

'I don't pray. Kneeling bags my nylons.'

(**Lorraine Minosa, *Ace in the Hole***)

The femme fatale is the most well-known film noir antagonist. She is a siren: sexy, seductive, and well aware of her ability to ensnare men. She is also deceptive and conniving with an ulterior motive (or two or three). The femme fatale is also unknowable – it may seem that she has been redeemed by love for the protagonist, but it is never clear whether she is merely feigning redemption. The femme fatale has been disillusioned and hardened by her past, but the stories she tells the protagonist about those who have done her wrong may be exaggerations or lies – it is impossible to know if she is telling the truth. The narrative is typically presented from the protagonist's point of view, and we are rarely given the chance to directly assess her stories or actions without the filter of the protagonist's judgement. She uses men to get what she wants and her success at manipulation encourages men to fear her as she has made them vulnerable.

The antagonist might also be male, but deception and betrayal are key. In film noir the antagonist is camouflaged in some way and secret enemies are often more powerful than those that make themselves known. The protagonist's adversary may also be a self-destructive vice such as drinking or gambling or an event from the past that has sent him on a downward spiral and comes back to claim him.

Type of Plot or Story Pattern: The focus of any film noir is deception and betrayal. The protagonist is either persuaded to do something criminal, usually murder, to assist the femme fatale he has fallen for, or he may be on a quest to halt the destruction of another person or himself, a task that seems futile from the beginning. The narrative is often non-linear and complex with the use of flashbacks or a 'bookend' structure, beginning in the present and flashing back to recount most of the story, then returning to the present to conclude the narrative. The deception and subsequent fall of the protagonist can occur in many ways: from a relationship with a woman; from being falsely or wrongly accused; from being double-crossed; or all of the above. The femme fatale love story pattern is the cynical version of the rom com in which boy meets girl, loses girl, and wins girl back. In the noir 'love story', boy meets girl, girl seduces boy into committing a crime, girl double-crosses boy. In a film noir with a quest element the falsely accused protagonist may be forced to prove his innocence or to escape some negative element from his past, both of which threaten to pull him under.

- *Act I:* We are introduced to the disillusioned protagonist's world, sometimes with the aid of his voiceover, which is then disrupted by an event. It may be a meeting with the femme fatale love interest, the discovery of a murder, or something negative resurrected from his past. He is then locked into his quest by promising to help the femme fatale, the desire to clear his name, or the need to discover the identity of the (true) murderer. The protagonist is typically reluctant to get involved but has either been seduced or forced into action.

- *Act II:* Focuses on either the planning and preparation for a crime dreamed up by the femme fatale or a desperate investigation to uncover the true murderer or the protagonist's attempt to prove his innocence. Nothing is what it seems and the protagonist is challenged to work out who he can really trust; typically he gets it wrong. There is a sense throughout that the protagonist is a victim. There are numerous twists and turns to the plot, emphasising the idea that there is no way out. The protagonist may be presented with clues that the femme fatale is lying or manipulating him, but he is blind to them. If fighting to clear his name or solve a murder, the protagonist may chase a red herring. By the end of Act II, the protagonist is ready to put the femme fatale's plan in action or it may look as if he will be successful in his quest to clear his name or solve a crime.

- *Act III:* The femme fatale's plan is put into action and all looks to be going well, until the femme fatale double-crosses the protagonist, leading to a less than happy ending or, perhaps, his murder. If he survives, the femme fatale often dies, but the protagonist finds little joy in her demise. If the protagonist has been falsely accused of a plan and knows who the true perpetrator is, then the third act is about proving it. He may succeed in this, but might lose his own life or something dear to him. If the protagonist survives his ordeal, he is more cynical and disillusioned than ever and likely to self-destruct in some uncertain future.

Narrative style: A film noir typically deals with a crime of physical violence, often murder, but the focus is on the emotional violence even more than the physical. When a femme fatale is the antagonist, there is a sexual intensity between her and the protagonist. The sexual flirtation is very knowing rather than innocent and there is a sense of doomed passion. In classical stage film noirs, both the protagonist and antagonist smoke cigarettes, a flirtation strategy that adds to the femme fatale's sexual allure and to his tough guy image. Children rarely appear in film noirs as they represent hope and the future whereas 'noir' is about desperation and deception. Film noir dialogue is sharp, wise-cracking, fast talking, and full of double entendres with sexual subtext. There may be a voiceover narration from the protagonist, which puts the focus on the narrator's point of view, and it may be unreliable. There are often scenes of plotting (typically of a murder), driven by the protagonist's lust for the femme fatale followed by a revelation to the protagonist that he has been betrayed. The revelation does not surprise him and adds to his sense of disillusionment. Concealed weapons are the norm, used to threaten or double-cross the protagonist. Physical violence is mixed with emotional violence, which is normally more devastating for the protagonist, even if expected.

Timeframe/Pace: Often time is compressed in a film noir through the use of ellipses, flashbacks or voiceover. The protagonist may fall for the femme fatale very quickly – a kind of *amour fou* – but the time taken for her to seduce him into committing a crime for her is compressed, whereas the build towards the crime itself and the protagonist's destruction is much faster, a ticking clock towards the event which also signifies that the protagonist's time is running out.

Tone: Overall, the tone of the film is pessimistic, ominous, and often nightmarish, with a focus on deception and the worst characteristics of people. In many ways, there is a strong sense of realism in that characters and their intentions are not sugar-coated, and while we may hope for the best from people, it is perhaps not completely surprising when they act ignobly. The use of shadows and unusual framing emphasises that the line between truth and falsehood is intentionally blurred. In many ways film noirs play to our fears: of being deceived, of our pasts coming back to haunt us, of our weaknesses destroying us. The classic film noir voiceover adds an ironic edge; the protagonist is cynical and self-mocking, a strategy which undercuts the audience thinking him a schmuck as he tells us all his failings first. The tone is very different to that of a classic gangster picture, just as the gangster and noir protagonists are normally poles apart.

Setting and Mise-en-scène: Film noirs are associated with the shadowy, rain-swept, mean streets of the city, but they also take place in small towns and derelict spaces, which are presented as desolate and alienating. Much of the action occurs at night or indoors in a shadowy location that makes the time of day difficult to gauge. Film noir uses low-key lighting for a chiaroscuro effect and a canted camera or high angle shots to add to the sense of dislocation and unease. The interplay of light and shadow is key; characters emerge from and disappear into the shadows, which enhances an atmosphere of mystery, tension and mistrust. There may be someone lurking around the corner with intent or eavesdropping in the gloom. Slatted lighting, courtesy of Venetian blinds, imprisons the characters with horizontal rather than vertical bars. The unease of the setting adds to the unknowability of the characters and, indeed, is a reflection of them. The femme fatale may look elegant and demure, but she carries a gun in her handbag. Characters tend to be armed and it is not uncommon for the protagonist to be shot or at least threatened with a gun. The archetypal film noir costume for men is a trench coat and Fedora or trilby hat pulled low; cigarettes are smoked to enhance sex appeal and to obscure with a filter of haze. All in all, the film noir atmosphere is at once beautiful and unnerving, a deadly spider's web glinting in artificial dappled light breaking through blackness.

WRITING EXERCISE: SEDUCTION AS DECEPTION

Film noirs are about deception and, frequently, seduction. When there is a seduction, the protagonist often finds out that it was a deception. In both seduction and deception, character strategy is key, as is hiding one's true motivation. The most useful fall guy is one who gets involved willingly in a crime, little knowing that he is being set up.

- Briefly describe your male protagonist: name, age, background, whether he has a job and, most importantly, why he's on a downward spiral of self-destruction or complete ambivalence.

- Describe your femme fatale: name, age, background, job and, most importantly, who she wants 'out of the way' and why.

- How and where do your noir anti-hero and femme fatale meet? Is it by chance or does she engineer it?

- Write a dialogue scene in which your protagonist thinks he is seducing the femme fatale, but it is actually the other way around. She plays hard to get but, whenever he is in danger of giving up, she lures him back in. Within the scene, your femme fatale must mention the character she wants him to dispose of and she must win over his sympathy.

- Conclude the scene with the femme fatale being summoned by the potential victim (in person or 'remotely'). Describe her reaction to this summons, which is effective in winning the protagonist over to her side. The protagonist makes a decision to see her again and proposes another meeting. Again, she plays hard to get, but acquiesces.

- Try the same scene with a female protagonist and a 'l'homme fatale'.

....

THE TRANSATLANTIC WAVE: POETIC REALISM TO FILM NOIR TO THE NOUVELLE VAGUE

'There is no greater solitude than that of the samurai unless it be that of a tiger in the jungle... perhaps...'

(Opening caption, Le Samurai, 1967)

Just as expressionist cinema and poetic realism influenced the style and content of film noir, film noir was admired by filmmakers in Europe and inspired their work. A key example is French director Jean-Pierre Melville (1917–73) who was nicknamed the 'Garlic Gangster', 'Poet of the Underworld', and 'Father of the Nouvelle Vague'. He introduced elements of the gangster and film noir sub-genres into his films, and his work in turn had an influence on French filmmakers like Truffaut and Godard, revisionist American filmmakers such as Martin Scorsese and Quentin Tarantino, and Hong Kong director John Woo. The titles of his works have the same ominous quality as most American film noirs and, despite Melville's nickname, his protagonists tend to be more 'noir' than gangster, solitary trench coat and Fedora wearing criminals (or the associates of criminals), on a downward path rather than the rise. The quality of these characters is superbly captured by Melville's frequent collaborators Alain Delon and Jean-Paul Belmondo. *Le Samourai* (1967), starring an icy Delon, is the story of a hit man who couldn't be more noir, even if he finds redemption through his own death. *Le Samourai* heavily influenced films such as Walter Hill's *The Driver* (1978), John Woo's *The Killer* (1989), and Jim Jarmusch's *Ghost Dog: The Way of the Samurai* (1999). Most of Melville's other crime films such as *Le Doulos* (1962), *Bob le Flambeur* (1956), *Le Deuxième Souffle* (1966), *Le Cercle Rouge* (1970), and *Un Flic* (1972) have the visual conventions and tone of film noir, but revolve around an intended heist – often 'one last job'. These plans are typically unravelled by betrayal, leading to the protagonist's downfall.

REVISIONIST FILM NOIR STORIES AND A NEW LOOK AT THE DARK SIDE WITH NEO-NOIR

Gilda: 'I hate you so much that I would destroy myself to take you down with me.'

(*Gilda*, 1946)

Touch of Evil (1958) is sometimes cited as the end of the film noir cycle, but that would be to underestimate the influence of the sub-genre (or mode or style) of films made thereafter and to ignore films labelled 'neo-noir'. There were also revisionist noir films made during its classical stage, possibly the best known of which is *Gilda*. The set-up has all the usual hallmarks of a film noir – down on his luck gambler protagonist, femme fatale, decadent casino-owner husband, deception, betrayal, and labyrinthine plot, but it also has a happy (enough) ending for the reunited, adulterous lovers Gilda and Johnny. Protagonist Johnny is saved from his downward spiral and Gilda's husband, Ballin Munson, is no anonymous sap the femme fatale wants to bump off – he's a vengeful, powerful criminal with a sadistic streak who is killed while preparing to murder both Gilda and Johnny. The French labelled

Gilda a 'film gris' in light of its happy ending, although our knowledge of Gilda and Johnny's characters makes us wonder how long that happiness will last. Another important revisionist element to *Gilda* is that we the audience are given insight into Gilda's true feelings, which is unusual for a film noir – normally the femme fatale is alluring, feisty, intriguing and opaque. So an obvious way to revise the film noir sub-genre is to make the femme fatale the protagonist. Films like *The Last Seduction* (1994), *Bound* (1996) and *The Opposite of Sex* (1998) have done this. The challenge in making any 'anti-hero' (or, indeed, villain) the protagonist is to make him or her empathetic or fascinating. In *The Last Seduction* there is a key scene in which the money-hungry Bridget is slapped by her husband Clay. His brutality goes some way towards justifying her actions towards him – almost everything she does to her husband comes across as revenge after the slap. She would be a far more alienating character if Clay weren't so unpleasant and it helps that the money she steals from him is ill-gotten rather than hard earned. This is an important strategy to consider when writing anti-hero or villain protagonists; if their victims are corrupt, it tends to be easier to enjoy watching them be done over, and if the 'bad guy' protagonist has a sense of humour, even better. Violet is a femme fatale in *Bound* who seduces lesbian Corky and schemes to steal mob money from her husband. *The Opposite of Sex* is a comedy, but the sardonic teenager Dede Truitt certainly thinks of herself as a femme fatale as she attempts to seduce her gay brother's boyfriend and narrates her adventures in acerbic voiceover; the dialogue has all the sharp wit of film noir and we are presented with the point of view of a modern, if rather unsophisticated, femme fatale.

Another revisionist noir is *Brick* (2005), which has many classic film noir tropes, including wise-cracking cynical dialogue, but has a teenage loner as protagonist and is played out in a high school crime underworld. Writer/director Rian Johnson and star Joseph Gordon-Levitt teamed up again for *Looper* (2012) set in 2044. Anti-hero protagonist Joe is a hit man for a mob that operates 30 years in the future and sends its victims back in time to be whacked. *Looper* is primarily science fiction, but Joe is a classic noir anti-hero on a downward spiral until he meets a woman and finds redemption in death. Both films use film noir conventions in an innovative way and give an interesting quality to the protagonist.

'They don't advertise for killers in the newspaper. That was my profession. Ex-cop. Ex-blade runner. Ex-killer.'

'The report read: "Routine retirement of a replicant." That didn't make me feel any better about shooting a woman in the back.'

(Deckard's narration, *Blade Runner*)

Blade Runner (1982) is probably the best known film noir set in the future. Based on science fiction writer Philip K Dick's 1968 novel *Do Androids Dream of Electric Sheep?*, the story is set in a dystopian, rain and neon saturated Los Angeles circa 2019, a place where animals no longer survive and replicants – utterly life-like robots – live alongside humans. The main character, Deckard, is a jaded, solitary and retired 'blade runner' whose specialty was terminating replicants when their allotted time was up. He is called back to assist the cops in terminating four escaped replicants. Deckard is on a downward spiral until he meets the beautiful, mysterious, film noir-styled Rachael, who happens to be a replicant. Most of the characters in this world, whether human or replicant, are desperate. Deckard is essentially a hit man who falls in love with a mark. Rachael seems to fall for Deckard, or is she living up to her femme fatale costume and deceiving him to save herself? Despite the sci fi elements of the story world and the vivid neon colours dazzling the midnight blue night sky, the mise-en-scène, atmosphere and tone of Blade Runner are very film noir, as are its characters and the core plot.

Perhaps the big shoulder pads of 1980s fashion inspired something of a revival in erotically charged, fatalistic stories such as *Dressed to Kill* (1980), *Body Heat* (1981), *Body Double* (1984), *Sea of Love* (1989) and, in 1992, *Basic Instinct*, followed by *Body of Evidence* in 1993. These erotic thrillers are sometimes labelled 'neo-noir', but only *Body Heat* (loosely based on *Double Indemnity*) and *Sea of Love* have the strong dynamic of lust and mistrust between the protagonist and the femme fatale to come across as truly 'noir'.

A number of historical crime films – films set in a substantially earlier time – utilise classical stage noir tropes, albeit with more graphic violence and sex. *Chinatown* (1974), *Mulholland Falls* (1996), *LA Confidential* (1997) and *The Black Dahlia* (2006) are examples of this. *The Usual Suspects* (1995) is a thriller, but has a noir labyrinthine plot, an overall cynical atmosphere, along with plenty of deception and revenge. The resolution is downbeat for most of the ensemble cast. *Sin City* (2005) is based on Frank Miller's graphic novels, which are an homage to film noir in terms of characters, story, mood, mise-en-scène and visual style. The film itself is very faithful to the graphic novel and succeeds as neo-noir.

The best neo-noirs utilise film noir conventions in an interesting manner, often driven by a director's specific vision. David Lynch's *Blue Velvet* (1986) relocates a femme fatale and her abusive partner to small town America where a conservative young man, inadvertently embroiled in the mystery of a severed ear, has his reality unravelled as he tries to save the femme fatale. Frank Booth and Dorothy Valens's world – the dark underbelly of the American dream – is contrasted with the cheerful shininess of its façade. Lynch revisited and reworked film noir conventions in a very 'Lynchian' way to produce neo-noirs *Lost Highway* (1997) and *Mulholland Drive* (2001).

> *'Loneliness has followed me my whole life. Everywhere. In bars, in cars, sidewalks, stores, everywhere. There's no escape. I'm God's lonely man...'*
>
> **(Travis Bickle, *Taxi Driver*, 1976)**

Travis Bickle's words indicate that he has some of the characteristics of a film noir anti-hero, but it's soon clear that this protagonist is not just a disillusioned, self-destructive man 'scraping the bottom of the barrel', but rather a man on the edge of sanity. He has recently returned from war – in this case Vietnam rather than World War II – a destabilised insomniac who is isolated and unable to adapt to the new world he finds himself in. Scorsese is known for using voiceovers in his crime films; in this case the voiceovers are a kind of diary and emphasise Travis's isolation. He tries to fill his sleepless nights with work, driving his taxi all over New York City, taking paying customers anywhere they want to go, no matter how dangerous the neighbourhood. Travis dreams of 'a real rain [that] will come and wash all this scum off the streets' – the pimps, whores and hustlers viewed through his cab window. And then he meets two females: Betsy, whom he views as an angel who will somehow redeem him, and Iris, the pre-teen hooker he wants to rescue. Travis decides to shoot a presidential candidate, but abandons that goal after he is almost caught and instead kills Iris's pimp and other 'scum'. Almost by chance Travis avoids being imprisoned and vilified as an assassin; in a reversal of fortune, he is touted as a hero who rescued a girl from a predator. Despite this brief moment of glory, there is no real future for Travis and all will eventually end badly for him as is hinted with his final chance meeting with Betsy in his cab.

> 'Remember those posters that said, "Today is the first day of the rest of your life"? Well, that's true of every day but one – the day you die.'

> **(Opening voiceover, Lester Burnham, *American Beauty*)**

> 'I can't feel anything but gratitude for every single moment of my stupid little life. You have no idea what I'm talking about, I'm sure. But don't worry... you will someday.'

> **(Closing voiceover, Lester Burnham, *American Beauty*)**

It is perhaps difficult to see *American Beauty* (1999) with its suburban setting, bright colours, fluttering rose petals, and middle class American concerns as neo-noir. Consider, however, the prison bar visual motif that runs through the film – protagonist Lester Burnham is 'caught' in the bars of window frames, computer screen data, picket fences. Rather than chiaroscuro lighting, there are hyper-saturated colours, with red rose petals like blood. The film begins with a prologue of a girl in a grainy black and white video asking the cameraman to kill her father. Lester's voiceover is the biggest nod to noir; the opening and closing self-mocking monologue references *Sunset Boulevard* as the protagonist tells his tale from the beyond. Lester also notes that he is already 'dead inside'. His wife Carolyn considers him a loser and then a lost cause when he is fired from his job. Lester is certainly on a downward spiral until he meets Angela, a teenage femme fatale who flirts with him and pretends to be more 'fatale' than she actually is. While Angela doesn't goad him to commit a crime, his desire for her is trouble enough, even if she is over 16, and his quest to win her does inadvertently lead to his own murder. In borrowing key conventions from film noir – a self-lacerating voiceover, deception, blackmail, revenge, a femme fatale, guns, and murder – a fresh twist is brought to what might otherwise be called a suburban melodrama.

THE PARODY STAGE:
COMICALLY DECEPTIVE AND INEFFECTUALLY SEDUCTIVE

'Carlotta was the kind of town where they spell trouble T-R-U-B-I-L, and if you try to correct them, they kill you.'

(Rigby Reardon, *Dead Men Don't Wear Plaid*, 1982)

Film noir and its visual style are inseparable and this is the first thing that is parodied: black and white film with low-key lighting to produce a shadowy world with dramatic glints of light, whether outdoors on the dark, rain-slicked streets or inside shadowy rooms with Venetian blind filtered light. The men wear trench coats and Fedoras pulled low; the women are in figure hugging, shoulder-padded dresses. Both smoke copiously and their patter is enviably sardonic – or a comical attempt at classic 'hard-boiled'. The male protagonist attempts swagger, but utterly lacks the jaded noir protagonist's cool. The femme fatale either struggles to hide her disdain for the clumsy protagonist or is sometimes equally inept. Examples of film noir parodies include Carl Reiner's *Dead Men Don't Wear Plaid* (1982), starring Steve Martin as private eye Rigby Reardon who interacts with characters extracted from classic film noirs in a mystery/farce complete with femme fatale. *Kiss Kiss Bang Bang* (2005) is a noir parody but with a happy ending. As mentioned earlier, *The Big Lebowski* (1998) is an homage to *The Big Sleep* and parodies aspects of it for comedy. Animations such as *Hoodwinked* (2005) and animation/live action mix *Who Framed Roger Rabbit?* (1988) also spoof elements of film noir, making clear that its tropes are very recognisable to an audience.

....

WRITING EXERCISE: VOICEOVER AND THE VOICE

Screenwriters are often advised to avoid voiceover as it's bad practice. Too much 'telling' rather than 'showing' is not a good thing but, as some excellent films use voiceover, it's clear that, if used well, it can be a useful and interesting device, particularly if the character's voice is as engaging as the content itself. Character voice is an element that script readers often comment on. Does each character have an individual voice or do they all sound alike? Does the voice give an indication of a character's backstory and, perhaps, what he or she is truly like rather than the façade constructed to face the world? Experimenting with character voice is a good way to sharpen dialogue writing skills.

- Revisit your image kit and randomly pick a character.

- Access an extract of voiceover from a film, preferably a film you know. (It doesn't have to be film noir.)

- Rewrite the voiceover in the voice of the character you have selected. Consider the character's backstory, personality and current lifestyle. Think about how their dialogue reflects where they come from in terms of location, socio-economic group, their aspirations. Use regional dialect, slang, verbal tics. Is the character telling the truth or lying with the voiceover?

- Select a different character and repeat the exercise.

....

DESIGNING THE CRIME:
HEISTS AND CRIME CAPERS

'It's a very difficult job and the only way to get through it is we all work together as a team. And that means you do everything I say.'

(Charlie Croker, *The Italian Job*)

Jewels, gold, silver – the riches of kings have a perennial allure to thieves, not just because of their value, but also their beauty. These are the irresistible femmes fatale of heist stories. Stealing the big prize is a common objective in myths, folk tales and fairy tales, whether an object with magical or transformative properties such as the golden fleece and Medusa's head, or a cache of enormous value like a dragon's horde. Temptation and desire or desperate need are the protagonist's driving force. The perpetrator in a heist film may be anything from a gentleman (or woman) thief, a gang of ruthless professionals, amateur opportunists, or a reluctant robber forced to do one last job. The focus is on taking the big prize and the unique skills required to circumvent the obstacles to the prize without getting caught. The crime is often daring rather than murderous, although the two are not mutually exclusive. Often a gang pulls a heist and each member has a specific skill and temperament, which may lead to conflict and the potential for betrayal. It's important that the audience invests in the planning and preparation of the heist and, through that, the final, fraught execution of the plan. Normally we hope that the perpetrators (or most of them) will get away with it, and fear that it will all go terribly wrong. Ultimately it is easier for an audience to understand the protagonist's desire for riches than perhaps it is to understand a casual attitude towards murder.

SMASH, GRAB AND RUN: PRIMITIVE STAGE HEIST FILM

Vince Massler: 'If it's so fool-proof, why hasn't somebody done it yet?'
Danny Ocean: 'Same reason nobody's gone to the moon yet – no equipment.'
Jimmy Foster: 'And we're equipped.'

(Ocean's Eleven, 1960)

One of the earliest heist films is silent one-reeler *The Great Train Robbery* (1903), directed by Edwin S Porter, in which a group of bandits holds up a train and is pursued by the sheriff's posse. This film takes us right into the action and puts us on the side of the victims as we witness them being robbed and the good guys coming to the rescue. Porter's original version of the film famously concluded with the image of an outlaw aiming his gun directly at the camera and, therefore, the viewer. This was very innovative and the direct confrontation of the audience acknowledged its interaction with the characters on screen; the scene was also frequently edited out of exhibited versions of the film as it was deemed too violent. Primitive stage heist films tend to focus on the action of the robbery, the attempted getaway, and the pursuit by agents of the law. Normally justice prevails. These short films are the prototypes for what is normally Act III in a heist feature.

CLASSICAL STAGE HEIST FILMS:
STEALING OLD MONEY AND PLANNING TO GET AWAY WITH IT

'For a job with you he'll come. Cesar! There's not a safe that can resist Cesar and not a woman that Cesar can resist.'

(Mario Ferrati, *Rififi*)

In Europe there is a long tradition of heist films, beginning with the gentleman thief such as Arsène Lupin and organised gangs like the highwaymen robbers of the Newgate novels or Charles Dickens's Fagin and his young pickpockets. There is a clear difference between the two. The gentleman thief is after the prize, but overall avoids extreme violence, relying on his wits and the art of escape. He is a rather more sympathetic protagonist, an anti-hero or anti-villain, depending on his background and motivation. Conversely, the cut-purse, thug, or organised crime gang will slit a throat to get the prize, which makes these villains far less sympathetic characters. Classical stage heist films have certain parallels with detective stories and an audience derives a similar kind of pleasure from them. A successful heist requires meticulous planning, organisation, and skills not dissimilar to those needed by a detective attempting to unravel a mystery. (A planned heist is of course very different to an armed robbery driven by muscle and violence rather than brains.)

As already noted, many of Jean-Pierre Melville's films have a film noir protagonist, visual conventions and tone; he also made a number of influential heist stories between 1962 and 1972: *Le Doulos*, *Bob le Flambeur*, *Le Deuxième Souffle*, *Le Cercle Rouge* and *Un Flic*. *Bob le Flambeur* is one with a more upbeat ending for the 'anti-villain' and demonstrates why the audience often sides with the heist perpetrator/protagonist. Bob is a compulsive gambler and ex-con, something of a gentleman thief in that he is well-liked and has scruples. He is almost broke and plans one last heist so he can retire in comfort, his target being the huge quantity of cash held at the Deauville casino. He comes up with a complicated plan and assembles a gang, including young safecracker Paolo. Tension is added by the fact that Bob tried a heist before, which landed him in prison. Too many people blab about the plan, which gets back to Inspector Ledru, who likes Bob as he once saved his life. He hopes to warn him off the scheme, but Bob is on a rare winning streak at the casino and half forgets his plan. At the appointed hour, Bob hurriedly cashes in his considerable chips just as his gang and the police descend on the casino, triggering a shoot out. Paolo is killed and

139

Bob is arrested, his legitimate winnings loaded into the Inspector's car, but it is suggested that Bob will be set free or serve minimum time for his role in the aborted heist and will have his comfortable retirement after all. Here we have the likeable crook, an impersonal target that seems fair game, and a cop who must enforce the law, but doesn't forget when he owes someone – all elements that make us root for Bob.

Jules Dassin, an American director who worked in Europe after being blacklisted in Hollywood, was another highly influential film-maker who made noir films such as *The Naked City* (1948) and *Thieves' Highway* (1949) before the highly influential heist film *Rififi* (1955), which inspired the original *Ocean's Eleven* (1960). He later made the caper *Topkapi* (1964), a jewel heist set in Istanbul. Other classic heist films from Europe are Jean-Luc Godard's *Bande à part* (1964), Claude Sautet's *Classe tous risques* (1960), *The Friends of Eddie Coyle* (1973), *The League of Gentlemen* (1960) and *Touchez pas au grisbi* (1954). Classic caper *The Italian Job* (1969) revolves around a plan to steal a shipment of gold bullion in Torino by creating a traffic jam using very British Mini Coopers, Jaguars and a bus.

Classic Hollywood heist films such as the original *Ocean's Eleven* (1960) by Lewis Milestone have a lighter tone while *The Killers* (1946), *Criss Cross* (1949) and *The Asphalt Jungle* (1950) are more 'noir', as indicated by their titles. *The Asphalt Jungle* is about a jewel caper that goes wrong; *The Killing* (1956) features another precisely timed heist, albeit at a racetrack, also with a disastrous resolution for the gang.

CLASSICAL STAGE HEIST SUB-GENRE CONVENTIONS

'For what it's worth, I never stole from anybody who would go hungry.'

(John Robie, *To Catch a Thief*)

Protagonist: The heist story typically focuses on a gang that needs to work together to pull off the heist, but there is often a ringleader who drives the action by making the most decisions. This ringleader is typically male and a charismatic character, rather like the gangster, which makes us engage with his 'quest', or it may be revealed that he has a sympathetic motive for the heist. For example, he might be a reformed criminal who needs to do one last job to get out of the game for good; to save someone else; or because he is being coerced into it under threat of violence to himself or someone important to him. If the motive for pulling the heist isn't noble, the gang may be robbing a person or organisation that 'deserves it' due to being more corrupt than the gang. The heist might also be undertaken by a solo artist such as the gentleman thief, who tends to be charismatic with exceptional skills that allow him to penetrate the 'fortress' that protects the prize.

Antagonist: A representative of the law is often a force of antagonism, but the main adversary may be a rival gang ringleader who wants the same prize; a turncoat within the gang; or the 'victim' of the heist, who may be a bigger criminal than the protagonist. The prize itself and its location may be the force of antagonism. For example, it may be sequestered in a notoriously inaccessible location, or the prize might be cursed or have supernatural elements; it might even be a living being – an animal or human with its own views about capture.

Type of Plot or Story Pattern: The focus of the story is the protagonist and/or gang's efforts to take the big prize without getting caught. It is both a chase and an escape. The success or failure of the heist is often linked to the story's theme and controlling idea, the motives of the ringleader and his gang, and the character of the 'victim'. If the main idea behind the story is 'greed leads to self-destruction', the heist might not go well for the gang motivated by money-lust. If, however, the ringleader is plotting to reclaim or steal back an heirloom stolen from his family, the heist might have a more positive resolution.

- *Act I:* The 'call to adventure' is typically the idea for the heist or first articulation of the planned job. It may be the ringleader's idea or he may be asked or told to undertake the heist. The decision to commit to the caper, whether voluntarily or under duress, locks the protagonist into the plot to seize the prize. As before, the protagonist's motive for pulling the job is usually linked to this decision unless his true motivation is hidden as part of a plot twist. The idea of doing 'one last job' has become something of a cliché, but a very understandable one in terms of character motivation.

- *Act II:* Designing the crime. The bigger the prize, the more is at stake should the heist fail. A prison sentence is one possibility or the heist might involve a life or death situation depending on the power of the antagonist or the audaciousness of the plan. This means that much time is spent on planning the heist and preparing for the action. A complex job might need a gang with various skills in order to increase the likelihood of success and the ringleader will approach his crew, each of whom will demonstrate his or her special skill. We learn why they want to do this job and get a sense of each character's strengths and weaknesses. This genre tends to need a good amount of exposition in order to explain what the job is, why it's so difficult, the likely stumbling blocks, and the forces of antagonism. Often the heist is mapped out with diagrams, whether low or high tech, and the potential crime scene, any adversaries, and the escape route will be checked out and perhaps placed under surveillance. These scenes of planning and preparation encourage the audience to vicariously participate in the intended heist and to engage with the gang. The midpoint might bring a complication that sends the story in a slightly different direction. For example, someone finds out about the plan and wants in; a gang member is lost and must be replaced; or the plan has to be modified. By the end of Act II, the gang is ready to put the plan into action. The plan may be brilliantly designed, but the audience is aware that the tiniest slip up will make everything fall apart, so tension is high. Normally the audience has invested enough time in the charismatic ringleader and interesting gang members to hope that the plan will go well despite the myriad things that might go wrong.

- *Act III:* Action! We know what the plan is, why such a dicey job is being undertaken, and who the gang members are. Now the question is, will the plan work? And if the gang gets the goods, will they make a safe getaway? Will everyone get away, or will there be casualties along the way? Will there be a fall guy or a double cross? If the ringleader is carrying out the heist for someone else under duress, the 'mark' may be falsely presented in a negative light, which could provide a major twist in Act III. Does the ringleader then stay with the plan or change sides?

- *Resolution:* It is crucial for the audience to invest emotionally in the outcome of the heist, which should never go smoothly unless that is the surprise for the audience after much initial chaos. If the job seems too easy the audience will lose interest. As before, the resolution tends to depend upon the protagonist's motivation and the theme.

Narrative Style: The heist story has certain parallels with the police procedural in that a good deal of screen-time is spent gathering information about the potential crime scene, interviewing or researching people connected with the target, and putting together the gang. Obviously these events are the 'before' of the crime, whereas the police are investigating the 'after'. Classically, a heist story involves stealing objects of obvious value: money, gold bullion, jewels, art, contraband, a secret formula. Such objects are normally locked up in a safe or fortified room in a high security building with heavy surveillance and so a crack team must be assembled to capture the prize. Some of the skilled operatives found in a classic heist are the mastermind or logician, safecracker, forger, marksman, master of disguise, pickpocket, cat burglar, muscle, getaway driver. A modern twist on the safecracker might be the computer hacker or technology whiz. We expect to see the gang members' tools of trade put into action and to be impressed by them. Or we may find that the former expert's skills are rusty but he won't bow out or he may hide his debilitation from the group. Both options make us fear the strategy will fall about due to his weakness. Information about the objects of desire might be gathered from independent experts known to do business with the criminal underworld such as gemologists, antique dealers or art experts and, if the prize isn't money, a fence or shady dealer to sell on the goods. This stresses the value of the objects, but also emphasises the possibility of betrayal. The interaction of this band of peculiar characters needs to engage us; we expect some kind of conflict within the gang, which may come from unexpected quarters. The getaway is as important as the theft itself and rarely goes without a hitch.

Timeframe/Pace: A heist story is typically built around a specific window when it is feasible to snatch the prize. This may be when the object's owner is away from the location; when a 'horde of treasure' will be housed in a specific location; when weaknesses in a security system will occur; to coincide with exhibition dates at a particular venue. Or the heist might be scheduled around the getaway plan, which relies on certain key elements or events – for example, the tides, a new moon, a major snowfall. The protagonist may have had the venue of the heist under surveillance for years, but this is backstory information that we tend to hear about rather than see. The heist itself usually has a very tight frame of execution that needs to be precisely timed; the ticking clock and lack of room for error should keep audience members on the edge of their seats.

Tone: High adventure and daring. Even if the goal is negative, the audience should relish the audacity of the gang and find the interaction of gang members with disparate characters engaging. There may be an element of wish fulfilment for the audience, particularly if the target's owner/custodian is depicted in negative terms.

Setting and Mise-en-scène: As noted before, a heist necessitates the theft of an object or cache of value, which typically suggests invading some type of fortress that protects the prize: a bank, casino, jewellery store, art museum, wealthy person's estate. An unusual prize might be sequestered somewhere equally unusual, which brings originality to the sub-genre, but whatever the prize and its location, it must be as difficult to reach as Sleeping Beauty was to the various princes who died trying to rescue (steal?) her. If the prize is an object of beauty as well as value, there are shots of the object that allow us to covet it also: spectacular jewels, piles of gold bullion, stacks of money. The prize may also provide comic value. For example, a painting or artefact worth a fortune might be deemed ugly by its would-be thieves.

REVISIONIST STAGE HEIST DRAMAS: A TWIST IN THE TALE

'What you think this is, the wheel of fortune? You think you can make your dough and fuck off? Leave the table? Thanks Don, see you Don, off to sunny Spain now Don, fuck off Don. Lying in your pool like a fat blob laughing at me, you think I'm gonna have that? You really think I'm gonna have that, ya ponce? All right, I'll make it easy for you. God knows you're fucking trying. Are you gonna do the job? It's not a difficult question, are you gonna do the job, yes or no?'

(Don, *Sexy Beast*)

Most of the classic heist sub-genre conventions can be twisted to bring an original angle as the heist picture normally features a male protagonist and gang pursuing obvious targets: jewels, gold, money, drugs. An obvious place to start if making a revisionist heist film is to make the mastermind a woman, the gang all-female, or reassign a typically 'macho role' to a female: getaway driver, physical muscle, expert marksman, safecracker. (Surprisingly, this is still considered unexpected.) The protagonist might also be very young or elderly, have a role in life that makes them less suspicious (a nun or priest, a housewife, a doctor), or a personality that makes them an unlikely suspect (timid, scatterbrained, shy). As before, the prize might be unusual: computer code, a person, a rare plant, a deadly toxin, an artefact from the past or another world. The location and the time period will influence what the prize is, how the heist is carried out, and the skills of the gang members.

Alfred Hitchcock's *To Catch a Thief* (1955) features a reformed jewel thief, played by Cary Grant, forced to play detective in order to clear his name. The story of a protagonist falsely accused and struggling to prove the accusations false as the clock ticks is classic thriller stuff; making the protagonist a supposedly reformed jewel thief and acknowledging heist story conventions brings something new to the story.

Sexy Beast (2000) by Jonathan Glazer is a tense crime drama that utilises classic elements of the heist film. Protagonist Gal Dove has retired to Spain with his wife after a lucrative career as an expert safecracker, followed by nine years in prison after taking the fall for a botched heist. His peaceful existence is shattered when career criminal and psychopath Don Logan turns up and demands that Gal gets involved in 'one last job' back in London. Rather than Act II focusing on the planning and preparations for the heist, it deals with Gal's attempts to avoid doing the job and the repercussions.

Sam Peckinpah's *The Getaway* (1972) is about the aftermath of a bank job, focusing on the getaway. Similarly, Don Siegel's *Charley Varrick* (1973) is about a character on the run from a hit man after robbing mob-laundered funds from a bank. Homing in on one element of a crime – a shorter part of the crime continuum – can bring an original angle to a crime story.

British writer/director Guy Ritchie's films are often labelled gangster films, but *Lock, Stock, and Two Smoking Barrels* (1998), *Snatch* (2000) and *RocknRolla* (2008) all have complex plots that involve gangs of cartoonish criminals involved in planned or unplanned heists. In *Lock, Stock, and Two Smoking Barrels* a criminal quartet manages to lose £500,000 in a card game to a porn king who gives them a week to pay up or else. They come up with a plan to rob some hoods after they hold up some drug dealers, but their complicated plan goes wrong due in part to their own incompetence. *Snatch* involves the theft of an 86-carat diamond in an Antwerp heist and *RocknRolla* centres around a crooked land deal, but also includes a stolen 'lucky painting' and money. Ritchie's films deal with crimes gone wrong and his characters tend to be comical even when being 'hard', a style that has been imitated extensively.

THE PARODY STAGE: LAUGHING ALL THE WAY TO THE BANK

'I'm not talking about a life of crime, just a momentary shift in lifestyle.'

(Russ, *Palookaville*)

The obvious way to parody a heist film is to put together an incompetent gang who are deluded enough to believe they can pull off a heist well beyond their means. An early example of this is *Big Deal on Madonna Street* (1958) by writer/director Mario Monicelli, a comedy caper in which an all-star cast of bumbling thieves attempts to steal jewellery from the Madonna Street pawn shop. *Palookaville* (1995) features a gang of three friends who want easy money so they can leave their small town; despite a failed jewellery store heist, they decide to rob an armoured truck, inspired by an old movie.

Ealing Studios produced comedy heist classics *The Lavender Hill Mob* (1951) and *The Ladykillers* (1955), both of which starred Alec Guinness. The protagonist of *The Lavender Hill Mob* is Henry Holland, an unassuming bank clerk in charge of a gold bullion shipment. He devises a scheme to steal the gold, melt it down and remould it into Eiffel Tower statuettes so it can be smuggled out of the country. He entices three accomplices into the scheme, including a foundry owner. In *The Ladykillers*, master thief Professor Marcus rents a boarding house room from Mrs Wilberforce, where he meets with his accomplices to plan and prepare for a big heist. To hide his true agenda, he pretends they are a string quartet. The Coen Brothers made a remake in 2004, which lacks the sparkle of the original.

Wes Anderson's *Bottle Rocket* (1996) is an elaborate plan concocted by three friends to commit a robbery and go on the run. The film acknowledges the innocent allure of the heist through its characters. Woody Allen's *The Curse of the Jade Scorpion* (2001) has an insurance investigator and efficiency expert who despise each other hypnotised with the aid of a jade scorpion into stealing jewels.

Given the precise preparations, planning and execution that must go into a heist and how much of the tension is generated by the possibility of something going wrong, it's easy to see the comic potential of a heist film parody.

....

WRITING EXERCISE: DESIGNING A HEIST

- The Object of Desire: Use your image kit and choose an object – something that is not of obvious value. Write a backstory for the object that imbues it with extreme value for a specific person or group of people. For example, the object may be a vintage couture item; a religious relic; a modern art sculpture; or the missing item from a valuable collection. Decide where the object is kept and why it would be extremely difficult to steal.

- The 'Collector'/Employer: Create a character who will stop at nothing to possess this object. Write a very brief backstory. Why is the object so important to him or her? Why must he or she hire someone to steal the object?

- The Charismatic Thief Protagonist: Write a very brief backstory for him or her. Why does he or she want or need to accept the assignment to steal this object – what is his or her motivation? What is the protagonist's opinion of his/her employer? Give your protagonist four key traits: two positive and two negative. For example: loyal, quick-thinking, easily flattered, an addictive gambler.

- Utilise all this information when outlining the following heist scenario:

  Act I: Introduce your protagonist in his or her daily routine. The Collector approaches him or her about the heist. The protagonist refuses. Make clear the protagonist's opinion of the Collector. An event then happens that makes the protagonist change his or her mind about the job. The protagonist goes to the Collector and grudgingly accepts the job. Consider if there are any conditions attached from either side.

Act II: The object is so difficult to access that the protagonist will need to assemble a gang to pull off the heist. Think of three gang members. Assign each a specific skill, one positive trait and one negative trait. Know why each wants to get involved in the heist – his or her motivation. The protagonist puts together a plan, which he or she relays to the gang; the plan requires the key skill of each. How might they get caught and what will the repercussions be? The protagonist suffers a reversal when one gang member is forced to drop out. Consider what the circumstances are and how this makes the protagonist alter the plan. Will a new team member be recruited or will they try to manage without the former member's expertise? The gang prepare in earnest for the heist, which must be performed on a specific day (state why). The necessary equipment for the heist is assembled and the gang members rehearse elements of the plan. These rehearsals should make it clear what might go wrong in the heist. Finish Act II the day before the heist is scheduled to take place. The protagonist reminds the gang of their timeframe for the heist, how any error will get them caught, and what the punishment for their actions might be.

Act III: The plan is put into action. After a shaky start, the plan is going well, but the fast-ticking clock leaves no margin for error. At a crucial moment, the former gang member turns up and tries to hijack the operation. The protagonist must think on his or her feet and regain control of the situation by altering the carefully constructed plan. (Or did the protagonist have a plan B?) In a to-the-wire finish, the heist is completed and the protagonist and his gang try to make their getaway with the prize. Do they succeed or does the former gang member outwit them? And, if they do succeed, do they deliver the prize to the Collector? And, most importantly, how does your protagonist feel at the end of the entire operation?

....

OTHER CRIMES AND MISDEMEANOURS:
POP ART, COMIC BOOK CRIME,
THE AUTEUR'S VOICE

QUENTIN TARANTINO

*

'I steal from every movie ever made.'

'As a writer, I demand the right to write any character in the world that I want to write. I demand the right to be them, I demand the right to think them and I demand the right to tell the truth as I see they are.'

'Novelists have always had complete freedom to pretty much tell their story any way they saw fit. And that's what I'm trying to do.'

*

There are a number of auteurs who frequently work in the crime genre, borrowing from various crime sub-genre conventions and making films with their own identifiable stamp. One such writer/director is Quentin Tarantino who was catapulted into the public eye with his first feature *Reservoir Dogs* (1992). Like Scorsese, Tarantino is a formidable cineaste with encyclopaedic knowledge of cinema, which he puts to use through film references, stylistics and casting choices. His work is markedly 'revisionist', mixing conventions from different sub-genres to bring his own spin, leading to the term 'Tarantino-esque' to describe inevitable attempts to copy his work. His films are often called gangster films because they include criminals, but some of his characters are far more 'noir' anti-hero than gangster. He is a popular culture magpie, borrowing from a variety of areas such as old school pulp fiction and more contemporary graphic novels and comic books; American television and genre films; popular music primarily from before 1980; and world cinema. His films tend to be 'pulp' rather than realistic, imbued with humour, lashings of gore, verbose dialogue, and a certain amount of chaos. He successfully utilises techniques that screenwriters are frequently told to avoid: flashbacks, captions, random and lengthy dialogue, voiceover. Tarantino's style and content may not appeal to everyone, but his film knowledge and skill as a writer and director are undeniable, as are his use of crime sub-genre elements and conventions. *Reservoir Dogs*, for example, is about a jewellery store heist gone wrong, but rather than focus the story on the heist itself Tarantino shows the lead up to, and aftermath of, the heist, exploring the dynamics of the gang pieced together by Joe Cabot: Mr White, Mr Orange, Mr Pink and Mr Blonde, pseudonyms to protect the identities of thieves who don't know each other. The debates between the thieves about random subjects are enjoyable and develop character. *Pulp Fiction* (1994) references the golden age of pulp fiction writing and weaves together four stories through the escapades of three classic 'pulp' characters: two mob hit men on a mission for a gangster; the gangster's trophy wife; and an ageing boxer asked to throw a fight... for the gangster. Hit man Vincent Vega seems to be on a downward spiral; he takes heroin recreationally and seems not to care about much until he meets Mia, the femme fatale, and his boss Marsellus Wallace's wife. Vega and fellow hit man Jules Winnfield are trying to locate a stolen suitcase for Marsellus, which is a reference to the noir film *Kiss Me Deadly* (1955). *Jackie Brown* (1997), one of Tarantino's 'quieter' films, uses elements of film noir. Protagonist Jackie Brown could be viewed as a femme fatale and bail bondsman Max Cherry seems to be on a downward spiral and looking for redemption. The scam Jackie undertakes is a double cross. All in all, Tarantino uses conventions from a number of genres, from kung fu films to war stories to creative adaptations of westerns, but puts a personal stamp and identifiable style on his films.

THE COEN BROTHERS

*

'Many people think we're always referencing movies, but it's the books those movies are based on that are more influential to us.'

(Joel Coen)

'It's hard to develop a story without seeing where it starts.'

(Ethan Coen)

'Every movie ever made is an attempt to remake The Wizard of Oz.'

(Joel Coen)

'We don't give a shit about people's sensitivities.'

(Ethan Coen)

*

The Coen Brothers also utilise conventions from various genres, particularly for comic effect, and many of their films revolve around a crime gone wrong. They have made crime films that are serious in tone such as Blood Simple (1984) and Miller's Crossing (1990), whereas their crime comedies such as The Big Lebowski typically feature inept criminals or a somewhat ludicrous crime such as the theft of the Dude's rug (and the kidnapping of Bunny). Raising Arizona (1987) features a married couple who happen to be a female cop and an ex-con who desperately want a baby and decide to steal one. The tone is established as broadly comical from the beginning of the film, whereas the story could be played very differently as a serious thriller. *Fargo* (1996) is a black comedy in which characters do get hurt; at its core is a 'noir' sort of tale: a man has his own wife kidnapped in order to extort cash from his father-in-law. It all goes wrong thanks to two inept but violent (and amusing) criminals. As the kidnappers-for-hire kill innocent bystanders, the story becomes a police investigation led by a very pregnant cop. The Coen Brothers also did a remake of the much loved heist comedy *The Ladykillers* (2004), which failed to live up to the original. Their adaptation of Cormac McCarthy's *No Country For Old Men* (2007) was much more successful and contains several crimes: a drug deal ending in the murder of all concerned; the theft of the drug money by protagonist Llewelyn Moss; and various killings committed by psychopathic philosopher-hit man Anton Chigurh. Whether making a straight up crime story or comedy crime, the Coen Brothers know their genre conventions and use them creatively.

LOCK 'EM UP AND THROW AWAY THE KEY:
PRISON STORIES

'Those gates only open three times. When you come in, when you've served your time, or when you're dead.'

(Gallagher to Joe Collins, *Brute Force*, 1947)

Prison stories have one obvious thing in common: a 'detention centre' location. Frequently this is a conventional prison, but could be any other space designated for retaining criminals, such as a ship, an island, even conceivably another planet. The key thing is that the prisoner has been retained against his or her will and usually with other lawbreakers. Prison stories are included here as a crime sub-genre as imprisonment is potentially part of the crime continuum (*Figure 2*) if the 'getaway plan' fails. Prison stories fall into three very general categories, each of which has quite a different central focus:

- wrongfully convicted
- life inside
- the great escape

Elements from each category can of course be in the same film, but the core theme tends to determine the overall structure and character motivation.

WRONGFULLY CONVICTED: GUILTY UNTIL PROVEN INNOCENT

'Madge framed you. Madge wanted to hook you, and when she found she couldn't have you, she framed you, sent you up for life. We both know that.'

(George Fellsinger to Vincent Parry, *Dark Passage*)

The focus of the 'wrongfully convicted' prison drama is the protagonist's attempt to prove his or her innocence in order to avoid incarceration or to get released from prison; typically this type of story is a subset of either the social issue film, legal drama or thriller. If the protagonist has been falsely accused, then a crime has been committed either by an individual, an organisation, or the State. A quick review of the classic conventions of 'wrongfully convicted' prison films will show how they differ in focus from 'rightfully convicted' prison films.

The Protagonist: The protagonist who has been wrongfully accused and convicted of a crime has suffered a miscarriage of justice and is a victim rather than a perpetrator. If imprisoned, then the focus is on fighting for justice and release. Thrillers often feature characters accused of a crime they did not commit who go on the run to avoid incarceration while trying to figure out who has set them up and why. There is a sense of desperation, fear and confusion as the protagonist's life is turned upside down and his or her reputation is damaged. The protagonist often needs to play detective to clear his or her name and doesn't know who to trust.

The Antagonist: The antagonist is the person or organisation that has falsely accused the protagonist and, for some reason, wants him or her in prison. The antagonist is perpetrating a crime against the protagonist and the motive may not be clear. There may be a David and Goliath dynamic in that the forces of antagonism seem impossible to defeat. It's also possible that the available evidence has made the protagonist appear guilty and no one has set out to pervert the course of justice; in this instance the justice system itself, with its rules, regulations and procedures, becomes the force of antagonism.

Type of Plot or Story Pattern: The focus of the story is the efforts of the protagonist to clear his or her name; the protagonist or his allies may need to bring the true perpetrator to justice in order to do so.

- *Act I:* An ordinary person's ordinary world is disrupted. The protagonist's world is turned upside down when he or she is accused of a crime and is either imprisoned or must go on the run to avoid imprisonment.

- *Act II:* Guilty until innocence is proved. The fight to prove the protagonist's innocence and to find the true perpetrator. If a thriller, there are many twists and turns and a high level of tension. If a social issue film, there may be many legal twists and turns, bureaucracy, or prejudice that makes clearing the protagonist's name difficult. Foes are convincing and the judicial system may prove faulty. The protagonist's fate typically looks bleak at the end of Act II.

- *Act III:* Justice prevails after much struggle. Usually the protagonist's innocence is proven and he or she comes out of hiding or is released from prison. The true perpetrators are caught. The experience will greatly change the protagonist.

Narrative Style: If the protagonist is falsely incarcerated, prison is shown to be a potentially dangerous place for him or her. The protagonist may learn how to cope inside and be 'hardened' by the experience. Flaws in the legal and judicial system are highlighted. The protagonist finds allies and antagonists in unexpected places. Criminal activity may be highlighted as well as police or government corruption. In a prison situation, violence is used to maintain order; if a thriller, violent means are used in an attempt to capture the protagonist, with numerous chase sequences.

Timeframe/Pace: If set primarily in a prison, the timescale might be much more drawn out and initially slower paced to emphasise the dragging of time for the inmates; this may be followed by a fast-ticking clock if capital punishment is an issue. If a thriller, the pace is much faster as the protagonist is pursued and finds there is nowhere to hide. A fast pace adds to tension if the protagonist must clear his or her name before being killed or imprisoned.

Tone: Realistic, often gritty, with a strong sense of impending violence throughout.

Setting and Mise-en-scène: The main setting may be a prison, which the protagonist will find difficult to survive, or 'the road' if the main character is on the run. In an on-the-run thriller, the protagonist may either seek out anonymous places to hide (motels and the like) or sanctuary from people they trust, which may prove to be a mistake.

An early film of this type is *I Am a Fugitive From a Chain Gang* (1932), starring Paul Muni as an innocent man falsely convicted twice and subjected to the harsh life of working on the chain gang; the film shows how these miscarriages of justice ultimately condemned him to a life of crime thereafter, forcing him to steal to survive. In *Each Dawn I Die* (1938) James Cagney plays Frank Ross, a reporter falsely imprisoned after being framed for murder by gangsters; in *An Innocent Man* (1989) model citizen James Rainwood is framed by corrupt cops; and *The Hurricane* (1999) tells the story of Rubin 'Hurricane' Carter, a boxer wrongly imprisoned for murder. In *Double Jeopardy* (1999) Libby Parsons is imprisoned for the murder of her husband who set her up by faking his death; upon her release the film turns into a revenge thriller. *Dark Passage* (1947), starring Humphrey Bogart and Lauren Bacall, is a story about a man falsely convicted of murdering his wife who manages to escape from prison and must try to prove his innocence while eluding the authorities. *The Fugitive* (1993) is a thriller in which Dr Richard Kimble, a man falsely convicted of murdering his wife and sentenced to death, goes on the run after the prison bus transporting him is involved in an accident; to clear his name Kimble must identify his wife's actual killer. Hitchcock has addressed the issue of an innocent man falsely accused in several films, but arguably the most widely recognised of his films dealing with the subject, in part due to its visual set pieces, is *North by Northwest* (1959) in which Roger O Thornhill, an advertising executive (played by Cary Grant), is mistaken for a government agent by foreign spies and then framed for murder, forcing him to go on the run from the police.

LIFE INSIDE: SURVIVAL OF THE TOUGHEST AND MOST ORGANISED CRIMINALS

'I wish I could tell you that Andy fought the good fight, and the Sisters let him be. I wish I could tell you that – but prison is no fairy-tale world. He never said who did it, but we all knew. Things went on like that for awhile – prison life consists of routine, and then more routine. Every so often, Andy would show up with fresh bruises. The Sisters kept at him – sometimes he was able to fight 'em off, sometimes not. And that's how it went for Andy – that was his routine. I do believe those first two years were the worst for him, and I also believe that if things had gone on that way, this place would have got the best of him.'

(Red, *The Shawshank Redemption*)

This type of prison story focuses on the inner workings of prison and the protagonist's attempts to survive inside. It can be a social issue film, exploring criminal hierarchies inside and corruption within the prison system – showing that the line between offender and law enforcer may be blurred. It might also be used to debate the issue of capital punishment.

The Protagonist: The protagonist has been rightfully convicted of a crime, but may be a young or inexperienced criminal or the crime was a relatively minor offence, accidental, or out of character. The naive protagonist is typically unprepared for life inside and vulnerable to attack from other inmates, so quickly must work out the prisoner hierarchy. A criminal's background, ethnicity, religion or crime may also make him or her vulnerable and the protagonist must come up with strategies to counter this. Repeat offenders or established criminals may be separated from their gang and must quickly establish themselves as 'harder' than other convicts or risk being murdered by rival gang members or criminals. The protagonist may have taken the fall for his gang or criminal organisation and might have allies inside already. Often the protagonist finds a mentor who helps him or her survive – a long term prisoner who has the respect of other prisoners, an excellent strategist, or a gang leader who gives him or her protection at a price.

The Antagonist: Other prisoners are typically antagonists as are prison guards, most particularly corrupt ones. The protagonist's cell mate is often a particular problem. Choosing sides brings enemies as well as allies.

Type of Plot or Story Pattern: This is a quest for survival story until the prisoner is released or meets a tragic end. The prisoner should be on a reformative arc, but instead may become more corrupt or destroyed by the system.

- *Act I:* An Old Way of Life/Cause and Effect
  The protagonist commits a crime and is sent to prison. Sometimes the perpetration of the crime, the protagonist's arrest or sentencing is the inciting incident and the arrival at prison is the point of no return. This is often the case if the protagonist is convicted abroad. The inciting incident might also be the protagonist's arrival at prison and the point of no return is a confrontation with the main antagonist or some event that will be the focus of struggle throughout Act II. The prisoner is quickly made aware of a prison hierarchy and, by the end of Act I, knows that life inside is not going to be easy.

- *Act II:* The New World: The Will and Struggle to Survive
  The main goal of Act II tends to be survival and the protagonist needs to come up with a strategy. Antagonists are quickly

established and apparent allies may prove to be false friends. If a novice criminal, the struggle is to make sense of the 'system' and to work out who can be trusted and who to avoid. The obstacles facing the novice are bullying, pressure to join a gang, theft of personal objects, physical attacks. If the protagonist is an established criminal, the goal is to quickly establish power, assemble a gang, bribe prison guards, and obtain what is needed from the outside. The ultimate goal may be to take over any illegal operations run on the inside and to continue to manage his illegal activities on the outside. This struggle for power will meet with resistance from known antagonists, hidden enemies and law enforcers. If the protagonist is imprisoned abroad for committing a crime, he or she will be hoping for help from family, a lawyer, government officials or journalists; given his or her guilt, the best possibility is the opportunity to serve a sentence back home. Low points in Act II are typically betrayal by purported allies, or an important relationship on the inside or outside being severed. If the resolution is positive, then the end of Act II tends to be bleak; if the protagonist is on a high at the end of Act II, he may meet with the classic gangster's fall at the end of Act III. Arguably, most films that deal with issues of capital punishment and have a lawyer, social campaigner, or family member as protagonist are social issue films that have much of their action outside the prison. If the protagonist is the prisoner sentenced to death, the focus is much more on 'life inside' and the tension of waiting for either execution by the state or a possible reprieve from death.

- *Act III:* Release from the Imposed World
  Act III tends to have a ticking clock element. It may focus on the lead up to the protagonist's execution or release date. Aggression towards him or her may hot up if a release is pending. If the protagonist is new to the prison system, he or she may survive, but will of course be hardened by the experience and perhaps more of a criminal. If released, we will wonder if he will manage to stay free, particularly if 'the system' has conspired against him.

The established gangster may fall as in a classical stage gangster film, or win one battle only to go on to fight yet another, suggesting that his fall is inevitable.

Narrative Style: The basic narrative style is similar to the 'wrongfully convicted' prison set story. Obviously, locations within a prison are limited and certain scenes have become almost cliché (which isn't to say they're not truthful): conflict over sharing a cell, the mess hall confrontation, the prison yard sizing up, the shower attack or rape, the strip search, lock-down after a riot, and solitary confinement after brutalisation. Prisoners are shown bartering for goods and bribing wardens. If paid, corrupt wardens turn a blind eye on trouble. Contraband is smuggled in and messages are smuggled out. Prisoners are creative in making weapons and using them.

Timeframe/Pace: 'Life inside' films are often similar in scope to gangster 'rise and fall' films, with more expansive timeframes to emphasise the protagonist's need to adapt if he or she wishes to survive the brutality and monotony of life in prison. Riots or unexpected attacks increase the pace and raise tension.

Tone: Again, the tone is primarily realistic, with much violence. Many of these films are set in notorious prisons, which makes survival more difficult for the protagonist. The audience should genuinely wonder if the protagonist will survive.

Setting and Mise-en-scène: The main setting is the prison and its various components: prison cell, mess hall, exercise yard, showers, workshop areas such as laundry, visiting rooms and infirmary. The fortress aspects of the prison will be emphasised and the foreignness if the protagonist is incarcerated in an alien country. If Act I or a subplot takes place outside, this will often provide an extreme contrast to the prison.

An early prototype prison film is the docu-drama *Execution of Czolgosz with Panorama of Auburn Prison* (1901) by Edwin S Porter, which recreates the electrocution of Leon Czolgosz who assassinated American President William McKinley. This primitive stage film certainly depicts one potential outcome of being sent to prison when guilty of a crime.

An early classical stage prison drama that contains many tropes of a 'life inside' prison drama and includes two ultimately unsuccessful jail breaks is *The Big House* (1930), written by Frances Marion who was a correspondent during the Great War and visited San Quentin to get a realistic picture of prison life. The film focuses on the dynamic between the prisoners more than the planning for the prison break, juxtaposing Kent Marlow, a privileged young man convicted of manslaughter while drunk driving, with hardened career criminals Butch 'Machine Gun' Schmidt and Joe Morgan. Morgan actually escapes prison temporarily, but ends up back inside with a longer sentence. Marlow can't handle prison life and becomes a stool pigeon in a bid for early release. He informs Warden James Adams about a planned prison break, and the escape attempt ends in a hail of bullets with over 50 dead.

Hell's Highway (1932) depicts the abusive treatment of inmates in a southern prison, which is summed up neatly by the prisoners' uniforms which have a bullseye on the back. The film begins with the suicide of a prisoner in a sweatbox and the film's protagonist, Duke Ellis, gets involved in a prison riot that (in the original version of the film) results in his death.

Other examples of 'life inside' prison films are *Riot in Cell Block 11* (1954), *Birdman of Alcatraz* (1962), *Scum* (1979) and *Brubaker* (1980). *Cool Hand Luke* (1967) is another twist on the southern chain gang with Paul Newman as Luke, a self-destructive rebel who has similar qualities to RP McMurphy in *One Flew Over the Cuckoo's Nest* (1975), in which a mental institution is literally substituted for a prison when McMurphy talks himself out of the prison work farm by feigning mental illness. *Yield to the Night* (1956) focuses on a murderess's wait for execution by hanging as she contemplates the events that led to her killing her rival. *Dead Man Walking* (1995) also deals with a convicted killer waiting for execution or reprieve, but is more of a social issue film as the protagonist is Sister Helen Prejean who supports convicted killer Matthew Poncelet who certainly does not start out as an empathetic character, but is changed by their interaction. *Kiss of the Spiderwoman* (1985) is based on the novel by Manuel Puig and focuses on the relationship between two cellmates in a Brazilian prison, left-wing activist Valentin Arregui and homosexual Luis Molina who was imprisoned for having sex with a minor. Molina has made a deal with the authorities – early release in exchange for getting information about Arregui's political activities, but an unlikely friendship develops between the two as Molina tells Arregui the plot of a (fictional) Nazi movie *Her Real Glory*, shown as a film within a film.

The groundbreaking television series *Oz* (1997–2003), created and primarily written by Tom Fontana, focuses on life in Oswald State Correctional Facility, a fictional maximum security prison in what is probably intended to be New York State. The show is set primarily in 'Emerald City', an experimental unit of the prison, and is narrated by the wheelchair-bound Augustus Hill, dealing with the interactions between various inmate factions such as the African-American 'Homeboys', the Aryan Brotherhood, the Muslims, the Wiseguys, the Latinos, the Irish, and the Bikers. The show was one of the first made by pay-TV channel HBO and was much grittier than shows normally made for American television.

'Guilty prisoner abroad' stories tend to focus on prisons with appalling conditions and the added difficulty of being a foreigner who must adapt. These stories also tend to revolve around the idea of a character making one life-changing mistake. An example is *Midnight Express* (1974), based on the true story of Billy Hayes who was imprisoned in Turkey for attempting to smuggle hashish. The crime is minor when compared with murder, but the protagonist knowingly and stupidly makes the decision to break the law whilst abroad and struggles to survive the prison conditions and guards even more than the other prisoners. A variation on this type of story is when the main character or characters naively break the law or are duped or blackmailed into committing a crime in a foreign country and suffer the consequences as happens in French film *Force Majeure* (1989), later remade in 1998 in the US as *Return to Paradise*, and *Brokedown Palace* (1999). The focus on the 'fatal error' motivated by naivety or fear makes it easier for the audience to feel sympathy for the protagonist as the punishment seems particularly harsh. The audience appeal of this sort of tale is demonstrated by the success of British documentary series *Banged Up Abroad* (2006–), eight series to date), which features true stories of people imprisoned while travelling abroad, typically for drug smuggling. The series has been broadcast internationally and harkens back to the semi-documentary police films of the 1950s, mixing interviews and reenactments.

Prison dramas have not lost their appeal. *Un prophète* (2009) is a recent, critically acclaimed prison film in which the young protagonist, Malik El Djebena, begins a six-year prison sentence in Brécourt. There are two factions in the prison: the Corsicans and the Muslims. The Corsicans have the power, with prison guards in their pocket. Malik is not affiliated with any gang outside or inside, but quickly learns that to survive means doing what César Luciani wants. César is head honcho of the Corsicans, is well protected inside, and still runs operations outside prison. Malik is not accepted by the other Corsicans due to his ethnicity and the Muslims think of him as a traitor. César forces him to murder a Muslim inmate as a test and Malik goes on to deal drugs and has no choice but to work as a 'runner' for the Corsican gang. Life inside takes Malik from small time offender to criminal in order to survive.

EXPERIMENTS IN TIME AND PLACE

The Shawshank Redemption (1994), adapted from Stephen King's novella *Rita Hayworth and the Shawshank Redemption*, takes place over 20 years, beginning with Andy Dufresne's imprisonment for the alleged murder of his wife and her lover and culminating when Red, the narrator, is released from prison in 1967 and joins Andy in Mexico. Andy maintains that he is innocent of the double murder throughout the film and, in a surprise twist, manages to escape by chiselling his way out with a rock hammer, but the focus of the film is on life inside and dealing with long term imprisonment.

Ghosts... of the Civil Dead (1988), John Hillcoat's first feature, is set in Central Industrial Prison, which is located in the middle of the desert in a mythical country and explores methods of social control. It begins with the prison in lock down and then flashes back to show how life in the prison led to that situation, using the device of an investigating committee.

THE GREAT ESCAPE

Papillon: 'We're something, aren't we? The only animals that shove things up their ass for survival.'

(*Papillon*, 1973)

The focus of this type of prison drama is the human desire for freedom and, of course, the protagonist's attempt or attempts to get out of jail. In his or her efforts to escape, the protagonist is committing another crime. Again, a quick review of classic prison escape conventions will show how this basic scenario differs from 'wrongfully convicted' and 'life inside' prison stories.

The Protagonist: The protagonist may be innocent or guilty of the crime for which he or she was imprisoned; the key thing is his or her determination to escape. The motivation for the escape attempt and the reason for incarceration will influence the audience's feelings towards the protagonist and whether we hope or fear they will succeed in the 'getaway'. If wrongfully convicted, or if the protagonist committed a relatively minor crime and is under threat from other inmates or wardens, we are more likely to sympathise with them. The same may apply if the protagonist learns that a loved one is gravely ill and this is the last chance to see him or her, or there is a love story subplot. Conversely, if the main character is a killer or psychopath, we are likely to be less sympathetic, particularly if he or she wants to continue a killing spree or take revenge against an innocent party such as the person who testified against them. The protagonist is determined and may be driven by a sense of having nothing left to lose. He or she may also be the leader of a small gang that needs to work together to escape or must rely on bribing various people to make good their plans.

The Antagonist: The protagonist meets with a number of people who will attempt to thwart his attempts to escape. It is, of course, the job of the wardens to keep prisoners inside, but some wardens may be more sadistic than others. A prison official may have denied the protagonist various privileges and made life particularly difficult for him or her. Other prisoners may make the protagonist's time inside insufferable to the point that the protagonist feels he or she must escape or die. The prison itself is a type of antagonist if notoriously difficult to escape from.

Type of Plot or Story Pattern: Unsurprisingly, the escape story pattern has certain similarities to the heist pattern.

- *Act I:* Nothing left to lose...
  The protagonist is confined in prison. We get a sense of the daily routine there, which is likely to be difficult. The inciting incident tends to be an event, a discovery, or some kind of news that makes incarceration intolerable for the protagonist. By the end of Act I, the protagonist has committed him or herself to escaping – the point of no return.

- *Act II:* The best made plans...
  Escape will not be easy and the obstacles must be big enough for the audience to wonder if the protagonist will succeed or fail. The repercussions of escape attempts should also be clear as this raises the stakes. We might see a failed attempt by another inmate or the guards might operate a 'shoot first, ask questions later' policy. This failed attempt might be an opportunistic 'run for it' effort, which makes it clear to the protagonist that planning is

critical for success. The protagonist comes up with a very basic plan, but must make it more concrete. He or she may need to recruit other prisoners, bribe guards, or enlist help from the outside. If working solo, the protagonist will need to make a detailed plan without raising the suspicions of other inmates or prison wardens. These scenes of planning and preparation are similar to those of a heist and encourage the audience to vicariously participate in the protagonist's efforts to gain the big prize of freedom and to invest in the protagonist and gang. If the main character is a villain, his or her expertise at planning and preparing for an escape will make us fear all the more for his potential victims, should they escape. Knowing the layout of the prison in detail is essential, whether working as a team or solo. The escape route may be a disused part of the prison (sewer tunnel, vents...) and almost always involves some kind of physically onerous path, whether digging the way out, crawling through rat-infested or narrow tunnels, or climbing through ventilation shafts. Potential complications are numerous. The prisoners may need to source tools for digging or climbing, weapons, disguises for the escape, or clothes to wear once free. The protagonist must be fully aware of the prison routine and the timing of any patrol by prison guards. These routines are normally studied and timed over weeks to establish a pattern. At the midpoint, something normally happens that alters the plan: someone finds out about the plan and wants in; a guard must be bribed or is despatched; part of the escape route is impenetrable; there is a betrayal; an essential team member is incapacitated, murdered, or simply drops out. The plan is readjusted for the setbacks and the protagonist and team are ready to go by the end of Act II. Again, something often goes wrong with the plan and they are forced to improvise as it's now or never. This raises the stakes – will the protagonist and team survive the escape attempt or not?

- *Act III:* Will the plan work?
  The plan is carried out. Typically there are casualties if it's a team endeavour and there may also be betrayals. The main theme of the

film and the protagonist's motivation dictate whether the escape will be a success or not.

A variation on this basic structure is the serial offender escape artist who spends less time planning and more time escaping and being recaptured in Act II. If a prisoner has a life sentence, the threat of rejected parole means little.

Narrative Style: The prison escape story has a similar sense of tension to the heist story. Many of the things that can go wrong with a heist apply to an escape. If the protagonist is putting together a gang to escape, the focus tends to be less on an individual's technical skills than on friendship, trust, or contacts on the inside or outside. The escape story indicates that the biggest prize for a human tends to be freedom rather than material possessions, although the lust for money can lead to imprisonment. Escaping the prison isn't the end of the story; the protagonist must be able to cover his or her tracks and disappear.

Timeframe/Pace: Timing is key in a prison escape story; the planning and preparation might take years, but the execution of the escape tends to have a very specific window. Guards and hostile inmates must be out of range; tools needed for the escape might be smuggled in or available at a particular time; there might be flaws in the prison security at a specific time or from a particular location within the prison. Guards may be incapacitated for a short time; even the weather might be a factor. The audience knows the escape must go like clockwork or the prisoners will be caught.

Tone: Daring, desperate and tense. Depending on the nature of the protagonist, the audience should either hope for a successful escape, or fear it if his or her motivation is evil. The escape plan might be particularly audacious and dangerous with much objective drama.

Setting and Mise-en-scène: In a reversal of the heist scenario, the protagonist is within the fortress and the big prize is on the outside:

freedom. The security of the prison will be emphasised: the bars, heavy metal doors, armed guards, guard dogs, high concrete walls and fencing, any natural boundaries such as remote locations, vast forests, mountains, the sea, and an extreme climate.

The desire to escape from prison is very understandable, whether the prisoner is guilty or innocent; audience reactions to the escape attempt will depend on the characterisation and driving motive. If the crime the protagonist committed was minor and the prison conditions are harsh, it's all the easier for the audience to root for the prisoner to succeed in his or her prison break. The same applies to prisoners who receive bad news about someone on the outside they care for, which prompts them to attempt the escape – ultimately, risking their lives for love. This seems a heroic gesture and makes the villain protagonist more empathetic.

Jules Dassin's *Brute Force* (1947) focuses on an inmate who wants to escape prison to be with his seriously ill girlfriend. This emotive situation, along with an exceptionally cruel prison guard, gets the audience on side. *The Defiant Ones* (1958) centres on the aftermath of a prison break. It's set in the rural south and follows the travails of two escaped convicts – one black and one white – who are literally chained together, an ideal set-up through which to explore issues of racism.

Papillon (1973) is a study in the human desire for freedom. Henri 'Papillon' Charrière (Steve McQueen) and counterfeiter Louis Degas (Dustin Hoffman) are French penal colony prisoners; the two make a connection and are likeable characters who attempt escape and fail. The repercussions break Degas whereas Papillon suffers intolerable cruelty with his desire for freedom intact. Degas, a haunted man, becomes resigned to life on the inescapable French penal colony Devil's Island, but Papillon is both obsessed and determined. After watching the waves that buffet the island cliffs day after day, he deciphers a pattern and decides that it is possible to ride the seventh wave out from the island without being crushed. Degas humours Papillon as he builds a raft, which seems an exercise in futility by a man who has lost his mind. Papillon leaps with his flimsy raft into the sea and, while we do not see his final fate, according to legend he escapes the island and survives the long journey to land. However, whether alive or drowned, Papillon finally finds freedom through his final attempt to escape the inescapable.

Don Siegel's *Escape from Alcatraz* (1979) is similar to *Papillon* in its use of an extreme location as an obstacle that is allegedly impossible to overcome. The film is based on a true escape attempt on 11 June 1962 from 'the Rock', a prison on a tiny island off the coast of San Francisco. The escape was masterminded by Allen West who did not manage to get out of his cell on time, and the escapees were Frank Lee Morris (played by Clint Eastwood) and brothers Clarence and John Anglin. The trio sailed to either freedom or their deaths on a raft made from prison issue raincoats. In reality, their legend has grown as their fates remain a mystery – no bodies were found and they were never arrested again. The sale of the *Escape from Alcatraz* screenplay is also interesting from a writer's perspective. Screenwriter Richard Tuggle wrote the screenplay on spec after six months of researching the material and the script was rejected by a number of agents. Tuggle managed to get the script to Don Siegel's agent by pretending he had met him at a party and that Siegel had requested to read it; Siegel, who had written an unproduced treatment about Alcatraz years previously and clearly had an interest in the subject, brought the project to Clint Eastwood and it was quickly green-lit. Tuggle went on to write *Tightrope* (1984) for Eastwood.

A more recent prison escape drama with an original twist is the brilliantly tense *Cell 211* (2009). The protagonist is a newly hired prison warden who gets locked inside during a riot; in order to escape and survive, he must pretend to be a prisoner. His strategy is not surprising, but the film is so well acted and executed that it never seems boring or predictable.

The Next Three Days (2010) brings another twist to the prison escape drama. Rather than a prison inmate trying to abscond, John Brennan decides to break his reluctant wife Lara out of prison after his attempts to get her out by legal means fail, and he fears she will commit suicide. He enlists the help of an accomplished prison escapee and prepares everything down to the minute. Her fear and reluctance threaten to scupper the plan, which would mean prison for both of them and an uncertain future for their son.

The television series *Prison Break* (2005–09) ran for four seasons and, as per its title, focuses on the planning, preparation and execution of a prison break, but also includes conventions from 'unjustly accused' and 'life inside' prison dramas. The basic story revolves around Michael Scofield's attempts to help his brother Lincoln escape from Fox River State Penitentiary when legal recourse fails; Lincoln has been falsely accused of murdering the American Vice President's brother and faces the death penalty. Michael commits armed robbery so he too will be inside the prison and has the escape route literally tattooed to his body. The first series focuses on the classical stage Act II prison escape story pattern conventions of his attempts to break out of the prison with his brother after putting together a gang, with complications arising when unwanted prisoners discover the plan and demand to take part. Six prisoners and the two brothers escape at the end of series one. Series two focuses on life on the run and concludes with the two brothers reaching Panama; Michael and three of their fellow escaped convicts are caught and imprisoned in Penitenciaría Federal de Sona. Series three focuses on Lincoln's attempts to break Michael out of this prison, while series four is more focused on the political intrigue subplot and blackmail. The final two episodes and series finale were broadcast as a TV movie – *Prison Break: The Final Break*. Overall, the series managed to maintain an admirably high level of tension throughout until the over-complications of series four.

Prisoner of war films such as *Stalag 17* (1960) and *The Great Escape* (1963) tend to use a number of the tropes of prison escape films, but are arguably a sub-genre of war films as the 'crime' committed is usually that of being an enemy national fighting for the other side.

PARODY STAGE: THE FUNNY SIDE OF BEING LOCKED UP?

'A hundred and twenty five years! Oh God, Oh God... I'll be a hundred and sixty one when I get out!'

(Harry Monroe, *Stir Crazy*)

Being incarcerated is hardly funny, but life inside has been fair game for parody. Even early comic films utilised some prison story tropes and a good number seem to focus on 'falsely accused' elements, often through a case of mistaken identity, which quickly puts the audience on the side of the protagonist and allows for a contrast between a good guy in a bad situation, juxtaposed with real criminals who are often exaggerated in a comical way.

Buster Keaton's comedy *Convict 13* (1920) has him end up on death row in prison through a case of mistaken identity. In Charlie Chaplin's comedy *Modern Times* (1936), his Little Tramp character is mistakenly identified as a communist demonstration instigator and sent to prison where, after accidentally ingesting cocaine, he disrupts a jailbreak in progress and is released from prison a hero. The Richard Pryor vehicle *Stir Crazy* (1980) is a prison comedy with fish-out-of-water elements that features two characters from the east coast of America framed for a bank robbery who are incarcerated in a prison out west and end up participating in an inter-prison rodeo. The opening sequence of the Coen Brothers' *Raising Arizona* (1987) parodies some 'life inside' conventions as we are shown several of protagonist HI's stints in prison as a way of introducing his criminal past and setting up the escaped prison thugs that come to threaten him and his police officer wife. Their film *O Brother, Where Art Thou?* (2000) is a reinterpretation of *The Odyssey*, with a gang of escaped convicts on the run and searching for hidden treasure, with conflict and tension generated by the lawman in pursuit. *Chicken Run* (2000) parodies many facets of prisoner-of-war film *The Great Escape*, but it's basic structure follows the prison escape story pattern.

....

WRITING EXERCISE: OUTLINING THE GREAT ESCAPE

This basic escape scenario can provide the basis for a prison break or an escape from a more psychological or emotional prison. Try it first with a physical prison.

- Write a short biography of your protagonist: age, family background, ethnicity, religion, home town. What crime did he or she commit or were they falsely imprisoned? What is his or her motivation for escaping from prison, besides the desire for freedom? Give your protagonist four key traits: two positive and two negative in terms of pulling off a big escape.

- Who is his or her greatest antagonist? A fellow prisoner or a prison guard? Someone on the outside? Is the antagonist a known or hidden enemy? What does he or she have against the protagonist and why will the antagonist do anything to keep your main character in prison?

- Describe the prison. Is there something specific about its location? Is it old or modern? What sort of prisoners are held there?

- Use this information when outlining your prison escape scenario:

  Act I: Introduce your protagonist in his or her daily routine. Something happens that makes life in prison unbearable for your protagonist. At the end of Act I, your protagonist decides to escape and to go it alone.

  Act II: Your protagonist comes up with a basic plan to escape after spotting what he or she thinks is a vulnerability in the prison. For example, the actual prison structure or how outsiders come and go. Your protagonist then realises that he or she needs assistance and must talk a fellow inmate into helping. The inmate demands to come also. Consider what the pros and cons are of two people escaping. Your protagonist and ally put together a plan and assemble the necessary tools – describe what they are and how the two will escape. They have a short timeframe to put their plan into action or the opportunity will be missed and they will get caught. Just as they are about to put the plan into gear, the main antagonist shows up. How does the protagonist adjust his or her strategy?

Act III: The revised plan is put into action. Everything is timed and there is no margin for error. Consider how your protagonist has integrated the antagonist into the plan (with the antagonist's knowledge or not) and if either will try to double-cross his or her enemy. Work out all the key logistics of the escape – at least three things they have to achieve. Who (if anyone) escapes and, if caught, how and why does it happen? If the protagonist escapes, what is his or her plan to avoid future recapture? If caught, what are the repercussions of the escape attempt?

....

SERIAL KILLER STORIES:
MEETING THE MONSTER

'Murder is an insidious thing. Once a man has dipped his fingers in blood, sooner or later he'll feel the urge to kill again.'

(Sherlock Holmes, *The House of Fear*)

Crimes of passion, revenge killings, a mob hit, murder for money – all are terrible crimes, all are motivated by the darker human emotions: jealousy, malice, vengefulness, envy, greed, lust for power. But what of the murderer who kills randomly, apparently without motive, and goes on to do it again and again? Such killers are termed 'monsters' and 'inhuman'. While it may be possible to reason with a potential killer motivated by negative emotions, if a murderer has no motive beyond the desire to kill, there seems little potential for negotiation. Coming face to face with a serial killer is like meeting a dangerous beast in human disguise, the great white shark of the human world. This is part of the uncomfortable allure of serial killer films – they are an amalgam of the crime and horror film genres. A screenwriter who wants to write a gripping serial killer film must create a villain who is both frightening and horribly fascinating, using key research by criminologists and psychologists for the necessary realism, or the story is likely to be more horror than crime.

PRIMITIVE STAGE SERIAL KILLER FILMS: THE POWERFUL ANTAGONIST

'...And I'm pursued by ghosts. Ghosts of mothers and of those children... they never leave me. They are always there... always, always, always! Except when I do it, when I... Then I can't remember anything. And afterwards I see those posters and read what I've done, and read, and read... did I do that? But I can't remember anything about it! But who will believe me? Who knows what it's like to be me? How I'm forced to act... how I must, must... don't want to, must!'

(Hans Beckert, *M*)

Is the serial killer story a sub-genre? The term 'serial killer' is relatively new; criminologist and former FBI agent Robert Ressler is attributed with coining the term in the mid-1970s. Various experts seem to define serial killer in slightly different ways; the definition offered by the Federal Bureau of Investigation is that serial murder is the unlawful killing of two or more victims by the same offender(s), in separate events. The FBI goes on to define a spree killer as a person (or more than one person) who commits two or more murders without a cooling-off period. Further, the definition of serial killer is constantly evolving. Certainly much has been written about the serial killer subsequent to the term being coined, and the more criminologists and psychologists learn about this type of sociopath, the more specific characteristics attributed to serial killers influence the plot and character interaction in crime dramas. The serial killer is such a powerful figure that police or detective stories following all the conventions of either sub-genre but with a serial killer antagonist are still typically labelled serial killer stories. The sub-genre did not exist in name before the 1970s but, just as serial killers existed in reality long before they were named, so did stories and films about them.

Figures of terror in folktales such as *Bluebeard* could be considered serial killer prototypes. Charles Perrault published a version of the tale in France in the late seventeenth century; Bluebeard is a wealthy nobleman whose beautiful wives keep disappearing until his eighth young wife defies his order not to enter a locked room in the chateau. She is horrified to find a blood-filled chamber where Bluebeard's murdered wives are hung up on hooks, like so many carcasses of meat. Bluebeard discovers from the blood on the door key that his wife entered the killing room and prepares to murder her, too, but she is saved by her brothers who kill Bluebeard. Many of the elements of this folktale could be found in a serial killer (or horror) film. A number of films were based on this folktale, the earliest being *Barbe Bleue* (1902), a short film by Georges Méliès. Later versions include *Bluebeard* (1944) by Edgar G Ulmer; Fritz Lang's *Secret Beyond the Door* (1948); *Blaubart* (1951) by Christian-Jaque; Claude Chabrol's *Bluebeard* (1963); Edward Dmytryk's *Bluebeard* (1972) and, more recently, Catherine Breillat's *Barbe Bleue* (2009).

Two early documented cases of serial murder were committed by Gilles de Rais and Erzsébet Báthory; both killers have been referenced in literature, film, plays and music. Fifteenth-century Breton nobleman Gilles de Rais was executed after confessing to luring numerous young boys to his residence where he raped and murdered them. In the early seventeenth century, the Hungarian 'Blood Countess' Erzsébet Báthory was imprisoned for killing 80 young girls, although it was rumoured that she murdered more than 600 victims through her lifetime. She escaped execution due to her nobility.

Newspaper articles helped bring multiple murders into the wider public consciousness, particularly when the police were conducting a manhunt. The most widely known multiple murderer in nineteenth-century England was Jack the Ripper whose nickname suggests a demonic, inhuman figure bridging the gap between crime and horror. He escaped justice as his true identity was never proven and this anonymity made Jack the Ripper the stuff of legend. A number of films have referred to him or his crimes, the earliest being GW Pabst's *Pandora's Box*, starring Louise Brooks, which has her die at his hands when she is reduced to working as a prostitute. Alfred Hitchcock's *The Lodger* (1926), based on Marie Belloc Lowndes's novel written in 1911, deals with artist Walter Sickert and the Ripper; the novel inspired three other films. Early historical crime films based on notorious perpetrators of multiple murders typically focused on the attempts of the police to apprehend the killer antagonist. Fritz Lang's film *M*, made in Germany in 1931, is about a police hunt for a (serial) killer of children who whistles 'In the Hall of the Mountain King' to attract his victims. The murderer has a specific modus operandi, which has become a known serial killer convention. In the manhunt for the perpetrator, other criminals join in, which accurately reflects how other criminals who operate 'with motive' feel about child molesters and killers.

The controversial *Peeping Tom* (1960), directed by Michael Powell, is about voyeurism and serial murder. When initially released, it was harshly received by critics, but attracted a cult following and now is considered a masterpiece. Main character and multiple murderer Mark Lewis films his female victims as he stalks and murders them, which we witness from the camera's point of view. The police notice that all the victims expired with an expression of horror on their faces, and we understand that this is because Lewis has attached a mirror to the top of his camera so the women witness their own deaths. Lewis's backstory is revealed in conversation to explain his motivation – his psychologist father used to perform psychological experiments on him, testing Mark's reactions to fearful situations, which clearly had a very negative impact on his adult mental state.

Another film that associates the parent with the serial killer's irresistible urge to murder is Alfred Hitchcock's *Psycho* (1960), based on the 1959 Robert Bloch novel of the same name. Bloch had made his name as a horror writer, but discovered, as Edgar Allan Poe had before him, that the horror of a disrupted mind is often more terrifying than the supernatural. In an interview with Douglas E Winter, Bloch states that: 'By the mid-1940s, I had pretty well mined the vein of ordinary supernatural themes until it had become varicose. I realised, as a result of what went on during World War II and of reading the more widely disseminated work in psychology, that the real horror is not in the shadows, but in that twisted little world inside our own skulls.' And so he wrote *Psycho*. Hitchcock was no stranger to making films about characters with unbalanced minds; he self-financed the film as the studios considered the subject matter of the novel repellent. It was loosely inspired by Wisconsin murderer Ed Gein, also known as the Plainfield Ghoul or the Mad Butcher, who murdered two women and possibly also his own brother. Gein also robbed graves of female body parts that he turned into macabre household objects and a suit of tanned human skin to wear himself. (This directly influenced the character Jame Gumb in *The Silence of the Lambs*.) In Bloch's novel and the film, it is revealed that lonely motel owner and devoted son Norman Bates murdered his mother and her lover, thieving secretary Marion Crane, and Detective Arbogast, a high enough body count to label him a serial killer. The film proved to be hugely popular, in part due to Hitchcock's clever publicity for it, but also because of its innovative story structure that successfully manipulates the audience into empathising with what would normally be seen as unsympathetic characters. In Act I, secretary Marion Crane is set up as the protagonist; she steals $40,000 from her arrogant boss and goes on the run in hopes of using the money to start a life with her cash-strapped boyfriend Sam Loomis. As she is motivated by love rather than greed, and her boss is so unpleasant and boastful of his wealth, we sympathise with her. The locking in point at the end of Act I sees her check into the Bates Motel during a heavy rainstorm and meet proprietor Norman Bates. This leads us to think that Act II will deal with all the obstacles to Marion's plan to evade the law and make a new life with Sam. She has dinner with the shy and likeable Norman who tells her that he is carer to his mentally ill mother; their conversation makes her feel guilty about her actions and consider returning the cash. It isn't until the midpoint of the film that Marion is stabbed to death in the shower by Mrs Bates. Norman discovers the murder and is in anguish; he decides to protect his mother, puts Marion's body in her car, and sinks it in a swamp. Despite the fact that Norman is breaking the law, it's not difficult to hope he gets away with it as he is cleaning up the evidence in order to protect his mother. With the initially established protagonist dead, it becomes Norman's story rather than Marion's and we wonder if he will succeed in safeguarding his unbalanced mother. Meanwhile,

Sam Loomis and Marion's sister, Lila, are concerned that Marion has not been in touch. Detective Arbogast goes in search of her, arrives at the Bates Motel and questions Norman, who comes across as overly nervous. At the end of Act II Detective Arbogast informs Sam and Lila that he is going to return to the Bates Motel to question Norman's mother; when he approaches Mrs Bates's bedroom, she stabs him to death. In Act III, Sam Loomis and Lila Crane take on the investigation of Marion's disappearance themselves, travelling to Fairvale where they question the local sheriff. He tells them that Mrs Bates died over a decade ago in a murder/suicide with her lover, but then we see Norman carrying his mother down into the basement as she protests his actions. Sam and Lila rent a room in the motel and try to find clues as to the cause of Marion's disappearance. In the third act twist, Lila discovers Mrs Bates in the basement, who is revealed to be a long dead corpse – and Norman emerges from the shadows dressed in a frock and wig, wielding a knife, the true murderer. Hitchcock manages to 'trick' the audience into empathising with both a thief and a murderer and makes the bold move of killing off the apparent protagonist at the midpoint and shifting the story to the (serial) killer's point of view. This is a clever and difficult achievement in terms of storytelling; it also has the effect of making the audience a victim of a serial killer who wears a convincing mask.

Notorious murderers with multiple victims continued to inspire writers and filmmakers and were retrospectively labelled serial killer movies after the advent of criminal profiling in the 1970s. Films made in the early 1970s could perhaps be considered on the cusp of classical stage serial killer stories as they utilised information from true cases, but criminal profiling had yet to influence storytelling conventions. Examples include *10 Rillington Place* (1971), based on the serial killer/necrophiliac John Christie, and Hitchcock's *Frenzy* (1972), adapted from Arthur La Bern's novel *Goodbye Piccadilly, Farewell Leicester Square*, which is about a serial killer called the Necktie Murderer, whose killings bear similarities to the London Nude Murders committed from 1964–65 by 'Jack the Stripper' who killed six to eight prostitutes but was never caught.

CLASSICAL STAGE SERIAL KILLER FILMS:
TO NAME SOMETHING IS TO GIVE IT FORM

'If we catch John Doe and he turns out to be the devil, I mean if he's Satan himself, that might live up to our expectations, but he's not the devil. He's just a man.'

(William Somerset, *Se7en*)

It could be argued that the primitive stage of the serial killer sub-genre is particularly long as conventions could not be established in films until they were recognised in reality. As criminal profiling developed in the 1970s and was used by law enforcement agencies in efforts to apprehend newly labelled serial and spree killers, the classic conventions we are now aware of from serial killer films and television series began to firm up as writers used these criminal profiling concepts when developing characters and any police procedural aspects of the plot. Some conventions overlap with gangster film tropes, but the 'classic' motivation of film gangsters is power over a gang and the accumulation of wealth whereas the serial killer's motivation is, very simply, to kill. Further, there are two types of serial killer: organised and disorganised. The organised serial killer is psychopathic/sociopathic, but sane with the ability to plan and carry out a murder and proclivity for enjoying the subsequent notoriety. The disorganised serial killer kills with little planning due to a 'monstrous urge' and is asocial and psychotic. All in all, classical stage serial killer films focus more on the serial killer as a character rather than an unknown monster pursued by police; the sub-genre explores the borders of horror and crime films – the idea of evil incarnate.

Classical stage serial killer films often revolve around a police investigation when it becomes clear that a serial killer is at work and must be stopped before he kills again. The main protagonist may come up with the serial killer theory and, for added conflict, his superiors refuse to believe him or, for some reason, he must pursue the killer on his own. An example of this is *Cop* (1988), based on James Ellroy's novel *Blood on the Moon*. James Woods plays an investigative cop who believes a serial killer is on the loose and untangles a web of corruption while trying to capture the perpetrator; *Cop* was one of the first films to use the term 'serial killer'. The murderer's modus operandi – method of murder – is often key in serial killer stories due to its specificity. Examples of this are David Fincher's *Se7en* (1995) and *Zodiac* (2007). In *Se7en*, two homicide detectives figure out that the killer's modus operandi is linked to the seven deadly sins, which results in macabre crime scenes. *Zodiac* is based on the serial killer who operated in Northern California during the late 1960s and early 1970s, murdering seven people. He taunted the police with letters containing cryptograms and signed off as 'Zodiac'; the film features a cartoonist who plays amateur detective as the police try to track down Zodiac. Historical crime serial killer story *The Raven* (2012) focuses on Edgar Allan Poe's stories as the basis for the serial killer's modus operandi and has Poe as protagonist, supporting the police in their pursuit of the killer. Other examples of films about law enforcers pursuing serial killers are *Jennifer 8* (1992), with a killer who targets blind women, and *Citizen X* (1995), with a Russian serial killer who murders and eats children.

Thomas Harris's four Hannibal Lecter novels have been adapted into five feature films and one television series to date, indicating what a gripping character Thomas Harris created. Dr Hannibal Lecter, a brilliant psychiatrist and cannibalistic serial killer, plays antagonist to several different FBI agent protagonists in *Manhunter* (1986), *The Silence of the Lambs* (1991), *Hannibal* (2001), *Red Dragon* (2002), *Hannibal Rising* (2006) and TV series *Hannibal* (2013–). The most memorable of the five films is probably *The Silence of the Lambs* with Jodie Foster playing rookie FBI agent Clarice Starling and Anthony Hopkins in the role of Dr Lecter; their interesting relationship portrays the ability of organised serial killers to manipulate others.

Rather than the cop/serial killer, protagonist/antagonist dynamic, *Copycat* (1995) pits two women, police detective MJ Monahan and criminal profiler and serial killer expert Dr Helen Hudson, against a copycat serial killer, with the added twist that Dr Hudson is an agoraphobic afraid to leave her apartment due to being previously attacked by now imprisoned serial killer Daryll Lee Cullum, who we discover in a coda is manipulating serial killers outside of prison to carry out his crimes.

Television series *The Following* (2013–) uses a similar device. Dr Joe Carroll (played by James Purefoy), university lecturer and expert on Edgar Allan Poe, murders 14 female students before being imprisoned. From his cell and through his charismatic personality, Carroll has managed to attract a 'following' of killers or want-to-be killers who do his bidding. Former FBI agent Ryan Hardy (played by Kevin Bacon) is brought in as a consultant when Carroll escapes prison; Hardy was stabbed through the heart by Carroll when he originally captured him, which led to his retirement through disability as he now needs a pacemaker to survive. Carroll is caught and returned to prison in the pilot episode, but then it becomes clear that his 'following' will do anything, including murder, to please him. The series was created by Kevin Williamson and the basic pitch is: 'The FBI estimates there are currently over 300 active serial killers in the United States. What would happen if these killers had a way of communicating and connecting with each other? What if they were able to work together and form alliances across the country? What if one brilliant psychotic serial killer was able to bring them all together and activate a following?' Again, this deals with the notion of a serial killer as a charismatic, persuasive, 'hypnotic' individual adept at manipulating others.

Another ongoing television series that frequently deals with serial killers is *Criminal Minds* (2005–) which follows the FBI's Behavioral Analysis Unit, a team of expert criminal profilers who work with local police to solve extremely violent crimes, often perpetrated by serial killers. The show is reminiscent of *NCIS* in terms of a specialist team that works for a government agency, but the focus is on using psychological profiling to predict the serial killer's next move and then bring him or her in.

CLASSICAL STAGE SERIAL KILLER SUB-GENRE CONVENTIONS

Dr Hannibal Lecter: 'Why do you think he removes their skins, Agent Starling? Enthral me with your acumen.'
Clarice Starling: 'It excites him. Most serial killers keep some sort of trophies from their victims.'
Dr Hannibal Lecter: 'I didn't.'
Clarice Starling: 'No. No, you ate yours.'

(***The Silence of the Lambs***)

Serial killer films embrace both crime and horror film genre conventions as they deal with the crime of murder and meeting the 'monster' – a character that seems through his or her actions less than human. Serial killer and horror films both focus on the darker sides of life (and death) and are designed to unsettle and shock us; they invoke our hidden fears and make us feel squeamish. Both horror and serial killer films makes us fear death, mutilation and dismemberment; in some ways the serial killer film may be more frightening as the 'monster' is human rather than supernatural.

As the serial killer sub-genre is quite new due to the recent advent of criminal profiling and 'defining' common traits of this specific sociopath, serial killer character conventions are also quite new and based on the most current theories about such killers. A number of primitive stage serial killer films do paint an accurate portrait of these killers based on the writer's ability to translate reported fact into credible characterisation, but writers are now expected to incorporate current research about serial killers into their stories. It will be interesting to see how this relatively new sub-genre develops. Serial killers are normally depicted as the antagonist, particularly in a story with police procedural elements, but there has been an increasing number of films and television series with the serial killer as protagonist. This might just be a revisionist strategy for innovation, or might perhaps indicate that the sub-genre is developing in a similar manner to the gangster sub-genre. The serial killer certainly has strong enough character conventions as derived from casebook studies for this to be the case.

The Protagonist: The Demon Battler

The main character is normally an agent of the law, which means that he or she has a code of conduct to adhere to; the protagonist may be a criminologist with specialist knowledge of serial killers who has been called in specifically to help capture the perpetrator. If this is the case, he or she may be on loan from another agency or may be an independent expert who must work with local police and this may cause conflict. Equally, the protagonist may be a law enforcement officer without specialist knowledge who must learn on the job and has a more emotional relationship with the perpetrator and his actions as he or she is deeply disturbed by the serial killer's crimes. The serial killer may specifically taunt the protagonist, which drives him or her to solve the case, but also to make mistakes. The serial killer often tells the protagonist that 'we are the same', a comment that horrifies the protagonist because it contains some truth. It's important to note that the protagonist is also a potential victim of the serial killer, as is the case in a horror film. If a 'civilian', then the protagonist's goal is to escape, but at some point he or she must face up to the serial killer monster. If the protagonist is an agent of the law, escape can only be a temporary goal as the protagonist's role is to vanquish the monster – to apprehend the serial killer. As in a horror film, a number of secondary characters normally become the serial killer's victims. There is frequently the threat that at least one of these victims will be close to the protagonist, either a work partner, family member, or a love interest.

The Antagonist: Organised or Disorganised?

As noted earlier, the serial killer is broadly categorised into two types: organised and disorganised, and most serial killer conventions are derived from the research of criminal profilers. He – for, typically, the serial killer is a white male – may be a charismatic, compelling figure with a façade of normality or a character dissolving into violent psychosis, lacking any social graces. The disorganised serial killer tends to have clearer similarities to a horror film antagonist, a figure of menace who is visually recognisable as not quite fitting into society.

The organised serial killer has the skills to blend into his community; in many ways that makes him more dangerous and fascinating, in a similar way to the violent gangster. But while the gangster might kill to achieve or steal power and to obtain material success, the serial killer is motivated by the compulsion to take a life and the power he associates with that. He may also kill to protect himself from capture. The serial killer, whether organised or disorganised, has little empathy for fellow human beings. The organised serial killer is anti-social, narcissistic and has a superiority complex. They are also manipulative, cunning, and may wear a 'good citizen' mask, have a tidy outward appearance, and be married with a family. While the victim rarely tends to do anything specific to cause the serial killer to murder them, a stressor event in his everyday life often provokes his compulsion to kill. The organised serial killer tends to plan his crimes in detail; he may have a 'kill kit' with items of restraint or murder weapons, and may have a specific modus operandi that supports the fantasy world that drives him. The organised serial killer often monitors a specific area for 'prey', then stalks the potential victim who tends to be a stranger and may be of a specific type. The serial killer is skilled at persuading his victims to accompany him away from the meeting spot and, after the kill, he tends to hide the body in a new location. Normally extreme care is taken to eradicate any evidence and the killer may be adept at staging the crime or disposal scene to suggest a specific motive for murder such as robbery or rape to help divert attention from himself. He also tends to take 'trophies' from the victim, rather like victory spoils, which he uses to relive his crime and further enhance his fantasy world. The organised serial killer monitors any police investigation into his crimes, may play games with the police, and tends to believe he is too smart to get caught.

The disorganised serial killer is driven far more by compulsion than organisation. He may live alone or with an emotionally or physically abusive parental figure, has few social skills, may have nocturnal habits, and is recognised as odd by others. The disorganised serial killer lacks the methodology of the organised killer and does not consider the consequences of his actions. This means that he may murder family or close neighbours and tends to operate in an area he knows well as this gives him a sense of security; he does not attempt to conceal the body and may mutilate and essentially dehumanise it in a frenzied attack of overkill. Any staging of the crime scene is done as part of the disorganised serial killer's fantasy rather than in an attempt to confuse investigators, and he takes little care about erasing any evidence. The organised serial killer is often of above average intelligence (and often of exceptional intelligence in serial killer books and films), but his disorganised counterpart may be of lower than average intelligence with substance abuse problems. He may also take trophies and have a hiding place in his home for them; the disorganised serial killer is often fixated on the crime scene to help him relive his kill.

The serial killer tends to be a somewhat exaggerated character in films. If of the organised type, he is an extremely brilliant and often talented 'evil genius', which raises the stakes and makes him much more difficult to defeat. A disorganised serial killer is often depicted as something of a horror figure with almost supernatural skills and an unstoppable urge to kill in a horrific manner.

Type of Plot or Story Pattern: The focus of the story is the efforts of the agent of the law to apprehend the serial killer, or the potential victim to escape the killer.

- *Act I:* Introduction to the Monster
  Normally a murder is committed early in Act I and something about the crime scene or the way the victim has been killed bears similarities to another recent killing or notorious murders from the past. Typically the specifics of the murder or the crime scene are particularly disturbing and memorable. A second murder often happens near the end of Act I that strongly suggests that a serial killer is at work. Equally, the killer might send a goading letter to the protagonist's place of work (typically a law enforcement agency, but could be a private practice) or a newspaper threatening to kill again. It becomes the protagonist's mission to capture the serial killer, whether due to being assigned the case, some past history, or because his or her superiors refuse to believe a serial killer is

at work. If the main protagonist is a 'civilian' rather than an agent of the law, he or she is a potential victim and the main goal for Act II is to escape. Often a specific connection is made between the protagonist and the serial killer, if only through the protagonist making announcements to the press or by his or her presence at the crime scene, which is noticed by the serial killer who has been observing the police at work.

- *Act II:* Battle with the Monster
  The power and skills of the serial killer are the focus of Act II – he seems impossible to defeat. As the agents of the law attempt to discover who the perpetrator is and to capture him, information as to how serial killers are meant to operate is disseminated, typically through exposition from the police team and experts, but also through the particularly gruesome crime scenes. The serial killer's modus operandi tends to be a point of focus. If the protagonist is a civilian and potential victim, he or she may spend much of Act II in flight and developing a survival strategy. As Act II and the investigation progresses, a relationship tends to develop between the serial killer and the main protagonist, often with the taunt, 'we are the same', which to the observer has a certain ring of truth about it. Whereas the police procedural tends to focus on the gathering of evidence and, through that, fathoming suspects and motive, in the serial killer film the focus is on mind hunting – working out the psychology and motive of the serial killer. During this process, however, it tends to be the (organised) serial killer who gets inside the head of the protagonist, manipulating him or her in unexpected ways. If the antagonist is a disorganised serial killer, his crimes may escalate, becoming more horrific, which puts additional pressure on the protagonist. The ticking clock throughout is the threat of further murders. At the end of Act II it may seem that the serial killer will prevail.

- *Act III:* He Who Fights With Monsters...
  By this stage, the serial killer may seem invincible. In a twist, something crucial is often revealed about the serial killer that

gives some advantage to the protagonist. A showdown between the protagonist and the serial killer is expected, but victory must not come too easily for him or her. Often this showdown will occur in a remote or isolated place to preclude assistance from third parties. Normally the protagonist prevails, but equally (as in a horror film) it is shown that the serial killer has the means to escape custody or has managed to do so. It is also clear that the protagonist will be changed – perhaps scarred – by the events as in a horror film.

Narrative Style: A serial killer story obviously deals with the crimes of the perpetrator, his modus operandi, and psychology; normally a convincingly realistic portrait of an investigation by law enforcement officials is presented. The murders themselves may be particularly horrific. Elements of the police procedural are typically included such as evidence gathering, interviewing witnesses, interrogating suspects and autopsies, but the 'mind hunt' is the central focus, utilising the expertise of criminal profilers. The serial killer will often taunt his pursuers through messages or at the crime scenes. There are usually cat and mouse chase sequences between protagonist and antagonist; there is often a nightmarish quality to this struggle, as in horror films. Just as horror films may deal with magic objects and talismans, the serial killer might collect trophies. Mystery, suspense, surprise or fear through use of dramatic irony are heavily used.

Timeframe/Pace: A serial killer by his or her nature has a number of victims and the scope of the narrative must accommodate this. As in psychological horror, there is normally a focus on character arc and the mental disintegration of the character. As the serial killer's behaviour escalates, pace increases as more victims fall prey to his attacks and the protagonist must work harder to stop him – or escape him.

Tone: Violent, aggressive, suspenseful, nightmarish – a mix of police hunt and horror tropes. The serial killer's overriding goal is to kill and he will stop at nothing to do so.

Setting and Mise-en-scène: In reality, serial killer stories happen in small towns and suburbia as much as in big cities (if not more so). There is something frightening about meeting the monster in a seemingly safe environment. The sub-genre also embraces ideas of crazed killer in a remote location (where no one can hear you scream).

Overall, the serial killer film tends to have similar conventions to the police story murder investigation combined with some horror film tropes. Horror films are designed to provide the audience with a cathartic experience – after all the fear and distress generated by the monster, 'the horror' is defeated and normality returns (if only for a time…). The serial killer film would seem to provide less of a cathartic experience as the monster is human and the question of 'why' is rarely answered – the chill is more lingering as it is rooted in reality.

REVISIONIST SERIAL KILLER STORIES: THE MONSTER'S POINT OF VIEW

'If you shoot someone in the head with a .45 every time you kill somebody, it becomes like your fingerprint, see? But if you strangle one, stab another, and one you cut up, and one you don't, then the police don't know what to do. They think you're four different people. What they really want, what makes their job so much easier, is pattern. What they call a modus operandi. That's Latin. Bet you didn't know any Latin, did you kid?'

(Henry, *Henry: Portrait of a Serial Killer*)

Typically, Hitchcock was ahead of his time; Norman Bates's point of view is presented to the audience, even if in a rather deceptive way, as he acts out his own psychosis and is labelled 'psycho' rather than 'serial killer'. The most obvious revisionist strategy for classic conventions of the serial killer sub-genre is to make the serial killer the protagonist rather than the powerful antagonist. This has the effect of humanising the serial killer to an extent and moving him further from horror genre monster to the human culprit of the crime genre.

Henry: Portrait of a Serial Killer (1986), directed by John McNaughton, is an early groundbreaking example of this; the protagonist is loosely based on serial killer Henry Lee Lucas and the movie's tagline was: 'He's not Freddy. He's not Jason. He's real.' This cleverly indicates what is particularly frightening about serial killer movies. The $110,000 budget used to make 'Henry' was originally for a gory horror film, but McNaughton thought the budget too small for convincing horror effects and, after seeing a news item about Henry Lee Lucas, decided to use his crimes as the basis for his film. While the film was shot in 1986, it was not released until 1990 due to problems in rating it, given the violent content.

American Psycho (2000), based on Bret Easton Ellis's novel and directed by Mary Harron, has a psychopathic investment banking executive as the main protagonist who descends into his own violent fantasies and has a secret life as a serial killer. It is as much an indictment of the 1980s culture of avarice as it is a tale of an escalating serial killer.

Patty Jenkins's film *Monster* (2003) is based on the life of prostitute Aileen Wuornos who turned serial killer after being violently raped by one of her tricks and was executed in 2002 for the murder of six men. Charlize Theron won an Oscar and 16 other awards for her portrayal of Wuornos.

Perfume: The Story of a Murderer (2006), based on the novel by Patrick Süskind and written and directed by Tom Tykwer, is the story of Jean-Baptiste Grenouille, impoverished and abused from birth, but with an incredible sense of smell, who learns the fine art of perfumery and takes to murder in his bid to create the perfect scent. The novel follows Grenouille's life story and the film, while compressed, includes backstory about Grenouille's birth as that encourages audience sympathy with the protagonist.

The television series *Dexter* (2006–) is based on the novel *Darkly Dreaming Dexter* by Jeff Lindsay. Dexter, the protagonist of the series, is a Miami Metro Police blood spatter analyst; he is also a serial killer who kills other killers who have evaded justice.

Spike Lee's *Summer of Sam* (1999) provides another variation on the serial killer story. It focuses on an Italian-American community in the Bronx in the summer of 1977, where David Berkowitz – dubbed the Son of Sam – carried out multiple homicides over the course of a year, creating intense unease and local vigilantes. In the film, fear ultimately drives the community to criminal behaviour.

Les Revenants (2012) is a French television serial set in an isolated mountain town in which the dead mysteriously come back to life and try to resume their roles in their families and the community – horror blended with realism. It also has a serial killer subplot; attacks with a specific modus operandi resume after several years cessation. While this may happen if a serial killer has been imprisoned and then released, in this instance it seems that the killer has died and was released from the prison of death.

SPREE KILLER AND MASS MURDER FILMS

Spree killers and mass murderers differ from serial killers by definition, but are often associated due to the perpetrator's attitude towards murder and certain overlaps in character. As noted earlier, spree killers commit two or more murders without a cooling off period; these murders may occur in several different locations. This suggests a rampage as opposed to the careful planning of the organised serial killer. According to the FBI definition, the mass murderer unlawfully kills four or more persons during a particular event with no cooling off period between the murders. Typically the murders are committed in a single location by one or more perpetrators. Many acts of mass murder end with the death of the perpetrator, by either suicide or agents of the law. Examples of spree killings are Badlands (1973) and Natural Born Killers (1994). Badlands, written and directed by Terrence Malick, follows the on-the-run escapades of young lovers and spree killers Holly Sargis and Kit Carruthers, characters loosely based on killers Charles Starkweather and Caril Ann Fugate who murdered 11 people in Nebraska and Wyoming between December 1957 and January 1958. In the film, Holly's eerie voiceover presents her peculiarly emotionless point of view. Natural Born Killers (1994) is the story of two lovers who go on a killing spree, which is glorified to extremes in the media. The poster strapline states: 'The Media Made Them Superstars.' The script was originally written by Quentin Tarantino but was considerably reworked by director Oliver Stone, and the film also caused much controversy due to its extremely violent content.

Elephant (2003) and We Need to Talk About Kevin (2011) are about mass murderers. Gus Van Sant's Elephant is loosely based on the Columbine High School massacre that occurred in Littleton, Colorado in 1999 when two students, Eric Harris and Dylan Klebold, murdered 13 people and injured 24 more before they both committed suicide. The film received the Palme d'Or at the 2003 Cannes Film Festival. We Need to Talk About Kevin is based on Lionel Shriver's epistolary novel, which focuses on a mother's attempt to cope with the fact that her son is a mass murderer. The film begins with murderer Kevin Katchadourian in prison and flashes back to show the events that led to him being imprisoned as remembered by his mother Eva. It's an effective approach that explores Eva's sense of guilt and her attempts to understand what made Kevin a monster.

PARODY STAGE: LAUGHING AT WHAT WE FEAR MOST

'You know, you're bigger than Freddy and Jason now, only you're a real person.'

(Birdie to Beverly, Serial Mom)

The advent of criminal profiling threw a spotlight onto the serial killer character and psychology, so an obvious convention to spoof in a serial killer parody is the serial killer character, making a surprising character the serial killer. Examples of this are Eating Raoul (1982), Serial Mom (1994) and Sightseers (2012). The serial killer protagonists in Eating Raoul are a debt-ridden, prudish married couple – Paul and Mary Bland – who resort to murdering swingers for their money in hopes of opening their own restaurant. The murders begin after a drunken swinger tries to molest Mary, and Paul hits the attacker over the head with a large frying pan. The frying pan then becomes their weapon of choice in the subsequent murders, which brings a slapstick lightness to the killings. (Pedro Almodóvar uses a similar tactic in *¿Que he hecho yo para merecer esto!!* [1984] when Gloria accidentally kills her brutal husband after hitting him over the head with a large ham leg.)

John Waters's *Serial Mom* pokes fun at American middle class bigotry and stars Kathleen Turner as perfect housewife and serial killer Beverly Sutphin who murders those who insult her or have different values. (She famously murders a character played by Patty Hearst for wearing white shoes after Labor Day, a fashion faux pas.)

Ben Wheatley's *Sightseers*, written by and starring Alice Lowe and Steve Oram, has the tagline: *'Killers Have Never Been So Average.'* When Chris and Tina go on their first holiday together, caravanning in the north of England, they discover a mutual love of… murder. Again, the black comedy pokes fun at the idea of organised serial killers being able to construct an ordinary façade as well as the very minor irritations that drive Chris and Tina to kill.

C'est arrivé près de chez vous (*Man Bites Dog*) (1992) takes a slightly different approach; it's a mockumentary in which a film crew follows around a serial killer called Ben and documents his everyday life and exploits. The crew are unable to remain objective and get caught up in Ben's murders – until someone begins to take revenge on Ben and on them.

As unsettling as serial killer stories are, conventions have been effectively parodied in black comedy form where characters certainly get hurt (murdered), usually by unlikely killers with unusual murder weapons, or set off by peculiar stressors.

....

WRITING EXERCISE: WRITING THE MONSTER

Part A

As we have seen previously, many crime stories are based on true crimes and a number of serial killer films are derived from the crimes of actual predators, which are often so brutal and unusual as to seem fabricated. A writer of serial killer stories should be able to create a convincing killer by utilising current knowledge of psychological profiling; basing characters on real perpetrators can be a useful starting point to help create a serial killer figure that seems realistic rather than an exaggerated horror film antagonist. The more realistic the character, the more chilling his or her crimes seem due to an inherent lack of humanity. (The following exercise and research is not for the faint-hearted!)

- This is a list of ten serial killers from various time periods and locations, some well-known, others less so. Choose one.

    i.   Maria Catherina Swanenburg
    ii.   Jeffrey Dahmer
    iii. Yang Xinhai
    iv.   Dennis Rader
    v.   Edson Isidoro Guimarães
    vi.   Joachim Georg Kroll
    vii. Anatoly Onoprienko
    viii. Dennis Nilsen
    ix.   Ted Bundy
    x.   Charles Sobhraj

- Research your chosen perpetrator online and complete the following short 'profile' details as best you can:

    i.   Name
    ii.   Date of birth – date of death
    iii. Nickname: derived from his or her crimes
    iv.   Nationality/birth place

    v.   Relevant backstory (information about parents/family, socio-economic group, religion, education, standing in community, work, and so on)

    vi.   Years active as serial killer (what triggered first kill? how frequent were the kills?)

    vii. Main locations of crimes

    viii. Number of confirmed victims or number of victims convicted of killing

    ix.   Suspected or confessed total number of victims

    x.   Usual victim type (age, sex, hair colour or body type, and so on)

    xi.   Modus operandi

    xii. Trophies (if taken)

    xiii. Possible motive or stated motive:

    xiv. Date of capture/how that occurred

    xv. Imprisonment or execution (when and where)

    xvi. Memorable quotes

- Outline a scene of introduction – the first time we see the serial killer onscreen. Make it a subtle but revealing scene in which we know something isn't quite right about the character, but we are not yet aware that he or she is a serial killer. Ultimately the scene should be quite chilling in tone and, later, in content when we understand more about the character.

- Choose a character from your image kit as 'victim'. If the serial killer targeted has a specific victim type, choose accordingly. If he or she murdered at random, then choose your victim randomly.

- Outline a second scene in which serial killer and potential victim first meet. Think about a shift in tone or in the balance of power. If this is the scene in which the serial killer will attack the victim, make it surprising and chilling. Try to refrain from using gore for effect. Think about character and more surprising effects or images.

Part B

Now repeat the above exercise after creating a profile for one of the three serial killers noted below who have yet to be identified and captured:

- The Zodiac Killer
- The Doodler (San Francisco, 1970s)
- The West Mesa Bone Collector (Albuquerque, New Mexico)

Obviously this will entail a mix of research and extrapolation. Really consider how the perpetrators have managed to avoid detection – is it through cleverness on his or her part; sloppy procedure by investigators; or just luck, with the answers hidden in plain sight?

....

AN INSIDE JOB:
THOUGHTS AND EXPERIENCES OF INDUSTRY PROFESSIONALS WORKING IN THE CRIME GENRE

'I demand that a film express either the joy of making cinema or the agony of making cinema. I am not at all interested in anything in between.'

(François Truffaut)

'I always ask myself one question: what is human? What does it mean to be human? Maybe people will consider my new films brutal again. But this violence is just a reflection of what they really are, of what is in each one of us to certain degree.'

(Kim Ki-duk)

VICKI MADDEN

Vicki is the director of Australian development consultancy and production company Sweet Potato Films and has extensive international experience as a television and feature film script editor, story producer, show runner and writer. She brought her script editing skills to crime series such as *The Bill*, the classic British television police procedural that ran from 1984 to 2010, and Lynda La Plante's

Trial and Retribution. Vicki also wrote Australian tele-movie *Blood Brothers*, based on the 1993 murders of Jeffrey Gilham's family, and has been writer and show runner on several crime series. Vicki spent two years as a script executive for Nine Network (Australia), so she knows how to develop concepts that sell and find an audience. She continues to use these skills as a 'gun for hire' brought in to redevelop television shows with declining ratings and to assist producers in putting together concept documents. In addition to her own projects in development, Vicki offers script consultancy services and runs an online course for emerging writers, *'Into the Box'*, through the Australian Film Television & Radio School.

www.sweetpotatofilms.com.au

*

Any thoughts as to why fewer detective and police story features seem to get off the ground as features when they are so popular on television? Or would you disagree with this?

Television has mastered the police procedural/detective genre so well that it is hard for a feature to sell itself as simply a police story or a detective story. Audiences want more bang for their buck when they go out and pay money. There are, of course, still plenty of feature films that are dressed up as something else, but, at their core, they are police procedural and detective stories. Even Batman is a cop show – just so happens the top detective wears leather and has an unhealthy interest in bats... Cross-genre films (and TV) are the big thing now so, while a studio or network may dress a film up and sell it off as an action thriller (*The Bourne Identity*, *Die Hard*, *Batman*, *The Matrix*, etc), or superhero film (*Batman*, *Spiderman*, *Superman*, etc), ultimately these are all stories where good versus evil and all the standard tropes of the detective and police procedural genres are used. *House MD* is a good example of the cross-genre. It's a medical show but uses the tropes of a detective show – only the perpetrator is a germ or virus. House is a detective – they base him and Wilson (his off-sider) on Holmes and Watson. There are many clues within the show itself but primarily it's a detective series.

Would you briefly summarise what your work as a television script editor entails and how that differs from script editing a feature? And, from an insider's perspective, what skills are required to be a successful crime series writer who works well with script editors?

The television industry has become a huge hungry beast for money and unfortunately very few people who run TV networks have any interest in the business as entertainment. It is just another business they run to make money. The pressure on producers, then, is to trim down budgets to their core essentials and speed up the turnaround process. I started my writing career at Crawford Productions – at that time, and for many years, it was one of the largest and most prolific production companies in Australia. It was the training ground for the majority of our industry but sadly it is now closed. Hector Crawford ran the place and he was more passionate about TV than anyone I've ever met since. I remember he called me down to his office one day. I had only been working at the place for a month and was training on *The Flying Doctors* as a trainee script editor. I was terrified before the meeting as Hector was, and still is, legendary in the business. However, it was one of the most amazing meetings. He told me he wanted to pass over some knowledge to me and to ensure that, as I moved forward with my career, I would always keep the passion and understand the importance of our role in bringing stories to the small screen. He told me to have pride in my work – never release a script with one single typing mistake in it (I always remember that!) and never send it out until it was the very best script it could be.

That message has long been lost and finding people like Hector Crawford in the TV industry any more is almost impossible. I say all this because it is relevant to your question – what is the role of a script editor in television and how does it differ from feature work?

In television a script editor's role was to work in-house, exclusively on one particular show, and help guide the script from its conception to delivery, under the guidance of a story editor/script producer or show runner (depends what country you're working in). This is the role I normally work in as well as writer, but I also script edit when necessary (read: starving). Why? Because script editing is the most under-valued, over-abused job in television. You are the proverbial meat in the sandwich trying to please the requirements of the show and the fragile ego of the writer. No one really wins (but the show will make a profit from all the stunts and locations you just cut out).

Whereby the script editor in TV used to be the mediator and note giver and 'sounding board' for the writer, they now become furious re-writers, putting in all-nighters trying to keep up with the relentless, breakneck speed and demands made on them by the show's producers.

As a feature script editor, the job is more hands-off and the script editor provides notes for the writer and the relationship is more intimate – they work sometimes even before a producer is onboard. They can work more as a team – the writer has more control and the script editor's role is not to serve anyone else but the writer, to see their vision and, hopefully, contribute to it. They can be invaluable and they can be a curse.

I would like to digress here for a moment and give you my humble opinion on a couple of key issues that also contribute to the 'scathing hatred' a lot of writers have for script editors. It is a fundamental problem that the TV industry and some writers actually fail to recognise (usually the writers who bang on and get so upset). And it is this: just because you can write, that doesn't mean you can tell a story...

There it is. A simple fact. Not all storytellers are proficient writers. They are vastly different skills but barely acknowledged or recognised by producers. So, what happens is this – someone can write a good script so suddenly a producer will hire them as a show runner/ story producer. The show flops. The blame-game starts. But no one recognises this simple fact. I've worked with top-shelf writers who cannot plot to save their life. I've seen brilliant storytellers struggle with writing – but producers think they are one and the same.

To counterpoint that, there are a few writers who can do both, and they are invaluable in television, but I could count them on one hand. Until producers understand the roles within the script department, that problem will always exist.

There is barely any acknowledgement of the important role of the story producer in the UK and Australia – no training or very little – and no understanding or respect for this role by producers who don't like being told how the script should be. Everyone thinks they are a writer and story producer and, for some strange reason, everyone in TV seems to be allowed to have input. In one job I did in Ireland, and I kid you not, a producer asked an on-set nurse to go into the edit suite (that I hadn't been into as story producer) and asked her if she thought the scene worked. She didn't, so they cut it.

Do you think that the training a writer receives working on a crime series – following a specific format, with a script editor and producer along with tight deadlines – is a plus when writing features? Or are there any negatives? I also ask this as some well-known television writers have found it difficult to get feature projects off the ground. Can a feature script be 'too TV'?

There are always positives and negatives when writers go from TV to features and vice-versa. Television teaches you discipline. Discipline can mean the difference between success and failure – no matter where your talent sits. I know a couple of amazingly wonderful writers who have never completed a feature through lack of discipline and won't touch TV because they don't want to be known as a TV writer – go figure. Writing for TV also teaches you to think quickly. You learn to hold on to and juggle many stories at once and somehow, mentally, you start to plot them all in your head.

Downside – you become used to the speed and that produces shallow writing. You have 'go-to' clichés that work in TV but are not acceptable in features – however, with the standard of TV going up thanks to HBO, Foxtel, etc, the demands on TV writers are increasing. We're also seeing a flood of film writers turning to TV now and that is changing the way we view TV shows.

TV writers also find the breadth of features, in terms of story as well as length, difficult to grasp at times and I have read quite a few feature scripts written by TV writers that are just too – well, television.

The Bill *(sadly now defunct)* had a reputation as a series that offered new writers an entry into television writing; few other series today seem to offer that in the UK. Any interesting new writers you worked with on The Bill? Any that made the transition to writing crime features? What marked them out in your opinion as particularly noteworthy?

Soaps in the UK are excellent training grounds and *The Bill* was especially because it was an hour-long format. I can't remember any new writers especially, as it was back nine years ago, but there were a couple of writers who stood out – those rare ones who you could trust with a story, to plot it out and write it in fast turnaround – a godsend for the furious pace in which we had to work. I do remember a couple in particular: Jake Riddell and Tom Needam. They saved my butt a few times, I can tell you!

You've worked with Lynda La Plante who has a knack for coming up with commercial hits; given your own experience with commissioning projects and 'rebooting' ailing series, where does she go right?

Lynda La Plante is probably the most inspirational woman I have ever met in my professional life. She is also a wonderfully eccentric and smart and intelligent woman who I am lucky to call a friend. (Jimmy McGovern and Paul Abbott are the most inspirational men.) Lynda has a natural gift – I don't mean she's just good, it's a gift, for storytelling. Her gut instinct is spot on, and she can sniff a good story a mile away. She is a natural born storyteller. Even when you spend time with her outside of work (and I was lucky enough to often spend weekends at her house) she would regale you with wonderful stories about people she's met (from A-list celebrities to hard-core crims) and she would have you mesmerised, leaning across the table as she slowly built up anticipation... She'd pause for effect, carry on, building the story up, and then she'd hit you with a zinger of a twist or a reveal that would leave you totally awestruck. She is also a mastermind at getting people to open up. You end up laying bare your whole life – like she has some magic that makes you want to tell her everything and she gets it. She understands human nature. Lynda's observational skills are also needle-sharp. She can almost read people – and she is particularly sensitive to women who end up in prison. Even though she is criticised at times for making money out of victims' stories (as some UK papers once stated), she also gives back. Not many people know this about Lynda, but she is extraordinarily giving and generous.

I remember one particular story we were trying to crack; Lynda had read about a woman's hand that was found in a river somewhere and in a flash had sketched out an idea for a *Trial and Retribution*. The problem was, a hand doesn't equate necessarily to a murder, so there was no reason for our heroes to be in on the case up front. We worked well into the night – myself and Jacqueline Malton (the amazing ex-cop, now a writer, who was the inspiration for Jane Tennison in *Prime Suspect*), along with four other experts in some field of forensics, criminal behaviour, criminal law, etc. It was relentless, but Lynda wasn't going to budge. She had this story in her head and it had to work – and it did... eventually, after not much sleep and a lot of pizza!

I used to stay at Lynda's place on weekends as I was new to the UK and didn't know many people. She would often be off doing talks, attending dinners and making appearances, etc, so I had the run of her viewing room which was like a candy store for crime addicts like myself, and her dog, Bates (Norman), a gentle giant of a Great Dane, who used to bring a teddy bear in his mouth and jump up on the sofa (don't tell Lynda that) with me – and I would end up sitting on the floor. Sadly he has passed on, but I have so many wonderful memories.

Former cops writing police procedural novels really paved the way for police procedural series in the US. **Prime Suspect** *and* **Policewoman,** *the 1970s series starring Angie Dickinson, were ground-breaking cop shows featuring women. You mention working with Jacqueline Malton, the inspiration for Jane Tennison. It can't be easy to become* *a television script consultant and crime writer after such a notable career as a police officer.*

Jacqueline Malton is an extraordinary woman and sharp as a tack. She did the hard yards in the police force as a woman toughing it out. A lot of what you see in Jane Tennison is there in Jacqueline. She has an amazing gift for story and is excellent at creating characters – probably because of her life as a cop working with so many varied and troubled types. She often worked as a consultant on various police shows, from Lynda La Plante's *Company* to *The Bill* and even *New Tricks*. I'd work with her in a flash if I was over there.

Do you think a certain type of person/writer is better suited to crime writing? For example, someone who reads lots of crime literature or a very analytical person...? Might this vary with crime sub-genres? Murder mystery versus gangster saga, or amateur detective versus police story?

You have to be genuinely interested in the nature of crime, I believe, or the psychology of crime in order to write a good crime story. There are many films and TV shows that really just service a simple plot with no attempt to get underneath the story and characters, to see what makes them tick. It's very unfortunate how much we glorify criminals (not to mention dangerous), and I personally don't like writing stories about career criminals – druggies or gangs, etc. They don't interest me at all. I am interested in domestic crime – why a man kills his family over a small issue like cereal (obviously not the main cause) but the trigger – and digging back into this character's life in order to understand the psychology behind it. So, I read a lot of true crime – it fascinates me in a way I don't understand myself. If I was smart enough, I would be a criminal profiler. (Though I did do very well in an FBI course I attended on criminal profiling!) The lecturer was a die-hard FBI hard man and the course was made up primarily of cops and social workers, lawyers, and one TV writer. I managed to sneak in because I had worked with the professor of criminology at the university previously. He was sitting in and thought it was hilarious that the one person who put their hand up more than anyone when the lecturer was asking who knew of the cases he was talking about and what made them special was the TV writer. He actually interrupted the guy and told him who I was. The FBI guy was impressed but no one else was. At morning tea I was mobbed by smart-aleck cops who wanted to tell me how shit the show was that I was working on at the time (about undercover cops!).

Some people are naturally interested in certain sub-genres and, therefore, they tend to lean towards these; however, in TV especially, you kind of need to be across as much as you can in order to stay working. I study TV shows and films a lot in order to understand how they work. I break them down, work out every aspect of how they work – especially if I like them. At the moment I am watching everything Scandinavian. *The Killing* is totally addictive and yet a simple story based around a simple theme – the nature of friendship – but told within a complex and riveting story world. *Borgen* is another one, and *The Bridge* – all with complex female characters imbued with male characteristics that turn expectations of women on their head. Good yarns where the stakes are about as high as you can take them.

With respect to your commissioning and packaging work, are there any crime sub-genres you are particularly drawn to? And when you read a script are there formatting issues or ways of writing that really turn you off? Or crime clichés? Can you give some specifics about writers you thought were the 'real deal' as soon as you read their work, even if you didn't particularly like the story?

I love thrillers and the UK produces more of my favourite shows than anywhere else. I love *Spooks*, *The Shadow Line*, *Whitechapel*. But then, when *Life On Mars* came out, followed by *Ashes to Ashes*, I started to become intrigued with sci-fi crime. I thought the end of *Ashes to Ashes* was one of the most satisfying ends of any series I'd seen. I absolutely loved it. I also discovered something about myself after developing a mad crush on Gene Hunt.

I hate boring characters and scripts that are simply plot-driven with no character exploration.

In terms of uncovering 'gems' in terms of writers, when I worked in Ireland on a TV series as a script editor in my first season, I was quickly told who were the 'best' writers on the show. I was surprised when I read them as they were, to be honest, pretty mediocre. It was a particularly harrowing time because of a particular personality, and so I found myself stressed to the eyeballs waiting for one writer to deliver. It was a Friday night and I needed a weekend off, but given the conversation I'd had with the writer (I hadn't met him) a few days earlier, I figured I'd be doing notes all weekend. He wasn't happy with the story and had to try and do what he could with it, etc. When it arrived (about 5pm) I was almost too stressed to read it, but I sat down and thought I may as well just see what I was in for (you can usually tell after a couple of scenes). I read the whole script clean through and knew this was the very best writer on this series who, for some reason, had been lost in the pile. The writing was clean, tight, and the skill with which this writer had me turning pages was a gift. I knew then I'd unearthed a gem. This was Peter McKenna.

The following series I was asked back to recreate the series as story producer and I asked Peter if he would be my gun writer. I wanted him to come in-house so he could understand more how production worked and why he got annoying notes. He was hesitant at first, but I talked him into it, and I was paid back in spades. We went on, along with Ciaran Hayden, another special find of mine, to create the highest rated series to date. Peter was fantastic, and we made a good team. He is one of those few writers who can plot and write in equal measure, and he fights a good fight. He went on to apply and win a place in the BBC Writer's Room and is now writing for both UK and Irish TV. It's one of my greatest pleasures to discover a writer – I add them to my collection with plans to one day create the ultimate Writer's Room!

How do you find juggling the editor's and writer's hats? Pros and cons? Do you self-censor too much or has your experience editing made the writing much faster/more efficient? Is there a methodology that works well in your opinion?

There is a fine line to walk as a script editor, and this is where editors really have to check themselves. It is much better for a writer if the script editor is either a writer or story producer so they can value-add to the script and not just implement notes given to them by hordes of others. A good script editor should be able to challenge notes and fight the good fight on behalf of the writer – but, sadly, a lot of them just tow the line and make their lives easier or, equally as bad; they don't know what makes a good or bad script. A good script editor should serve the writer in many ways. If possible, they should never over-write, they should suggest but not impose their own ideas on the writer – they need to try and help the writer realise their own story. This can be hard at times – writers have itchy fingers. They sometimes just want to get in there and write it themselves.

Being a TV writer is like riding a roller-coaster. In Australia the writer has absolutely no power and they often find themselves caught with a bad story or so many restrictions they can't perform their duty well. They often have to write under pressure (faster) due to production problems and, when they deliver the script, they are criticised. It's demoralising and, sadly, the best writers in Australia have opted out of TV altogether, preferring to live on funding body grants and teaching – it's a harrowing occupation, and you need really tough skin to survive. It's the injustice of it all that can hurt the most. I think we would all put our hand up if we felt we hadn't nailed a script, but to be cut off through bad organisation inside the show really, really sucks.

I like to think, as someone who divides their time between story producing and writing, that I bring a perspective that serves everyone. I understand the importance of scripts coming in on time and being production-friendly. I sit in all production meetings and am very aware of the shooting restrictions on any show I work on. I keep an open communication with the production office (when they don't like you it's like working in Hell), and I make myself known to all HODs. Most importantly, I try to keep the writers calm and happy. If an editor tells me a writer is complaining about the story or is having any kind of problem, I immediately tell them to come in. A good writer on your team is worth more than anything else. Good scripts make a good show – end of story.

PHILIP PALMER

Philip is a novelist, playwright and screenwriter, originally from Port Talbot, Wales. A number of his radio plays have been broadcast on Radio 4 and he has written for crime television series such as *The Bill*. His feature film *The Many Lives of Albert Walker* has a crime at the heart of it and he is currently producing a film noir set in Wales. Philip has also written five published novels: *Debatable Space*, *Red Claw*, *Version 43*, *Hell Ship* and *Artemis*. He describes himself as '..a glamorous hyphenate: writer-writer-toolazytogetaproperjob-writer'.

*

I'm proud of the fact that for many years I've made a living from crime. My first TV job was working as a script editor on a crime/thriller series called *The Paradise Club*, about two brothers in the East End who owned a nightclub. One of them was a gangster; and every week there'd be a heist or a scam to savour. After that I was a regular writer on the ITV series *The Bill* in the days when it was made up of half-hour episodes. That's when I did most of my research into crime – hanging out with coppers, going to crime scenes and mortuaries, interviewing criminals, and so forth. And I've also worked on a pseudo-detective crime series (*McCallum*) – this means any show where the protagonist isn't a detective but *behaves* like a detective, however improbable that might be. More recently I've been working on a film noir feature film.

What sort of crime genre films (sub-genres) are you particularly interested in? Any sub-genres you aren't so keen on?

A lot of the shows I worked on when I was a TV script editor were serial killer stories; at one point, I was working on a project about a serial killer who kills serial killers. And I think I did suffer from Serial Killer Overkill. For that reason, I tend to avoid writing about serial killers these days – I prefer corrupt cops, psychopaths (who may or may not be serial killers) and ordinary people who just happen to become, er... murderers.

Do you think a certain type of person/writer is better suited to crime writing? Might this vary with sub-genres?

It's an interesting question. I also write science fiction and, by and large, SF fans tend to have a cerebral side; they're interested in ideas and stories which teach them about new worlds. Crime fans, however, are more interested in character: character plus mystery. And, though the who-dun-it element of crime stories is often paramount, I would say that all crime stories – including Agatha Christie's – really tap into our human desire to investigate *other people*: their quirks; their eccentricities; their possible motives for murder.

I believe curiosity is the most powerful human drive – nudging ahead of sex and greed – and that's what crime taps into. What has happened, and *why?* Why does this person behave in this way? What kind of life did the murdered person have? It's nosiness, with blood.

I remember on one occasion – when I was researching for a crime story – I was sitting in the office of an East End detective, about to sip a glass of malt whisky from a bottle he had concealed in his desk drawer. (Ah! Those were the good/bad old days!) Then the phone rang and it was a 'shout'. A woman had been murdered; did I want to come along? The rush of adrenalin I felt then was astonishing. I was taken to the murder scene, I saw the slain woman in situ. I was able to look at her face, and I felt of course a terrible sadness. But I also felt a yearning to know – what were you like? Who did this to you, and why?

That crime was solved because the murderer – idiotically – had left his own bloody fingerprint on the victim's skin. So much for detection. For the truth is, most murderers are stupid; most criminals are banal. The real life Moriartys do exist but they are in a minority.

On another occasion, I was introduced to an armed robber, who had come out of jail and reformed, and who invited me on a guided tour of his former blaggings. I spent the day tootling around London in my little Fiat Panda, with an ex-armed robber in the passenger seat, driving to the various banks this guy had robbed over the years. We also went to Wembley Stadium, where the blaggers had robbed a charity event by dressing as coppers to gain entry – before brandishing their shooters. They then ran away, changed into civvy clothes, and piled into their cars, which were loaded with all the paraphernalia of a family holiday – suitcases, surfboards, wives and children. The wives, bless 'em, had been told where to be at a particular time and weren't given any option about being the de facto getaway drivers. Brilliant really; what cops in hot pursuit of bad 'uns are going to stop a car full of kids and a husband and wife glowering at each other? But also, not that clever; not if you want to have a happy marriage.

Crime fascinates me; indeed, even when I write science fiction, I often write crime. My third novel *Version 43* is a detective drama with blaggers and serial killers (sorry, I lapsed!) and a sleazy criminal demi-monde – but set on an alien planet with a cyborg as the detective.

Anything you'd like to say about The Bill *or other crime series that gave an opening to new writers?*

Sadly, *The Bill* is no more – it was a great way in for writers. Now the main entry-level show is *Doctors*, which is a fine series in its way, but doesn't train you in writing suspense and action.

You've written in various crime sub-genres for radio and television in particular. Any reason for starting your literary career with sci-fi novels? I ask as there seems to be a push from agents and/or publishers to make a writer work in one genre/arena. And it seems that producers tend to hire the 'usual suspects' when looking for a writer for a certain genre.

I wrote an SF novel because I love SF – it didn't occur to me I'd be branded as an SF writer. But that's absolutely how the process works. In fact, often you can't be a 'genre writer'; you have to pick a particular sub-genre within that genre. That's branding; it's the business.

More recently, my drama agent has, quite rightly, persuaded me not to offer up such a wide range of stories to commissioners, but to focus on thrillers. So far, that's paying off. So the truth is: writers are pigeonholed, and you do need to pigeonhole yourself.

How would you define The Many Lives of Albert Walker *in terms of* sub-genre? *(Obviously a crime takes place...)*

This was my *Harry Hook* TV movie. It's a strange mix of fact and fiction – Albert Walker is a real person, convicted of murder, but the detective in the story, played by John Gordon Sinclair, is a fictional character. It's kind of a faction meets detective drama.

Do you think more thrillers get made as features rather than detective/ police films? Or are they just labelled as thrillers for marketing purposes? How would you define the difference?

There are definitely more thrillers out there than pure crime. *Blitz*, based on a Ken Bruen crime novel, is one of the rare exceptions; it's got its idiocies but it is fundamentally a cracking crime drama. It's thrilling, yes, but it's not a 'thriller' in the way that *Bourne* is. The action thriller is the preferred genre of sales agents and distributors, which is fine if you love them, which I do, but it is limiting.

What about the film noir feature you are currently developing? Any thoughts on noir as a sub-genre? (I presume you think it is one?)

It's called *Inferno* and is set in South Wales. It was inspired partly by classic American noirs like *Double Indemnity* and *Body Heat*, and partly by an Italian version of an American noir, namely Visconti's *Ossessione* – set in Italy but based closely on James M Cain's *The Postman Always Rings Twice*.

Noir is definitely a genre, and it can't in my view be defined in terms of weather or moody lighting (*Chinatown* is one of the greatest of noirs and takes place in blazing sunshine). I think a noir is an existential thriller; it's scary, not because of the violence, but because of the *anticipation* of violence, and the intimations of our own mortality that come along with that.

Clouzot's *The Wages of Fear* is a noir by that definition; no guns, just one girl briefly glimpsed, no bad guys; but noir through and through.

JACKIE MALTON

Jackie is a writer and UK television script consultant with credits for over 500 episodes of crime drama, including *Prime Suspect*, *The Bill*, *Jury II*, *Trial and Retribution*, *Messiah* and the 2012 film *I, Anna*. She was previously a senior detective and the inspiration for DCI Jane Tennison, the main character of the *Prime Suspect* series, written by Lynda La Plante, who describes Jackie as 'the most important person I have ever met'. Jackie is also an addiction counsellor and Chair of Trustees for YES +. www.primecrime.com

*

You carved out an impressive career in the police force, working in the Flying Squad, Murder Squad, Fraud Squad and becoming one of only four female Detective Chief Inspectors in the UK. How did you begin working with Lynda La Plante when she was first developing Prime Suspect *and what was it about the project that inspired you to continue on as a consultant?*

There were only three female DCI's in the Metropolitan Police when Lynda La Plante spoke with me about my experiences. The initial response was this is 'therapy', a cathartic experience, and the more I talked the more she changed the character.

You left the police force in 1997 to pursue further work as a script consultant on a number of crime shows such as Cracker *and* Band of Gold, *and also to write yourself. Was it something of a culture shock moving into television work? Had you always been a (secret) writer or did working on* Prime Suspect *spark that interest in you?*

When working as a detective I often thought, 'Oh, that would make a great story.' Not because of fast cars, action, gory murders, but because of character. Lynda was kind enough to say I was a great storyteller and had a gift in knowing what writers needed. I decided to develop this 'gift' and am thankful to her for inspiring me.

Would you outline the process of working as a story consultant on a crime series? For example, when are you brought in to work on a project – at concept, outline, draft script stage? When do you 'sign off'? How wide is your remit? Do writers ever get lazy and think you'll fix the specifics of police procedure?

I prefer a blank page best of all… and we worked in this way as members of the story team on *The Bill*. In individual projects, a writer will obviously have an idea and a character and we go from there. I enjoy developing the stories and characters and enjoy least being given a script to check over. Writers can be reluctant to take notes at this stage. They become over identified with, and possessive about, their work. I do understand, although there seems little point asking a consultant to check it over and not wanting to hear what I have to say. That is the human condition!

Writers seem to think that police procedure is not necessary. It can be used dramatically if the writer takes time to try and understand and use it properly. Their answer, sometimes, is to cheat and jump over the difficulties. This makes the script unbelievable. I appreciate that the drama is the most important aspect. What I am saying is the drama could be better without the cheat.

With respect to your addiction counselling work, you state on your website that: 'In understanding and exploring the messiness of the human condition I continue to be inspired by those who are willing to show their fragmented selves, representing the best and worst of human nature.' This could be a writer talking about her characters – realistic characters. You were the inspiration for DCI Jane Tennison and clearly Lynda La Plante created a character that really speaks to audiences. Where do you think she went right in terms of creating such a compelling character? Are there any other characters in crime films or series that you find particularly interesting and why?

Lynda did listen to my experiences for a number of weeks, which then translated into the character of Tennison. It was a long process and this, of course, exposed the character's strengths and flaws. We all have them whether we are a criminal or cop.

Detective Inspector Sarah Lund in *Forbrydelsen* (and homicide detective Sarah Linden in US remake *The Killing*) is a brilliant character: enigmatic, contained, an avoidant in relationships, intense, insular. All of these characteristics, however, are not suitable to leadership, team building, fulfilling the role of a senior investigating officer, etc. Yet we are compelled by her, precisely because of those characteristics.

Any practical recommendations for screenwriters who wish to write accurate police procedurals?

The best way is to Google… the answers are all there!

What is your position on procedural accuracy and realism versus suspension of disbelief/dramatic effect? For example, in CSI *and similar shows, the actors rarely seem kitted up properly when testing evidence. Do you find that annoying, amusing, or okay if the audience buys it?*

I cannot watch *CSI* – It is ridiculous! I appreciate that drama is far more important than the police procedure. I have always known that, so poetic licence is not a problem for me if it is for the benefit of the drama. *CSI* is all poetic licence and no reality. My whole persona is rooted in reality.

On your website you describe yourself as a 'voyeur, with a taste for the darkness of life'. It's a tantalising statement and sounds like a useful prerequisite for being a crime writer and crime story consultant. Would you elaborate a bit on this?

I do believe that it would benefit a writer to do some inner work on themselves. I suspect more USA writers are in therapy than UK writers, and you can see that in the writing, with characters who are deeper, more complex, struggling with their own demons, etc. I have worked for a number of years in a male prison and witnessed men truly trying to connect to themselves to show their vulnerability, their deepest fears, shame, unworthiness. I do think a writer needs to do a bit of their own psychology.

Having worked with writers for a number of years, I took myself off to university and did an MA in Creative Writing. From that I discovered I enjoyed writing radio plays and my first one was transmitted on BBC Radio 4 last September. I have written a second play and am still waiting to hear!

JON GILBERT

Jon has been writing and directing short films since 1994. For the past 11 years, he has worked as a reader for companies like Universal, Industrial Scripts, the Film Council and The Works International, as well as being a freelance script editor. Jon's script *The Sculptress and The Thief* came third in the 2005 'Final Draft Big Break!' screenwriting competition and is in development with Trudie Styler's Maven Pictures. His debut feature film as screenwriter, co-written with director Vincent Bal, is an adaptation of David Grossman's children's detective novel *Nono, The Zig Zag Kid*, which premiered to great acclaim at the 2012 Toronto Film Festival ahead of its European release. Jon is represented by Independent in the UK and Elevate Entertainment and the Gersh Agency in the US. www.wildhoneyfilms.com

*

You've worked in various areas of feature film development and production; could you explain a bit about your career trajectory in film and how the different areas you've worked in enhance each other – or not!

My interest in pursuing a career in the film industry began from an early age. Growing up on a diet of old black-and-white movies shown on BBC2, and more European fare on Channel 4, I initially (like most kids who get into film) wanted to be an actor. It was only once I spent some time in Paris as an 18-year-old that I learnt what a director did and realised that was what I really wanted to be. While at university, I was lucky enough to get a summer job working as a runner at Hat Trick Productions, which led to some work running on a Channel 4 feature called *Like It Is* in the late nineties. It wasn't until 2002 that I got my first job as a script reader. I'd been working at a company called The Film Consortium, one of the original franchise organisations picking films for the Film Council, for around six months as an office runner, and had got to know the Head of Development, who let me read scripts and report back informally. This then became a little more official, with me writing coverage for her and the other executives; and when one of her regular readers left I immediately offered my services, which got me going as a freelance reader.

Over the next few years, I built up my client base reading for other companies such as The Works, The Film Council, The Script Factory, and then Universal Pictures and Industrial Scripts, who are my main sources of reading and consulting work today. With my writing career taking off in tandem, I've had to pay equal attention to both strands of my work without letting one overwhelm the other. Script reading has led to script editing, which is more unpredictable but ultimately more interesting and rewarding work, collaborating one-on-one with writers to develop and improve their projects; I've also got into teaching and running workshops for actors and writers. Overall, the reading work has really helped enhance my understanding of: a) how scripts are put together, from the point of view of a writer's craft, but, just as importantly, b) which projects get green-lit and which ones remain forever unproduced. As you'd expect, it's not always down to the quality of the writing but rather a whole confluence of factors to do with cast, director, producer, subject matter, genre, money and marketability. While this hasn't influenced me in terms of making me 'sell out', it has definitely encouraged me to identify early on which of the projects I'm developing has a greater likelihood of going the distance.

You have secured representation as a screenwriter both in the UK and the US; no easy task. How did you manage this?

Although I'd written scripts before I became a reader, it was only when I went freelance that I really started to devote myself, not just to writing every day, but also to learning more about the craft of screenwriting. It was here that I began to realise just what a long and daunting task it was bound to be, but that also encouraged me by acting as a challenge. In 2004, I was fortunate enough to have a project get picked up for an excellent development scheme run by the (now sadly defunct) First Film Foundation. Over three, week-long sessions spread out across nine months, I and eight other writers got to learn about screenwriting from some of the best teachers around whilst also developing our projects through group discussion and mutual support. At the end of the scheme, I had significantly improved my one script and, encouraged by people's feedback, I submitted it to two US screenwriting contests. In one, it failed to make the top 250; in the other, it came third! (This is testament to the importance of luck as well as hard work, persistence and, a very distant fourth, talent as the key factors in a screenwriter's success...)

The prize for this particular contest, the Final Draft Big Break award, was to be flown out to Hollywood, put up in a five-star hotel, driven round in a limo, and taken to a ceremony where prizes and awards were handed out – an incredible experience that I mistakenly thought meant I had 'arrived'. Although this *was* the beginning of my entrance proper into the film world, it was very much that: a beginning. The vocal support of one particular judge on the contest's panel helped me secure an agent back in the UK, but although this judge (a well-established American director) became attached to my project, it sadly didn't result in the film getting made. However, his seal of approval and my new-found representation in the UK did mean I started to get meetings, commissions, and to get projects optioned for the first time back home.

All this was a big surprise to me, as the script was essentially an art film I had originally planned to try and direct myself on a micro-budget; discovering that big-time Hollywood directors and well-established UK producers were interested in making it made no real sense to me. In retrospect, it's clear that the script had two things which helped to make me appealing as a writer: some interesting and original characters and a strong genre component. The story begins as a crime film (it's set in the immediate aftermath of a heist) and throughout Act One follows the standard trope of a thief on the run with the loot who is forced to hide out somewhere unexpected. From there on in, the narrative mixes further crime film tropes as both cops and criminals search for our anti-hero, with a more character-driven core story that ends up becoming a kind of twisted romance. Though I had no conscious idea of what I'd done, this unusual take on a standard genre piece was almost certainly exactly what made the project appealing to agents, directors and producers, and from an industry perspective it started to put me on the map (even though the project still has yet to get made!). Similarly, the same script helped secure me an agent and manager in the States, something that came about purely by accident as a result of links already forged by my agent over here. The project has opened a number of doors in Hollywood, but has also brought home the importance of being able to follow up those opportunities with other well-developed ideas in order to cash in on meetings. The more projects you have on the go, and that you're ready to pitch, the better!

Your first produced screenplay was for Nono, The Zigzag Kid; *how did you get attached to the project, which was originally in development with Belgian writer/director Vincent Bal?*

Nono, The Zigzag Kid is a Dutch/Belgian co-production adapted from an award-winning children's book by Israeli author David Grossman. Like so many things in the film industry, it came about not because of my actual writing but because of getting to know a director with whom I happened to get on well. Personal connection counts for so much in such a collaborative industry, so although it's true that a writer can spend a huge amount of time locked away working alone – and that many writers (myself included!) feel much more comfortable in their own imaginary worlds than in the real world – getting out there and meeting people (let's not call it networking but socialising, but just connecting with other human beings, which sounds a little more achievable) is of huge importance. I met Belgian director Vincent Bal on a European development scheme I attended as a script editor. He was already developing *Zigzag Kid*; indeed, he'd been working on it for several years (there's that key word 'persistence' again) and had reached the point where he wanted fresh eyes on it.

Despite never having read anything of mine, he invited me to write a new draft, collaborating with him but essentially taking three previous drafts he'd worked on, plus the original novel, and trying to forge them together. We worked very well together, both by email and in person, his vision for the project being so clear that it made it relatively easy to see what would work and what wouldn't. The script continued to be developed even after I stopped working on it in 2007, and it wasn't until 2011 that the film was finally shot. However, the end result turned out extremely well, screening in Toronto in 2012 and Berlin in 2013, then going on to win a Young Audience Award at the 2013 European Film Academy. What's interesting about the film from a creative point of view is the way it melds a kids' adventure movie with conventions from the crime/detective story, telling the tale of a boy trying to piece together the truth about his late mother (the book's heartbreaking emotional core) through the prism of a 1970s caper movie that features cat burglars, torch singers and a French Riviera setting. This element of parody contributes a huge amount to the light-hearted, fun feel of the film, which helps to leaven the heavier aspects of the deeper character journey for Nono, the protagonist, as he comes to understand his place in the world.

With genre-mixing an increasingly important part of screenwriting, the main thing to recognise when mixing two or more genres is whether it's going to double your audience's satisfaction or halve it. A film like *Attack the Block* covers the teen audience, horror fans, and comedy lovers, and it works because none of these audiences is mutually exclusive. Andrea Arnold's reworking of *Wuthering Heights*, on the other hand, struggled commercially because the audience for period drama is almost diametrically opposed to that for British social realism. This is not to say that experimenting in this way can't produce artistically powerful statements, but it requires careful thought in terms of how it will reach an audience.

Given your extensive work in feature film development and screen-writing, I was surprised to learn that your original ambition was to write and direct. How or why did script reading, editing and writing become the main focus of your career up until now?

One point worth raising about my experiences in film to date is the extent to which a creative career can be driven by chance as well as design. Becoming a script reader was never especially part of my plan – I didn't even know the job existed until I started working at The Film Consortium – but equally my original intention was always to be a writer-director rather than to focus so much more heavily on screenwriting specifically. Despite my passion for cinema, I only first started making short films at a youth centre when I was 18. I loved it from the start and pursued my interest at university, helping to set up a filmmaking society at Nottingham University alongside Christopher Ross, who went on to be the cinematographer on films like *London to Brighton* and *Eden Lake*. One film I made there won a small award at a local film festival, which spurred me on to continue directing once I moved back to London. Chris and I set up a company (Wild Honey Films), for the purposes of getting insurance, and made several shorts, first on 16mm, then on 35.

It was the second of these, *The Confidence Trick*, that really pushed me into wanting to learn more about screenwriting. Up until that point, although I'd read a few books on the subject (notably *Story* by Robert McKee) and watched lots of films, I was writing mostly on instinct. Though I was happy with the results of *The Confidence Trick*, I knew the story didn't work as well as it could have done, and I wanted to find out why, something I could only do by making a concerted effort to try to understand screenplay structure in much more depth. This was particularly important since I wanted ultimately to direct a feature and therefore needed to feel fully confident about how stories work technically. Because one of the screenplays I was working on as part of my learning curve got picked up for a development scheme and then got me an agent, I was always seen as a writer rather than a writer-director, and this caused me slightly to stray off my original path, with the majority of my subsequent work being writing rather than directing. I suppose this illustrates the importance of being very clear about what you're trying to achieve in your career. At the same time all these experiences as a writer have been invaluable in helping me understand story at a deeper level, which should ultimately pay off at a later stage.

PETER CARLTON

Peter is head of Warp Films Europe with a remit to develop and produce distinctive British and European originated film and television fiction stories for the international market. Prior to that he spent six years as senior commissioning executive at Film 4, Channel 4 television where he executive produced over 30 feature films, including innovative, award-winning films such as *Four Lions*, *Submarine*, *Hunger*, *Garage*, *Death of a President*, *Better Things*, *This is England*, *Dead Man's Shoes*, and *Me and You and Everyone We Know*.
http://warp.net/films www.film4.com

*

When you asked me to do this, I thought, 'I don't know bloody anything about crime.' And then I thought, looking at the movies I've made, actually a huge number of them have a crime at their heart. So if I'm an expert at anything to do with the crime genre it's in making shows that don't have police in them. That's the common denominator. And I realise that applies, strangely enough, to my most recent project. I've actually moved into producing television series. *Southcliffe* is written by Tony Grisoni and directed by Sean Durkin – it's a four by one-hour crime show with a difference. We were in production at the same time as *Broadchurch* – there must be something in the water at the moment about making crime shows in small seaside towns in the UK.

And Broadchurch *was a big success story for ITV...*

Broadchurch had nine million viewers and is ITV's most successful show since *Downton Abbey*. It's an eight-part serial – a whodunit – and audiences tuned in each week. An interesting thing about *Broadchurch* is that the writer, Chris Chibnall, had the idea ten years ago and wanted to set it in a recognisable place similar to where he lived. When *The Killing* came along, it kind of gave him permission to do it. He wrote it on spec. What was interesting for us in watching it is that it deals with location and place and all of those things. Like *The Killing* its central character is a cop, but it's also very focused on relationships and a number of people around them.

***Would you explain a bit more about* Southcliffe?**

Southcliffe is about a spree killing, a four-part serial. The killing happens in episode one so it's not a whodunit because you know who did the killing – it's much more about the effect on the community. Hopefully the spree killing in episode one is such an impactful moment that you identify with or empathise with those families as you go through the experience with them.

So it's not a traditional police procedural?

It doesn't have any police as major characters. It has a journalist as a key character, doing what journalists do, but the story is not the investigation, and they're actually really quite bad at investigating. It's almost as though the initial act of the killing is the rock dropped in a pool and we follow the ripples moving out from that – looking at what happens to all these people connected to the event. And that's quite challenging as the perceived wisdom is that you need one driving mystery at a serial's heart. But this isn't a whodunit, whydunit, or did he do it – while those questions are lurking in the background, they don't drive the narrative.

You said we begin with the spree in episode one. Can you talk a bit about the structure?

The narrative in the first episode is 'how's it going to happen' and then it mucks about with time. Although the spree occurs in the first episode, you don't know who some of the victims are. So when we wind back in time and get to know some of the characters, you actually don't know if they will be living at the end of the episode. It dispenses with investigative mode – no cops, etc. So what drives you is what's going to happen to these characters and when you gradually unravel who's been killed and who hasn't the next question is, what's the effect going to be short term and longer term on the community.

So the focus is on character and, in a way, the audience plays detective rather than following a detective's investigation?

It's profoundly character driven in that the motor is empathy for the character and what may or may not happen to these characters rather than a bigger whodunit – your reasons to stay there are because you empathise with these characters. If you don't, you won't watch it to the end. It's tougher when making series or serials not using the investigative motor – that crutch is useful.

Looking at what you've made at Film 4 and now Warp, it seems that you choose to work with filmmakers who make crime films that twist genre conventions in an original manner.

Or they extrapolate from genre conventions. The *Cahiers du Cinéma* take on auteur theory came from genre really – auteur films are like genre films but better because someone has done something interesting with them. We identify the revisionist twist with being the genius of the auteur. People forget that the 'New Wave' was obsessed with crime, genre driven but twisted. Art house cinema is meant to be pure navel gazing and genre is meant to be all about gearing it towards the public and following convention – that's the worst case scenario of both. But the reality is that to make a story work or get it financed, it's important to look at it through a pair of genre glasses and consider whether maybe a few cliffhangers should be added or maybe a few more recognisable genre tropes to help the whole thing hang together better. Some filmmakers use genre conventions to make their interests more acceptable and others use their own interests to subvert the genre. It's weird to say the good stuff is in the middle ground and basically nods to genre and messes with genre at the same time, but most of the stuff that in any way moves the genre on is exactly that. Films that completely follow conventions – yes, they could make money when released, but probably no one will really remember them in ten years time.

I would also say that the filmmakers I work with aren't all that interested in recounting story as in plot. They're interested in 'what do people do in these circumstances'. And so one of the great things about crime and violence of some description is it turns the volume up and allows you to put in tension while examining character. I think the other thing is that most people I work with are interested in the notion of transgression. On a very basic level, the rules are there to be broken and, on a second level, looking at what transgression means – essentially, are we civilised beings or are we beasts?

One of the things that interests me in cinema and television on a fundamental level that the novel doesn't so obviously treat is the notion of immortality. Was it Cocteau who said, 'Cinema is death in process'? Cinema is temporal; what you're watching on screen happened previously in actual life as it's a recorded medium. You can literally be watching dead people on the screen. And the technical treatment of time – whether through cutting, jumps forwards and backwards in time, or jump-cuts – we're constantly dealing with that anxiety about the non-solidity of human existence. So if you try to make a film about immortality, you'll be lucky to end up in some side bar in Cannes, but if you just put a murder in at the beginning, people go: 'Oh, it's a crime film.' A large and violent inciting event in some shape or form – either the actual occurrence of it or the threat of it – is a great narrative motor. By utilising tropes from the crime genre, you can explore existential angst or peering into the abyss by putting it into palatable form. For me a key question is how few classic conventions can we use and still get away with it? What we don't want in our films is people getting in and out of police cars, taking case notes... none of that crap. We want to cut to the angsty chase. This could almost be a guide as to whether I would be bothered to read past the first ten pages. If I'm sent a script that doesn't go outside a police station in the first ten pages, there's not much chance that I'll read on. Of course these are rules to be broken. I really can't think of any police show – other than *The Killing* – that would attract my interest and, even then, I'm not most interested in cops. Maybe it's residual adolescent issues with authority.

If you were to give a writer advice as to how to approach a genre film creatively, what might that be?

The important thing is to know enough about genre to write it and play with it. There might have been an intellectual start to experimenting with a genre piece, but it has to mean something to you as a writer. The genre pieces that I loathe feel obviously derivative or when everyone is trying too damn hard to make it clever – or jumping through hoops to find new twists. It needs to be felt and genuine for the story to feel fresh.

For example, before writing *Southcliffe*, Tony Grisoni spent four months with a researcher interviewing people connected to spree killings – people who had lost loved ones through violent death. There was a massive depth of research in place when he went to develop the characters. I think convincing writers have a reason for homing in on a particular story; maybe it addresses something they know or are concerned about. If I said, 'You can always tell if somebody knows what they're writing about' – that isn't quite true. But you kind of can. Writers don't have to write about what they already know. Obviously they can research material. But there's also the bit about inhabiting it. There's two important combinations: getting the detail right and also having an authentic attitude.

You mentioned that you like The Killing *– Scandinavian crime shows have really connected with UK audiences. Any thoughts as to why?*

I think there is also a certain amount of exotic distance with *The Killing* (*Forbrydelsen*) for British viewers, and we feel slightly cleverer for watching it. The comforts of style and exoticism are not to be underestimated. But primarily I think it's because Detective Inspector Sarah Lund – the representative of the law – is an identifiable person. She is flawed and weak, but tries to do good things. Essentially, despite all her faults, she is trying to live a decent life. We feel the influence of the crime on her, which makes us like her. Wallander is similar – you see the pain on his face. He wakes up in the morning and the pain is there – we understand it without backstory. It's very attractive the fact that he is somehow working through pain... but it's not explained. We just witness it. And in both *The Killing* and *Wallander* the main characters are rarely in the precinct and both spend time with grieving families. And somehow you totally believe the original Swedish *Wallander*, but the British one feels acted out – it doesn't feel lived.

I think that's one of the things we did with *Southcliffe*. We weren't actively trying to subvert genre, but we wanted that element. I introduced Sean Durkin, our director, to *Edge of Darkness*; I'd looked up some reviews of it and one noted that it was the most sustained portrait of grief ever to be shown on British television. It was something Tony Grisoni and I were aware of as a kind of influence for *Southcliffe*. Even if our series dispenses with the investigation and dispenses with the conspiracy, in some ways it's a four-act portrait of grief. In an art movie context, you might get something like *La Vie de Jésus* by Bruno Dumont, which has a murder in it, but it's about existence more than about killing.

In France audiences apparently prefer to be led in to the darker aspects of crime dramas through the character, which requires longer to set up. Haut et Court, a French company we're currently working with, made *Les Revenants* (*The Returned*), which was the highest rated series in France. It's based on an art house film they made ten years ago and is set in a small village in the Alps where the dead come back – not as dripping flesh-eaters, but to take their place again amongst the living. They don't realise they're dead either. For example, a 15-year-old girl returns three years later and her twin sister is about to sleep with her boyfriend – she has aged whereas the dead twin has not. In another story, a woman has remarried and has a child – then her beloved husband returns from the dead. The story focuses much more on our feelings about death rather than plot and we wonder what the dead want. Most of the 'returned' are arguably benign... but one is a murderer. So even in that series, there's a crime motor. The project broke the mould in French television and has just been bought by Channel 4 and will be put out on primetime – the first time they've shown a subtitled show on primetime in 20 years.

Looking at the films you've produced and executive produced, a number of them have a crime within them even if you might not categorise them as a crime film. Dead Man's Shoes, for example.

Dead Man's Shoes does contain a series of crimes, but you'd probably think of it as a revenge thriller or a Western. I don't think anyone who loves crime films would go and watch Dead Man's Shoes because it was a crime show. It's not a whodunit or a why-dunit – the narrative drive has nothing to do with either solving a crime or trying to prevent one. But, on one level, structurally it's similar to Se7en. The main character is a serial killer, and we wonder if anyone is going to be able to stop him – or if he'll be able to stop himself. It's interesting, because I didn't previously think of it as a serial killer movie, but it is. Plenty of serial killer stories don't have police in them. Snowtown, co-produced by Warp X Australia, is a good example. There's no police investigation, and it's not a why-dunit. I suppose it deals with the inevitability of death unfolding. And of course when we say 'crime' we usually mean 'death' in a crime film. If you remove the police – the force of the law – the focus is on the pressing inevitability of mortality being replayed on a day to day basis, and can we create any kind of survival in the face of the fact that we are going to die in some arbitrary way at some point? I think that's a really fundamental philosophical question that crime procedurals fudge – they're existential angst light. But in a serial killer movie – when you take the police out of it – it feels artier, but actually it's cruder. It's more unmediated. We're dealing with horrible death. Off we go. Without the investigative element, you are watching a series of deaths unfold, and it takes you to the abyss. Is the whole world going to collapse into this bloodbath or will we be able to pull some sort of sense out of it? Thinking about it, that trope is followed by *Snowtown* and Ben Wheatley's film *Kill List*, which Warp X produced. They have classic horror elements – once we've unleashed the horror or the evil, can we pull it back in? For example, *Kill List* is about a contract killer and a series of grisly deaths. We know the motive: money. The film mutates into horror. In serial killer films there's a fine line between crime and horror if they follow that classic trope wherein the serial killer gets the upper hand and draws you into his universe. The contract killer in *Kill List* is a serial killer in one sense – he's just getting paid to kill.

So they're acknowledging that evil and horror exist in real life as opposed to the horror film exaggeration of evil?

Yes, the darkness at the centre. I suppose that's why I balked at acknowledging that I had made any crime films in the sense that I'd almost classify them more as horror films on some level. In my head a crime film or series is about whether you can solve or prevent the crime, and none of the things I worked on, or am working on, is actually interested in that. They're interested in contemplating what these deeds mean at the heart of human behaviour. Although I suppose horror films are interested in preventing the horror from spreading... so perhaps I'm just not interested in the preventative bit.

We've talked about crime films typically dealing with murder, but there is also a strong tradition of heist films in Europe. Any thoughts on that sub-genre?

The heist is a transgression, but it's definitely a lighter crime; it's easier to be on their side than in a murder. People do tend to get killed in heist movies, but they don't cross the existential line – heist films are usually about an attempt at betterment and the punishment is curtailment of freedom rather than death. The moment you have a film that deals with murder or a series of murders, the whole thing becomes about mortality, which is fundamentally different.

Are you currently developing any other crime films or series at Warp?

We're developing an international crime series to be shot next year called *Barbarians* and that starts with a crime – a very lengthy diamond heist. At the moment it's six episodes, but it might end up being eight. It has a complex structure – a kind of 'layers of the onion' structure in that we go forwards and backwards in time and go outwards from the epicentre. So we follow the diamonds, moving forwards with them, but also move backwards to find out where they came from – and all this leads us into other crimes. There's a new crime or heist each week but not a new case. Basically, as you follow a new character, you discover a crime in their past or we may follow characters into situations where they are perpetrators and victims of crimes. And there's a prison break. All in one series!

SALLY GRIFFITHS

Sally and writing partner **Rachel Cuperman** have co-written a number of feature film scripts. To date, they have written three episodes of the popular British crime drama *Midsomer Murders*: 'A Sacred Trust'; 'Death and the Divas'; and 'Wild Harvest'. Sally has worked as a reader for many of the UK's leading film companies, and her first radio play, *Haunted*, was nominated for the prestigious Richard Imison award; Rachel was associate producer of a number of Samuelson Productions movies including *Tom & Viv* and *Wilde*.

*

How did you get started writing crime drama for radio and television? Any particular writers who influenced you?

I've always read crime fiction for pleasure, beginning with Agatha Christie when I was a teenager. I love the quirky, much-underrated Margery Allingham, Dorothy L Sayers, Magdalen Nabb, even Gladys Mitchell, though she's very much an acquired taste. Mostly female writers, I guess – though I also like Michael Dibdin and the late, great Rex Stout – and generally those who focus on character and atmosphere as much as plot and menace, and write with a bit of wit. I don't care much for novels which dwell in great detail on forensics and gore, or those seeking to expose the dark underbelly of society; crime is my holiday reading, essentially, and therefore has to be intelligent but not too demanding. So *Midsomer Murders* has proved quite a good fit for me.

You and co-writer Rachel Cuperman have to date written three episodes of the classic UK crime series Midsomer Murders. Could you talk a bit about the series and expected episode structure?

It's a two-hour drama, shown between 8pm and 10pm on ITV. The action takes place in Midsomer County, an idyllic part of the world with a murder rate to rival that of downtown Baltimore. There's no strict formula, but almost all episodes have more than one murder, and fewer than five; the focus will be on a community rather than a household – so, unlike Christie, for example, these aren't 'country house murders'.

There are a number of comedy writing partnerships, but there seem to be far fewer crime writing collaborations. What are your co-writing strategies/methodology? And how is working with a script editor, particularly as you have script edited quite a few projects yourself?

I write with Rachel Cuperman, and our approach is essentially the same as when we're writing screenplays: we start with the characters, and try to create people we find interesting, amusing, sympathetic, or marvellously awful. The show is approaching its hundredth episode, so it can be a challenge to find murder methods that haven't been used before. (The episode that seems to be most people's favourite – not written by us, sadly – had a wine lover staked out on his own croquet lawn, being pelted to death with vintage bottles fired from an antique form of catapult; so the stakes are quite high.) It can be hard to find interesting motives, too, or, rather, variations on the standard motives of money, fear and revenge. (There's plenty of sex in *Midsomer*, much of it extra-marital, but sex killings – as opposed to those motivated by sexual jealousy – are virtually unknown.)

We have 90 minutes in which to set up and develop the mystery, establish up to a dozen characters – new victims and suspects in every episode – lead the audience down several wrong paths, and provide a satisfying conclusion via a climax which should, if possible, include some immediate jeopardy. (Poirot-style gatherings in the library to unmask the killer are not Detective Chief Inspector Barnaby's style.) It should all be a little strange and exotic and yet, in context, believable, and rooted in something that's recognisable as modern country life.

In real life, murder is mostly sickening, banal, and profoundly traumatic for the family of the victim. In *Midsomer*, it can't be any of those things, but nor can it be taken for granted. Every death has to be a shock, and while it's fine to have one victim whom everyone hated – so everyone's a suspect! – there has to be grief and upset too, because an episode devoid of any positive emotion will be arid and alienating.

It's a collaborative process, right from treatment stage: between Rachel and me, of course, but also with the producer and script editor and, later in the process, the director. We've written three episodes to date, and in two of those the identity of the killer has been changed – fairly early on – at someone else's suggestion; and in both cases I think they were right. And in our current episode, someone who originally died in the teaser – the pre-credit sequence – now survives to the end...

It's a weird thing to do, to write fun stories about violent death; Rachel and I do much of our preliminary planning work in cafes, and we get some odd looks from neighbouring tables when the conversation becomes animated. As a partnership, we have to work everything out in advance, whatever we're writing; luckily, it's a method well suited to crime drama, where so much depends on clarity and logic. Once we have a detailed step-outline, we'll write half the script each, then swap and rewrite, so that, by the time we're done, it should be impossible to tell who wrote which bit.

You read for several major companies and funders. Are you sent many police or detective stories and, if so, is there a type of story or crime sub-genre that tends to secure your interest? And are there particular script weaknesses that encourage you to reject a project?

As a reader in the film industry, I encounter surprisingly few crime stories, although that wasn't the case when I was reading regularly for a TV company, when I used to get sent masses of crime fiction. Such crime screenplays as come my way tend to be gritty, noirish, small-time British gangster or semi-gangster flicks. I do get sent thrillers in novel form, but not so much what you might call straight crime, which is maybe regarded as more suitable for TV, perhaps because its essential neatness – every case has a solution – lends itself to the series form.

When I do read or watch crime drama, either professionally or for pleasure, I want it to be clever, but not show-off clever. The best possible outcome to a mystery is for the viewer/reader to think, 'Damn, I should have thought of that' – i.e. the outcome makes perfect sense and the writer has played fair, but you didn't see it coming. Which is much easier said than done. Whodunit doesn't have to be the issue – sometimes you know almost from the beginning, because the dramatic focus is elsewhere – but if the ending is meant to come as a surprise, it has to be a good one. I enjoyed the first series of *The Killing*, but was disappointed when the killer turned out to be someone I'd all but dismissed as too obvious. On the other hand, I guessed about halfway through who the guilty party was in *Broadchurch*, but it didn't matter, because the series was primarily about the emotional impact of the murder on the family and the community.

And never, ever make the killer the quiet guy/woman whom nobody suspected, because old hands will have been onto them from the start...

KEITH POTTER

Keith joined Bord Scannán na hÉireann/the Irish Film Board as project manager in spring 2013. Previously Keith was head of production at the Film Agency for Wales, where he was responsible for a slate of over 50 active feature film projects. Recent productions which he oversaw from development through to production and exploitation include *Kelly and Victor*, *Resistance*, *The Gospel of Us*, *We Went to War* and *Hunky Dory*. His first role at the Film Agency for Wales was as head of talent where he invested in the development of films such as *Submarine*, *Mugabe and the White African*, *Patagonia*, and *I Am Slave*. Before joining the Film Agency for Wales, Keith was head of development at independent production company Dan Films.
www.irishfilmboard.ie www.filmagencywales.com

*

Your work in feature film development and production has required that you find and work with both new and established screenwriters and directors. Would you note a few key things that make you sit up and take notice of a new writer's work? Any new discoveries you'd care to name, particularly crime writers?

One project that we developed when I was at Dan Films that hasn't yet been made, but is one of the best thrillers I've come across, is a script by Tom Rob Smith called *Pulled Together*, which is about amnesia in many respects. The main character's wife is murdered, and he is manipulated into committing a crime by a shadowy organisation, seemingly in revenge for her death. The writer really wanted to explore the notion: what is love? I found it interesting that he was exploring a very fundamental human emotion within the framework of a conspiracy thriller. Tom Rob Smith went on to write the novel *Child 44*, a best-selling crime thriller set in Stalin's Soviet Union. It's a cracking page-turner about a serial killer on the loose, and I believe it's been optioned by Ridley Scott's company, Scott Free. The crimes have to be investigated but, as it's set during Stalin's time and crime is not meant to exist as society is perfect, the investigations must be kept very quiet. The relationships are handled well in the novel – the main character and his wife, local gossip, people shopping other people to the authorities, and the strain this behaviour puts on the marriage – do husband and wife trust each other? What is particularly interesting about both his pieces from my perspective is the impact of the crimes on the characters and the dilemmas raised by these crimes.

(For more about Tom Rob Smith's work, see: www.tombrobsmith.com)

Is there a particular sub-genre of crime films that appeals to you and why?

What often fascinates about film noir – that hardy perennial – is that there's a doomed romanticism to it. It involves a lot of fairly macho characters, but often it's the women calling the shots. And the world is not as it seems.

I think in general when looking at scripts I'm most interested in the human dilemma posited at the beginning of the script that we keep returning to via the character interactions with each other and the dilemmas that they face – rather than an elaborately drawn tapestry of a plot that the characters revolve around.

Do you receive many police procedural or detective films? It would seem that not many get off the ground these days, despite their popularity on television.

I haven't received that many police procedural films. Gangster movies were very popular for a long time. Certainly in the UK there is more interest in looking at the criminal than the cop in movies. Maybe it's because cops here wear funny uniforms, or because television does cop shows so well. Clearly you have the high-brow *Morse* and *Midsomer Murders*, which are more like *Cluedo*, an intellectual exercise. And then you have the down and dirty, more accurate police procedurals. So perhaps the writers feel that sub-genre is already done, just in the same way you get few hospital-set feature films, whereas you can't move for them on the TV schedule. I think *Morse* worked very well because it was a filmic length and you started to wear the characters like a pair of slippers – in a good way. You get the feeling that Morse is dispirited by the evil side of human nature and there's an undertow to the piece that's quite sad. An example of a detective film that works in a similar way is the Argentine/Spanish co-production, *The Secret in Their Eyes*. The main character – a federal agent – is introduced as light and flirtatious, but then you see the expression on his face when he is at the scene of the brutal murder of a young woman. When you see a cop who is affected by crime, it has an impact.

Are there other crime sub-genre projects that are submitted to you regularly?

Quite a few prison dramas have come in through the years, but they're difficult; again, it's probably through character that a story seems fresh rather than derivative. Every once in a while something comes along like *The Prophet* with a seminal approach to the genre and it's hard to follow that. Prison break-out films tend to focus on specific prisons – the institution can become a character. *Escape from Alcatraz* is a very good prison escape movie, I think – the characters are memorable and interesting – that's what sets those movies apart. David Mackenzie's new film, *Starred Up*, is a prison film, which does sound interesting.

It's summed up as the story of a violent teenager sent to an adult prison where he meets his match – a man who happens to be his father. Instantly you wonder about the character dynamics.

Yes. For me the characters define the nature of the plot by their own missteps or contradictions. I respond to films that are emotionally intelligent rather than intellectually intelligent. I read a lot of allegedly complex pieces – very influenced by post-modernism/Tarantino –

WRITING AND SELLING CRIME FILM SCREENPLAYS

pastiches or with flashbacks within flashbacks. All that kind of stuff. But at the end of the piece you kind of feel it was a card trick you're not altogether sure has worked, but, even if it has, the emotions weren't really engaged. I can appreciate that you gave me four aces here, but I'm still not that impressed by the magic you showed me. My problem with the post-modern take on things is that you rely on the freshness of the post-modernism rather than what is happening to the characters, whereas the films that really work hook you with character dilemmas. Don't get me wrong, Tarantino's *Pulp Fiction* is very good, but I think *Jackie Brown* is his best film.

Any thoughts on other crime sub-genres and what you find appealing? Heist movies have traditionally been very popular in Europe and there seem to be quite a few serial killer stories about.

If you look at bank heist movies, they're almost companion pieces to prison movies with their focus on the minutiae of the planning and execution of the robbery. I still think the best film in that genre is Jules Dassin's *Rififi*. For a start, it does it all visually, with little speaking. I'd rather see a heist movie with a fresh angle – something like that or *Dog Day Afternoon*. As for serial killer films, people seem drawn to serial killers as they are fascinated with the nature of evil. The preacher character Robert Mitchum plays in *The Night of the Hunter* is a serial killer. It's possibly my favourite film of all time – a kind of fairy tale in many ways and Faulkner-esque, but with this psychotic killer in pursuit of the children. And *M* is probably the best serial killer film; it tries to address why the killer does what he does. I don't think many recent serial killer films bother with that. Having said that, I haven't read either script, so I wouldn't know how I'd react to them if they landed on my desk. Both *The Night of the Hunter* and *M* have terrific visual style, which engages you. The lighting, of course, and also the style of noir. Art Deco and nouveau are still very stylish and carry on in the memory; I'm not sure MFI decor would have the same impact. It's also a uniquely American genre. I would say Jacques Audiard's *The Beat That My Heart Skipped* and *Read My Lips* have been influenced by film noir and audiences seem drawn to that. And, of course, David Lynch is a master of neo-noir. Frank, the character in *Blue Velvet*, is one of the most imitated characters in scripts, but it's a law of diminishing returns when writers try to 'out-Frank' Frank.

You mentioned that you didn't know if the scripts for The Night of the Hunter or M would immediately grab you as much as the films do, as they are so visually compelling. What kind of things do grab you in a script – are indicators of good screenwriting in your opinion? And specifically writing for the crime genre?

I particularly like scenes that have incongruity and also show chinks in a character's armour – revealing scenes. They might be quiet moments or scenes without dialogue, but a good writer will know how to include them within a script so the emotion comes through. In *Point Blank*, for example, the Lee Marvin character is walking with purpose down this corridor – he's a big man and seems to take up much of the space. And when he enters his wife's bedroom, he unloads his gun into the empty bed. Apparently she is having an affair, and it's like he's unloading his own weapon. A good writer can write a scene like that in such a way that it can be visualised. In the film *Michael Clayton* there are some scenes that have nothing to do with the central crime, but go a long way to explain the characters. We don't get any backstory about the Tilda Swinton character but, in the scene in the hotel room, we learn a lot about her – what drives her. And, in the final scene, the expression on Michael Clayton's face reveals a lot. A film that Warp Films made, *This is England*, has a riveting scene like that – when the psychotic guy is banging his head against the windscreen. It is painful and upsetting and doesn't make his actions any more excusable, but it makes us dread what he is capable of. It provokes this strong infusion of emotions. In Kieslowski's *Three Colours: White* there is a great, primarily visual scene. The main character is so desperate, he asks a gangster to shoot him. The gangster shoots him – bang! And then there's this moment. The gangster finally says, 'That was a blank. The next one's real. Are you sure?' All of these are great visual and emotional scenes on screen, but they can be written convincingly.

The novelist Cormac McCarthy is one of the best writers I've come across in a while; his stuff is imbued with emotion. *No Country for Old Men* is like a movie in book form. The Anton Chigurh character shows what a good writer McCarthy is. When less accomplished writers write 'evil', they focus on 'evil' rather than what brought it about. It's not enough to write the guy with the tattoo on his neck. All in all, a crime screenwriter probably needs to be a good amateur psychologist, and the scripts they write need to be imbued with emotion.

AFTER ALL THE PLANNING
AND PREPARATION

*'Some of our most exquisite murders have been domestic, performed
with tenderness in simple, homey places like the kitchen table.'*

(Alfred Hitchcock)

It should be clear from the material presented herein that there are
certain audience and industry expectations from a crime genre film,
as well as tropes specific to the detective, police, gangster, film noir,
heist, prison, and serial killer sub-genres. It should also be clear that
these sub-genres are rather fluid, influenced by changes in society,
audience reactions, and experimentation from filmmakers. The best
crime genre films tend to contain recognisable tropes, but bring
something fresh to the genre. The writing exercises included here
should help stimulate thought and experimentation and are a good
way of sharpening character development, plotting, dialogue, and
basic screenwriting skills.

But what is the next stage after you've come up with an exciting
idea, you've developed it into outline form and then a solid draft,
taking on board feedback from trusted readers, all of whom think it's
a great script and ready to go out to potential producers?

Be your own toughest critic. First, make sure your draft script
is as professional as possible and be prepared to answer obvious
(and less than obvious) questions about the project. The following

information should seem incredibly obvious to most screenwriters, directors and producers, but, in my personal experience, this is not the case. I frequently receive scripts that make my heart sink due to unprofessional formatting and presentation, overly dense text, and plain old grubbiness, which does not make one feel enthused about what's inside the cover. While it's true that some scripts by well-known auteurs (in particular) are eccentrically formatted or overwritten, they can get away with it because they've proved their writing and directing skills, so the script presentation is less of an issue. This is never the case for a new(-ish) writer.

If your script is going to a public funding body, script contest, large production company, or some agents, it is likely to be given to a script reader to provide coverage on it. Script reading work is typically badly paid, which means the reader is likely to have a large stack of scripts to get through in a very short time period. Reading work is often an entry level position, which suggests a lack of script reading experience, or the reader is a mainstay at a company, has read an enormous number of scripts, and therefore is quite difficult to impress. Either way, do not make your script unpalatable to the reader (or script executive or producer). Your script should be professionally formatted and bound, tidy, with appropriate margins and <u>lots of white space</u>. Do not be tempted to try to make a 135-page script seem shorter by using a smaller font or margins, taking out spaces or doing strange things with the formatting. A script with lots of white space scans quickly and is more likely to seem like a 'page-turner' than a densely (over)written piece that is overly heavy on description, which obscures the plot and characterisation and ultimately is a very slow read. Readers with big piles of scripts to get through want to read something engaging and exciting, not turgid. My personal pet peeve is action description littered with 'we see' (this) and 'we see' (that). 'We see' is rarely necessary in action description and should be deleted to speed the read and allow the reader to visualise without an annoying external voice issuing instructions. Good writers also quickly learn how to write pithy action description, with few adverbs or adjectives, that manages to be descriptive and give a strong sense of character and emotion. The best crime novelists have this skill in spades; a crime screenwriter must also cultivate it. Superbly written action-description in a script is quite rare; study examples of it, learn the skill.

Many screenwriters dislike writing outlines and one page summaries, preferring to dive right into scripting. This is rarely a good idea as it's far easier to readjust a short 'treatment' than a 120-page script. When workshopping scripts in development, it's very common to go back to outline form to really work through the structure. Outlining your script is also a great help in terms of preparing to pitch and discuss it with potential producers or funders. When I worked for a funding body, I would spend most of my time at film festivals listening to project pitches and discussing script ideas. As the day wore on, it became increasingly difficult to listen to a badly told, unclear story with numerous digressions into 'great scenes' that may indeed be great, but are not relevant in such a meeting. Be able to summarise your story in one or two lines. Know what you want to say with the script; what is the core theme, what is your main character's dilemma and goal, what is the genre, and what is special about your project? Why should that script executive remember it after hearing dozens more stories that very same day? How does it use genre conventions in a way that will appeal to audiences, without being derivative? What is compelling about your main character and your antagonist? What is the hook that will make that funder really want to read your script and decide it's worth finding a substantial amount of money for the development and production budgets, while investing months (and normally years) of his or her life pushing to get your project off the ground? And once you can pitch and discuss your project in a convincing manner, reread your script and make sure all those elements are actually working in the draft.

And, finally, while it may seem that film funders, readers and producers are highly critical of scripts or even dismissive of much of what they read, most went into the film and television industries because they love the medium and most would love to discover that brilliant spec script and talented new writer. I think the personal comments of the 'industry insiders' make it clear that, while the creative team must work very hard to effectively develop the script before it enters production, the enthusiasm for the creative work and completed project is undoubtedly there.

*

'Oh, how Shakespeare would have loved cinema!'

(Derek Jarman)

INDEX